The Chinese Outbound Travel Market

with Special Insight into the Image of Europe as a Destination

The Chinese Outbound Travel Market with Special Insight into the Image of Europe as a Destination
ISBN: 978-92-844-1237-2 (UNWTO)
ISBN: 978-92-990050-2-6 (ETC)

Published by the World Tourism Organization and the European Travel Commission
Printed by the World Tourism Organization, Madrid, Spain
First printing 2008

World Tourism Organization
Calle Capitán Haya, 42
28020 Madrid, Spain
Tel.: (+34) 915 678 100
Fax: (+34) 915 713 733
Website: www.unwto.org
Email: omt@unwto.org

European Travel Commission
19A Avenue Marnix (PO Box 25)
1000 Brussels, Belgium
Tel.: (+32) 2 - 548 90 00
Fax: (+32) 2 - 514 18 43
Website: www.etc-corporate.org
Email: info@visiteurope.com

Table of Contents

Acknowledgements

This report was prepared by the European Tour Operators Association (ETOA), on commission to the European Travel Commission (ETC) and the World Tourism Organization (UNWTO).

The report, which forms part of ETC's ongoing Market Intelligence Programme, was carried out under the supervision of Mr Tom Ylkänen, Research Manager of the Finnish Tourist Board and Ms Lisa Davies (ETC) on behalf of ETC's Market Intelligence Group (MIG) in collaboration with Ms Sandra Carvão from UNWTO's Market Trends, Competitiveness and Trade in Tourism Services Section.

The members of the ETC Market Intelligence Committee who contributed to this exercise are: Mr Leslie Vella (Chairman MIG), Malta, Ms Lisa Davies (ETC Executive Unit), Ms Gaëlle Berréhouc, France, Mr Christian Ørsted Brandt, Denmark, Ms Alex Flack, United Kingdom, Mr Felipe Formariz, Spain, Mr Augusto Huescar, Ms Sandra Carvão and Mr John Kester, UNWTO, Mr Brian Maher, Ireland, Ms Carla Aguirre, Sweden, Ms José Nieuwhof, Netherlands, Mr Bill Richards, ETAG, Mr Joachim Scholz, Germany, Ms Judit Sulyok, Hungary, Mr Tom Ylkänen, Finland, and Mr Jernej Zajec, Slovenia.

Executive Summary

Summary of Key Market Trends

- China is one of the fastest growing outbound travel markets in the world. Thanks to rapid urbanisation, rising disposable incomes and relaxations of restrictions on foreign travel, outbound trip volume has grown by an annual average of 22.0% since 2000 and just under 15.5% since 1995 – reaching 34.5 million in 2006.
- In 1995, the World Tourism Organization (UNWTO) predicted that China would generate 100 million arrivals worldwide annually by 2020, making it the fourth largest market in the world (*UNWTO Tourism 2020 Vision*). In view of recent trends, it is on course to reach that target well before 2020.
- Nevertheless, much of the enthusiasm about China's potential as an outbound tourism source overlooks the fact that the vast majority of outbound trips (over 70%) are to the Chinese Special Administrative Regions (SARs) of Hong Kong and Macao. Around half of the rest are 'border visitors' on day trips to Russia, Vietnam or Laos for trade and/or shopping, or to gamble in casinos, which are illegal in China.
- Europe's share of China's outbound trip volume is difficult to determine as official outbound data only counts the first point of call. But the official count from the China National Tourism Administration (CNTA) was 1.8 million in 2005, unchanged over the previous year.
- According to CNTA, Europe attracted a modest share of 6% of total Chinese outbound trips/ departures in 2005 – down from nearly 10% in 2001, despite a 50% increase in trip volume over the four years.
- Over the last three or four years, the European tourism industry's attention has been primarily focused on the Chinese group leisure tour market, opened up as a result of the granting of Approved Destination Status (ADS) to most European countries in 2004. ADS is the scheme that authorises approved countries to receive leisure tour group travellers from China.
- However, it is proving difficult to generate sustainable and profitable business in a market characterised by low-priced, low-yield, multi-destination tours. Business, incentive and technical trips are showing better growth and, like independent (FIT) leisure trips, are seen as much more attractive for the longer term.

Operating Environment

- China is the third largest country in the world (after the Russian Federation and Canada) and the most populous (estimated 1.3 billion population in 2006).
- Although GDP is still only one-fifth the size of the United States of America's, and GDP per capita is a modest US$ 1,990 a year as against US$ 44,000 for the United States of America (2006), China's economy has been growing at an average of around 10% a year since 2000 – at a pace that is unprecedented in world history – and double-digit annual growth is set to continue over the foreseeable future.

- Among the drivers of outbound travel growth, one of the most important has been the rise in disposable incomes, boosted by the strong yuan/renminbi (which was unpegged from the US dollar in July 2005) and low inflation (1.3% in 2006).
- Most outbound travel is from China's three leading cities and surrounding regions – Beijing, Shanghai and Guangzhou – but, thanks to rapid urbanisation, the second-tier cities are also emerging as sources of growing demand.
- China's demographic profile is changing. The main source of the forecast growth in travel demand will be the young, affluent middle class that is emerging – from 175 million people now to around 500 million by 2025 – but the older 'working-age empty-nesters' are also a key segment of the market as their children have left home and they already possess all the home 'durables' they need.
- The majority of outbound, as well as domestic, trips are taken during the three 'Golden Weeks' – the official Chinese holiday periods – but paid holiday time outside these periods is expected to increase.
- There is a growing ability and desire among the Chinese to spend money on leisure, including tourism – as well as a greater willingness to use credit cards or to borrow money to do so.
- Despite significant liberalisation of outbound travel, China is one of the few countries in the world where outbound travel legislation continues to influence trends. These, coupled with the difficult, expensive and complex visa application process for many countries, are still a significant deterrent to growth.
- This also ensures that the vast majority of leisure tourists to Europe travel in organised tour groups to countries with Approved Destination Status (ADS), which is for many the least attractive segment of the market in terms of profitability.

Outbound Travel Trends

- The Chinese made 34.5 million trips abroad in 2006, up 10.5% over 2005, 90% of which were to other Asian destinations (and 71% to Hong Kong, China, and Macao, China).
- Although outbound travel has increased by 22% since 2000, the ratio of domestic to outbound trips is still 38:1, reflecting the huge growth potential.
- According to UNWTO, international travel expenditure by mainland Chinese residents topped US$ 24.3 billion in 2006, ranking China the world's sixth major spender on travel abroad, but average spend is still at a relatively modest US$ 704 per trip, or US$ 19 per capita. However, other sources confirm that, on long-haul trips, the Chinese are big spenders.
- Chinese leisure travellers are very price-conscious in terms of their outlay in terms of transport, accommodation, food and beverages, but they are big spenders on shopping.
- Excluding Hong Kong, China, and, the top destinations for Chinese outbound travellers are Singapore, the Republic of Korea, Japan and Thailand. According to the official outbound count from CNTA, the Russian Federation, Germany, Austria and Switzerland are the main destinations in Europe for Chinese (but, as mentioned, the count only includes first point of call on a trip).
- The ranking of leading destinations in terms of holiday travel – those most commonly offered by tour operators – suggests that Germany, France and Italy are the most popular destinations in Europe. The main competitors for Europe are the United States of America (which still attracts mainly students and business/technical visitors from China) and Australia.
- According to the trade interviews conducted in China and Europe, the average number of countries visited per trip is 6-8, although this is usually much lower for repeat visitors. The countries in

highest demand are France and Italy, with the French attractions of the Louvre, Notre Dame, the Eiffel Tower and Versailles Palace the most heavily requested by Chinese consumers.

- Around two thirds of all outbound travellers earn more than Rmb 5,000 a month (US$ 604 or € 486) and 35% earn more than Rmb 10,000.
- The proportion of male to female travellers is now quite balanced, with females outnumbering males by 53:47. But Europe attracts almost 50% more males than females (60:40), largely because of the higher than average share of business trips.
- Around 50% of outbound travellers are aged between 25 and 44 years, which is widely considered the age segment with the best growth potential. But a higher share of Chinese in the 45-plus age group travel to long-haul destinations, including Europe and Australia, and this age group is set to increase sharply in volume.
- Most travel to Europe takes place between the months of May and September, with more than 50% of tourists travelling in family groups and most of the remainder with friends.

Air Transport

- China will be the world's second largest aviation market by 2020, according to leading aircraft manufacturers Boeing and Airbus.
- Although excessive congestion at the main airports has resulted in recent cutbacks in flights, there has been a huge growth in international and domestic airline capacity in recent years – not least to Europe.
- In August 2007 there were 289 weekly flights to Europe, excluding flights from Hong Kong, China, with ten airlines operating more than ten flights per week (outbound only).
- International airlines face practical and political difficulties in raising their capacity in line with demand, but increased traffic rights and alliances are driving growth and helping them to secure their market presence.

Travel Distribution

- In 2006, more than 670 travel agencies in China were licensed to sell outbound travel.
- The vast majority of outbound trips, excluding those to Hong Kong, China, and Macao, China, are handled by travel agents.
- The ADS market is strictly regulated and agents who 'lose' tourists or otherwise displease the authorities are liable to be removed, temporarily or permanently, from the list of authorised ADS operators.
- The main travelling periods for tour groups sold by travel agents are around the three national holiday periods: the so-called 'Golden Weeks'. These are the Spring Festival at Chinese New Year, the May Holiday (first week in May) and the National Day Holiday (first week in October).
- Average lead-time for bookings placed with travel agents for leisure visits to Europe is 1-2 months. After receiving the booking, the agent may spend up to four weeks selecting inbound tour operators, who may not receive final confirmation until two weeks prior to departure.
- Consumer research on destinations is increasingly carried out online, but brochures and TV programmes are still popular.

- Price competition is rife, due in part to the willingness of Chinese agencies to use 'informal' networks of business contacts that bypass many of the normal requirements of group tourism. Furthermore, this growth has been sustained by the supply of spare capacity caused by the decline in demand for Europe over the past few years from the United States of America and Japan.

Online Travel

- In mid-2007, according to the China Internet Network Information Centre (CNNIC), China had approximately 162 million internet users, representing 12% of the population.
- Although this level of market penetration is still low, China ranks second only to the United States of America in absolute number of internet users, and the total is forecast to grow to around 250 million by 2011 (19% of the population).
- Research by ACNielsen has also shown that, within the 18-40 age group in the major cities, the market penetration level of internet users is 60-70% – and among university-educated Chinese of that age, the level is over 90%.
- Online travel companies are emerging but the market is heavily dominated by the two leading players, Ctrip and eLong.
- Except for domestic travel, the internet is used primarily for 'looking' (information gathering) than booking. This is likely to continue for the short to medium term because of the need for agents to help apply for visas.
- China's online travel industry will clearly undergo rapid transformation over the next few years. The appetite for the internet in China, together with the market's brisk enthusiasm for reducing costs, is certain to increase the proportion of those who book online.
- Driving this process forward will be the expansion of low-cost airlines, the increased use of credit cards, and the growth of the internet and of the Chinese economy. But it will not all be plain sailing for European suppliers since progress is likely to be inhibited by the continued requirement for visas from most ADS countries, restrictions on the ability of many Chinese to travel, and the tradition of relying on cash transactions.
- Eleven national tourism organizations (NTOs) from Europe offer websites in simplified Chinese.

Marketing to the Chinese Traveller

- Although the level of interest in Europe as a 'dream' leisure destination is high, demand will continue to be low and compromised by cost. The Chinese are surrounded by destinations with which they have greater cultural affinity, that are easier to travel to and offer excellent value for money.
- What demand there is for Europe remains dominated by the business sector, including the 'business tour'. This combines an ostensible business purpose with leisure activities such as shopping and sightseeing. As the participants are generally sponsored by their companies or partners abroad, normal marketing practices do not apply – as in the incentive travel market, demand tends to be dependent on commercial caprice and government edict.
- The ADS leisure tourist still represents a small share of total Chinese travel to Europe.
- Fewer than 30 foreign NTOs are established in China and, of these, 17 are European. Nine European NTOs have fulltime offices, including five which have offices in Shanghai as well as in Beijing. The remainder either share an office (the Scandinavian Tourist Board represents Denmark, Norway and

Sweden in Beijing and Shanghai), or are represented through their respective embassy, consulate, or local chamber of commerce.

Perceptions of Europe

- According to the surveys, trade interviews and focus groups carried out as part of the research for this study, the Chinese market is normally marked by regional differences in consumer behaviour. But the outbound travel market for Europe appears relatively homogeneous. There was no marked difference in the responses between the major visitor-generating cities. This simplifies marketing and advertising campaigns, which usually have to be adapted to suit the region in which they are being launched.
- Furthermore there is a strong perception of Europe as a unique destination, albeit with different regions and individual features. This has obviously been enhanced as a result of the Schengen visa and the euro.

What Sells?

- The favourite activity for Chinese visitors is shopping; this is preferred to visiting historic monuments.
- The Chinese travel trade interviewed for the purposes of this report felt that the features that best sell European itineraries are shopping, scenery, local customs, dining and outdoor activities. The European travel trade added brandname shops and the British royal family to this list.
- Both the travel trade and consumers suggested that marketing campaigns focus on traditional media sources and emphasise the diversity of Europe. Visual references should be to the more 'obvious' European iconic images such as the Louvre, Eiffel Tower and Colosseum.

What Does not Sell?

- The strongest negative associations among Chinese are that Europe is "arrogant", "expensive" and "lacking understanding of Chinese visitors".
- Chinese agents felt that features to avoid are long coach journeys, small countries and a plethora of churches and museums. European operators mentioned remote countryside, customer service and high prices as features that put Chinese clients off visiting Europe.
- This desire to have the positive features of escorted touring without the unavoidable shortcomings is common to many markets.
- When asked what Europe could do to be more welcoming to Chinese tour groups, respondents mentioned simplifying the visa application process, better quality Chinese food, a greater choice of itineraries, promotional and informational materials in Chinese and increased flights.

Conclusions

- Currently, available data on the Chinese market in European destinations is poor. Individual countries must try to differentiate between Chinese visitors and 'other Asians'. Information from visa issuing authorities would also be very useful for the travel trade in China, as well as for suppliers.

- Europe is perceived as an expensive destination, so it is important to devise some way of increasing the prestige of visiting Europe so that price becomes less of a constraint. If the goal for the industry is more visits from the Chinese middle class, this has to be seen as a long-term project.

- Despite increased use of the internet and of information channels such as television and newspapers, word of mouth has genuine authority in Chinese culture. A rumour that a particular visa-issuing office is asking personal questions can be sufficient to deter waves of groups from entering a country. One attack on a Chinese individual can blight a destination. How this can be countered by European NTOs remains a difficult question to answer, as it is not easy to allay fears without attracting attention to them.

- More effort must be made to make Chinese groups feel welcome. One negative impression that is gaining ground is the perception that Europe is unfriendly and lacking in understanding. One way of countering this is to ensure that more information is available in Chinese to visitors – in particular, explanations as to European customs and mores.

- The Chinese market to Europe is currently neither large, in terms of actual volume or short-term potential, nor easy to tap. The short-term prospects for Europe as a destination remain uncertain. But as China grows into being an economic super-power, finding a way to appeal to the potential Chinese visitor is one of the most pressing questions facing the European travel industry.

Scope of the Study

Why China?

In November 1983, Guangdong Province became the first province of the People's Republic of China to organise an outbound 'tour' to Hong Kong, China, primarily to allow its citizens to visit friends and relatives (VFR). By the following year, Chinese citizens were able to take regular 'tours' to both Hong Kong, China, and Macao, China, both of which are now Special Administrative Regions of China.

Leisure travel to non-Chinese destinations started in 1991, although the prime purpose was still VFR. Twenty-six years later, that trickle of VFR visitors from China has become a flood of leisure and business travellers, which is forecast to exceed 40 million trips abroad in 2007. The Chinese are now the sixth biggest spenders on international tourism, according to the World Tourism Organization (UNWTO), and are projected to continue to climb up the world spenders' ranking.

But how can Europe ensure it attracts a healthy share of this growth? The majority of European countries have had Approved Destination Status (ADS) – the scheme that enables them to receive leisure tour group travellers from China – for less than three years. Yet, more than 130 countries worldwide now have ADS (as at early 2007), and the competition from established and newly emerging tourism destinations is becoming increasingly intense. This makes it even more important to understand the market and to identify the main drivers of growth, so that destinations and suppliers can better target their marketing and develop the right kind of products to stimulate demand.

Objectives and Methodology

China is clearly an extremely important emerging travel market and both the World Tourism Organization (UNWTO) and the European Travel Commission (ETC) need to monitor the market on a regular basis to identify growth trends and any other developments that might affect growth in future.

ETC's main objective in commissioning this study, in line with the organization's Business Plan, was to improve its e-marketing through the visiteurope.com internet portal. Developing the right marketing messages for Chinese consumers is clearly a good way of attracting new tourism business for its member countries.

As the marketing activities of ETC are mainly focused around the development of the ETC portal, information on the image and image building of Europe is of central importance. But ETC recognises that, to be able to develop the right marketing messages for the Chinese consumer, it is not only the image of Europe that is important. It is also essential to have more in-depth information on Chinese consumers' experiences and their wishes concerning travel to and within Europe.

UNWTO's focus is clearly broader and its main priority in co-commissioning the study was to update the 2003 report (also published jointly by ETC and UNWTO), *China Outbound Tourism,* highlighting key trends in China outbound travel over the past five years or so – such as the market's size and value, growth in trip volume and spending, purpose of trip, the structure and role of the travel trade, online distribution, and other factors driving demand.

Also important for both ETC and UNWTO is information on government policy affecting outbound travel, such as the visa issue and operational difficulties related to the ADS scheme. All this information is critical to help NTOs and commercial operators plan ahead with greater foresight, providing guidance on both the short-term opportunities and the longer-term potential for investment in the Chinese market.

The study was required to comprise three distinct components, or phases:

- desk research;
- interviews with the travel trade, including travel agents in China and inbound tour operators in Europe; and
- focus groups with Chinese consumers – both those with European travel experience and those who had not yet visited Europe, but who planned to do so within a period of three years.

In addition, the European Tour Operators Association (ETOA) – the organization commissioned to undertake the study – felt it was appropriate to add a survey of Chinese travellers on coach tours of Europe. An innovative feature of this additional survey was that clients were asked for their perceptions both prior to taking their trip and then as a result of their trip, based on their experiences. This provided valuable insight into perceptions of Europe and the reality experienced by Chinese visitors.

The project team, led by ETOA, Europe's largest inbound trade association, included:

- Amber China Industry Insights: a Shanghai based business consultancy;
- Sustainable Solutions Worldwide: a United Kingdom-based consultancy;
- China Holidays, Kuoni Incoming Services, Gullivers Travel Associates (GTA) and Miki Travel: leading tour operators and members of ETOA which, together, control 70% of the Chinese outbound tourism market to Europe;
- Professor Ian Woodward: United Kingdom-based tourism consultant from Woodward Associates;
- Consumerdata: a market leader in consumer satisfaction surveys in the European and North American travel industries.

Data Sources

Several statistical sources were used for the compilation of this report, all of which are cited where relevant. Among the most widely used sources for the desk research phase of the study were the China National Tourism Administration (CNTA) for statistical data and other information on the Chinese outbound travel market, and UNWTO and ETC for data on inbound arrivals into Europe and other destinations. Statistics and other valuable information from ETC came either directly from its NTO members – listed at the end of the report – or via the TourMIS website (www.tourmis.info).

TourMIS, an information and marketing system, is a joint venture between the Austrian National Tourist Office (ANTO) and the Austrian Society for Applied Research in Tourism. Its development and ongoing operation are financially supported by ANTO and ETC.

Care must nevertheless be take in interpreting the statistics since different methodologies are used to measure outbound trips/departures and inbound arrivals, and there are even differences in countries' measurements of inbound travellers – as explained clearly in the report.

In addition to desk research, the information gathered for the overview of travel trends has also come from interviews with European and competitive NTOs, organizations specialising in economic and demographic trends, airlines, academics, consultants and the media. As already indicated, these are all listed in the Bibliography.

Further information on the Chinese market is available from ETC's Market Insight on China, which is updated every two years and can be found on ETC's website www.etc-corporate.org, as well as from UNWTO's 2006 report on China – part of the organization's *The Asia and the Pacific Intra-regional Outbound Series* – which is frequently referred to in this report.

Chapter 1

Introduction to China

1.1 Country and Population Overview

1.1.1 Geography

Situated in North-East Asia, the People's Republic of China is the third largest country in the world (after the Russian Federation and Canada), with a land area of some 9.6 million km^2.

It has 15 neighbouring countries. Russia and Mongolia lie to the north; the Democratic People's Republic of Korea to the north-east; and Kazakhstan, Kygyzstan, Tajikistan, Afghanistan and Pakistan to the west. India, Nepal, Bhutan, Myanmar, Lao PDR and Vietnam are situated to the south of China, and to the east and south, across the Yellow Sea, the East China Sea and the South China Sea, lie Japan, the Philippines, Malaysia, Indonesia and Brunei.

1.1.2 Population

China is the most populous country in the world, with a population of 1,314 million in 2006, according to the Chinese National Bureau of Statistics – of which the rural population accounts for some 58% and 42% live in urban areas. The total represents an increase of 140% since 1950. In its *2006 Population Revision,* the United Nations (which then estimated the Chinese population at 1,321 million) forecast that China's population would grow by 0.6% a year from 2005 through 2010.

The population density is about 137 per km^2. The household registration system is less stringent than it used to be, which is helping to improve the legal (and consequently economic) situation of 'illegal migrants' (migrants without residence permits, estimated to number 150-200 million) and will make the labour market more flexible.

The fertility rate (the average number of children per female) is estimated at 1.7. Infant mortality was 35 per thousand live births in 2000-2005 and life expectancy at birth was 72 years.

The birth rate has fallen to 13 births per 1,000, while the death rate has fallen much more steeply to 7 per 1,000, leading to the present population problem. The government introduced a law in the late 1970s setting a limit of one child per family. However, in rural areas the policy is more flexible, allowing families whose first child is a girl to have another baby. The one-child policy has inevitably led to social problems, to an imbalance between males and females (106 males per 100 females, compared with a world average of 102), and to the prospect of a population that will age very rapidly.

China is still keen to curb its population growth, and the controversial family planning policy is meant to limit urban couples to one child and rural families to two. But rising incomes mean that some newly rich couples in urban areas can easily afford to break the rules and pay the resulting fines. In fact, a survey in April 2007 by the National Population and Family Planning Commission found that the number of rich people and celebrities having more than one child was increasing rapidly, and nearly 10% of people in this category had three children.

The age split of the population in 2005 was, nevertheless, as follows:

Figure 1.1 Age Breakdown of China's Population, 2005 and 2020 (%)

Age (years)	2005	2020[a]
0-4	6.4	6.2
5-14	15.0	12.2
15-24	16.5	12.5
25-34	16.5	15.1
35-44	17.4	13.5
45-54	12.7	16.6
55-64	7.9	12.1
65-74	5.1	8.1
75-84	2.2	3.0
≥ 85	0.3	0.7

a) Forecast.

Source: United Nations Department of Economic and Social Affairs Population Division.

Although the data in the above table highlights the dominance of young people in China's population, the share of those aged under 30 years old declined from 56% of the total population in 1994 to 44% ten years later, according to Hong Kong-based Global Demographics. Despite evidence that some Chinese are contravening the family planning policy, Global Demographics also predicts that it will fall further, to 35%, by 2014. Meanwhile, Chinese citizens aged 60 years and over should have almost doubled their share from 1994 to 2014 – from 9% to 17% – and the 30-59 year-olds will have risen from 35% to an estimated 48% over the period.

Figure 1.2 The Ageing of the Chinese Population, 1994-2014 (%)

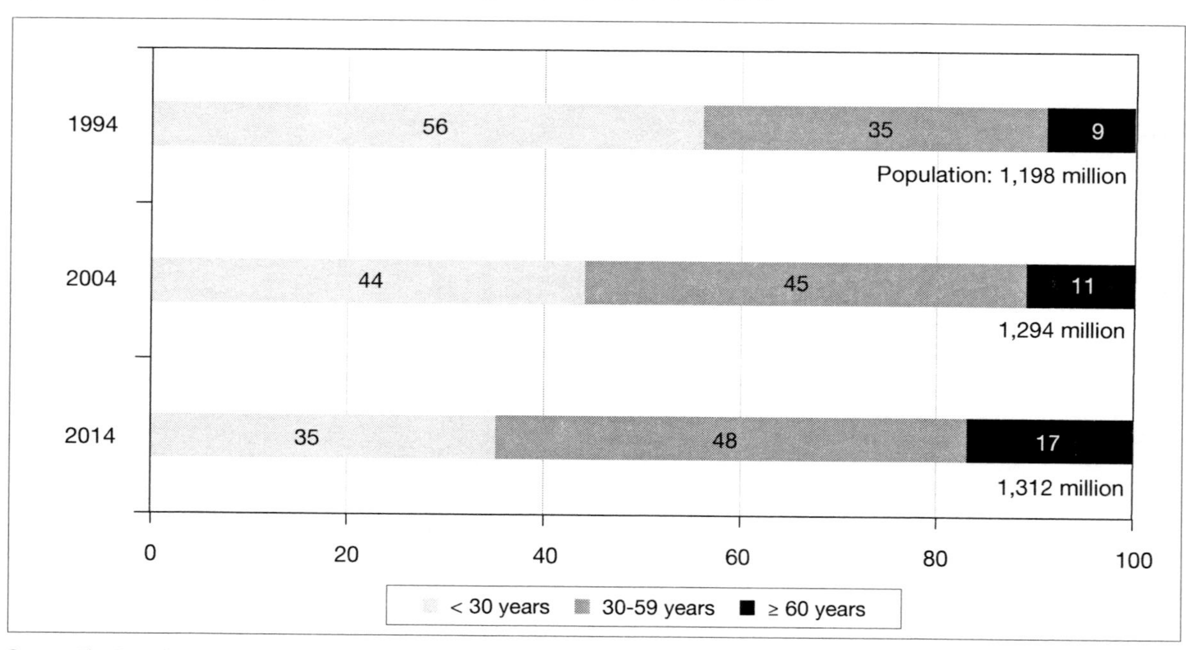

Source: The Travel Business Partnership, from Global Demographics data.

1.1.3 Language and Ethnic Groups

The national language of China is Mandarin (Putonghua), spoken throughout the mainland, and even increasingly in Macao, China, and Hong Kong, China, where Cantonese is the primary dialect, as it is in Guangdong Province. Other important dialects include Shanghainese, Fujianese, Hokkien-Taiwanese and Hakka.

About 92% of the population is Han Chinese; the remainder include Zhuang, Uygur, Hui, Yi, Tibetan, Miao, Manchu, Mongol, Buyi, Korean and other nationalities.

Buddhism and Taoism are two of the major religions in China, with Christianity and Islam having relatively small followings. China is officially atheist, but freedom of religious belief is protected by law.

1.2 Administrative Divisions

China is divided into 23 provinces, five autonomous regions and four municipalities. In addition to the 22 provinces listed in figure 1.3 below, Taiwan, Province of China, is also considered a province by the mainland government. The five autonomous regions are Guangxi, Inner Mongolia, Ningxia, Xinjiang and Tibet; and the four municipalities are Beijing (the capital), Chongqing, Shanghai and Tianjin.

Henan is the largest province in terms of population with over 97 million people. As many as 21 of the provinces have populations of at least 25 million people. The largest city in China is Shanghai with 12.9 million inhabitants, followed by Beijing with 10.8 million. Shanghai also has the largest population density with 2,646 people per km^2, while Qinghai Province in the west of China has just seven. The largest capital among the capitals of the provinces is Wuhan in Hubei with over 5 million people. Within China there are at least 25 cities with a population of over one million and 17 of China's cities rank among the 100 largest cities in the world.

China also has a number of Special Economic Zones (SEZs), which have flexible economic policies and offer attractive incentives for overseas investors. These include the five coastal areas of Shenzhen, Zhuhai, Shantou, Xiamen and Hainan Province. The Special Administrative Regions (SARs), which were reintegrated into mainland China after a period of rule by another country, are Hong Kong (relinquished by the United Kingdom in 1997) and Macao (retrieved from Portugal in 1999).

Figure 1.3 Administrative Divisions of China

Administrative divisions			Capital city		
Name	**Population 2000 (million)**	**Density (inhabitants per km^2)**	**Name**	**Population 2000 (million)**	**Share of division's population (%)**
Provinces					
Henan	97.2	546	Zhengzhou	2.1	2.2
Shangdong	89.9	587	Jinan	2.6	2.9
Guangdong	85.2	432	Guangzhou	3.9	4.6
Sichuan	82.3	169	Chengdu	3.3	4.0
Jiangsu	73.0	712	Nanjing	2.7	3.7
Hebei	66.6	329	Shijiazhuang	1.6	2.4
Hunan	63.2	301	Changsha	1.8	2.8
Hubei	59.5	317	Wuhan	5.2	8.7

Administrative divisions			Capital city		
Name	**Population 2000 (million)**	**Density (inhabitants per km²)**	**Name**	**Population 2000 (million)**	**Share of division's population (%)**
Anhui	58.9	422	Hefei	1.2	2.0
Zhejiang	45.9	451	Hangzhou	1.8	3.9
Yunnan	42.3	97	Kunming	1.7	4.0
Lioaning	41.8	277	Shenyang	4.8	11.5
Jiangxi	40.3	245	Nanchang	1.7	4.2
Heilongjiang	36.2	78	Harbin	2.9	8.0
Shaanxi	35.4	171	Xi'an	3.1	8.8
Guizhou	35.2	203	Guiyang	2.5	7.1
Fujian	34.1	277	Fuzhou	1.4	4.1
Shanxi	32.5	207	Taiyuan	2.4	7.4
Jilin	26.8	143	Changchun	3.1	11.6
Gansu	25.1	69	Lanzhou	1.7	6.8
Hainan	7.6	220	Haikou	0.4	5.3
Qinghai	4.8	7	Xining	0.7	14.6
Autonomous regions					
Guangxi Zhuang	43.8	199	Nanning	1.3	3.0
Nei Mongol	23.3	20	Hohhot	0.9	3.9
Xinjiang Uygur	18.4	11	Urumqi	1.4	7.6
Ningxia Hui	5.5	83	Yinchuan	0.5	9.1
Tibet	2.6	2	Lhasa	0.1	3.8
Municipalities					
Chongqing	30.5	372	Chongqing	4.9	16.1
Shanghai	16.4	2,646	Shanghai	12.9	78.7
Beijing	13.6	808	Beijing	10.8	79.4
Tianjin	9.8	872	Tianjin	9.1	92.9

Note: The 23rd administrative region of China is Taiwan, Province of China; Administrative Divisions are ranked by size of population.

Source: United Nations, *World Urbanisation Prospects* (2001 revision).

1.3 Infrastructure and Communications

China has about 57,600 km of railways, of which 90% are of standard gauge. The railways remain the backbone of inland transport and, like most parts of the transport system, are heavily congested. Significant investments are being made into expanding and improving the railways – the line to Lhasa in Tibet was completed in 2006, for example – including the urban systems.

In 2004, there were reported to be 34,000 km of motorways and 1.8 million km of highways. The country's major ports are at Shanghai, Qingdao, Dalian, Guangzhou, Ningbo, Qinhuangdao and Shenzhen.

There are a total of 330 airports (cf. chapter 3) in the country, with the main international airports at Beijing, Shanghai and Guangzhou. A huge programme of airport construction is underway – an estimated 86 new airports are due to open within the next decade.

The International Telecommunications Union (ITU) reports that, in 2005, China had 350.4 million main telephone lines (27 per hundred inhabitants) and 393.4 million mobile telephone subscribers (30 per hundred inhabitants). Between 2000 and 2005, the number of main telephone lines increased by 19% a year, and the number of mobile telephones by 30% a year. In 2005 there were about 53 million personal computers and 111 million internet users (cf. chapter 6).

1.4 Political System

China is a Communist state, under one-party rule. The most recent constitution was promulgated in December 1982. The Politburo (currently 20 members) of the Chinese Communist Party (CCP) sets policy and controls all administrative, legal and executive appointments. Its standing committee is the real focus of power.

A 15-member State Council (cabinet) is elected by the National People's Congress (NPC) and is responsible for drafting legislation. The State Council is headed by a president (head of state), who is elected by the NPC for a renewable five-year term. The government is headed by a premier.

Legislation is passed by the unicameral NPC (Quanguo Renmin Daibiao Dahui), which consists of 2,989 members elected by provinces, municipalities, autonomous regions and the armed forces. It elects the president and members of the State Council and members of the Standing Committee of the NPC, which meets when the NPC is not in session. Elections to the NPC are held every five years. The judicial branch is headed by a Supreme People's Court.

Presidential and State Council elections are held every five years. The last elections took place in March 2003. The CCP will hold its 17th Party Congress late in 2007.

1.5 International Trade

China's long quest to join the World Trade Organization (WTO), supported by the United States of America and the European Union (EU), came to fruition in December 2001. Membership has huge implications for many sectors, and these are already being felt – including by the travel and tourism industry.

Exports and imports are both rising extremely rapidly and are one of the most important factors in the recent strength of the world economy. The value of Chinese merchandise exports rose by 35% in both 2003 and 2004, by 28.5% in 2005 and by 27% in 2006 – to US$ 970 billion. The United States of America is China's single largest market, accounting for about a fifth of total exports, followed by Hong Kong, China, and Japan. China's principal exports include electrical and electronic goods, textiles, garments and footwear. Foreign-invested companies generate well over half of total exports.

The surge in textiles and clothing exports after the expiry of the Multifiber Agreement in January 2005, though widely expected, proved politically inflammatory, especially in the United States of America and EU (they negotiated temporary restraints on imports of clothing, which are due to be phased out by 2008). The size of China's trade surplus with the United States of America continues to exercise the US Government, which filed a suit against China with the World Trade Organization in February 2007, complaining about export subsidies and discrimination against imports.

Merchandise imports had been rising even faster – by 40% in 2003 and 36% in 2004. This growth slackened to just 18% in 2005 and 20% in 2006, bringing the total to US$ 752 billion. The increase largely reflects the demand for capital and semi-finished goods for export-oriented industries, but imports of consumer goods and food are also rising rapidly. China is increasingly dependent upon imported oil (and thus exposed to the vagaries of world oil prices). Imports come principally from Japan, the Republic of Korea, Taiwan, Province of China, and the United States of America. China has been investing heavily abroad to secure energy and raw materials supplies, notably in Africa, Latin America and Central Asia.

With the slower growth in imports, the surplus on the merchandise trade balance surged to about US$ 218 billion in 2006, and that on the current account to about US$ 250 billion (9.5% of GDP). The latter is expected to fall as imports of services and the profit remittances of foreign companies increase. However, the deficit in services fell from US$ 9.7 billion in 2004 to US$ 8.8 billion in 2006, and the deficit in income of US$ 3.5 billion became a surplus of US$ 11.8 billion. The surplus on current transfers – essentially aid, gifts and family remittances – increased from US$ 22.9 billion to US$ 29.2 billion. The influx of 'hot money' awaiting a revaluation of the yuan/renminbi in 2004-2005 has apparently ceased; outward-bound portfolio investment has increased very sharply, to US$ 110 billion in 2006.

Chapter 2

Operating Environment

2.1 Economic Indicators

2.1.1 GDP and Growth Rates

It is obvious that, as a potential market, China dwarfs most other emerging or developing countries, and its economy is growing at a pace which is unprecedented in world history. Its gross domestic product (GDP) is, as yet, little more than three times the size of, say, Australia's in US dollar terms, and only one fifth the size of the United States of America's. Moreover, it is so vast, diverse and problematic that it cannot sensibly be treated as a single market.

China's GDP is estimated to have increased by 17.9% (11.1% in real terms) to Rmb 21,087 billion (US$ 2,626 billion) in 2006.

Figure 2.1 Comparison of GDP across Selected Key Economies, 2000-2006 (US$ billion)

Selected key economies	2000	2001	2002	2003	2004	2005	2006
World	31,775	31,559	32,834	36,882	41,452	44,745	48,245
United States of America	9,817	10,128	10,470	10,961	11,686	12,434	13,195
Japan	4,669	4,098	3,925	4,235	4,608	4,557	4,366
Germany	1,906	1,893	2,024	2,447	2,749	2,796	2,916
China	**1,198**	**1,325**	**1,454**	**1,641**	**1,932**	**2,244**	**2,645**
United Kingdom	1,454	1,445	1,585	1,828	2,169	2,246	2,399
Russia Federation	260	307	345	431	592	764	985
India	462	473	496	575	666	779	874
Australia	390	368	413	528	639	713	756

Source: IMF, *World Economic Outlook*, October 2007.

In late 1978, the Chinese leadership under Deng Xiao Ping began moving the economy from a centrally planned economy to a more market-oriented system. He set a goal of quadrupling China's economic output by the turn of the 21st century, which implies annual real GDP growth of 7.2%. In fact, since 1978 the Chinese economy has grown at an average of 10% a year, led by extraordinary increases in investment, doubling per capita income every ten years. Such growth surpasses the experience of any other country in modern history.

Figure 2.2 Comparison of Real GDP Growth across Selected Key Economies, 2000-2006 (%)

Selected key economies	2000	2001	2002	2003	2004	2005	2006	AAGR[a]
World	4.8	2.5	3.1	4.0	5.3	4.8	5.4	4.3
United States of America	3.7	0.8	1.6	2.5	3.6	3.1	2.9	2.6
Japan	2.9	0.2	0.3	1.4	2.7	1.9	2.2	1.7
Germany	3.1	1.2	0.0	-0.3	1.1	0.8	2.9	1.3
China	**8.4**	**8.3**	**9.1**	**10.0**	**10.1**	**10.4**	**11.1**	**9.6**
United Kingdom	3.8	2.4	2.1	2.8	3.3	1.8	2.8	2.7
Russian Federation	6.1	5.1	4.7	7.3	7.2	6.4	6.7	6.2
India	5.4	3.9	4.5	6.9	7.9	9.0	9.7	6.8
Australia	3.4	2.1	4.1	3.1	3.7	2.8	2.7	3.1

a) AAGR = Average annual growth rate 2000-2006.

Source: IMF, *World Economic Outlook*, October 2007.

Figure 2.3 Real GDP Growth Indexed (2000 = 100) for Selected Key Economies, 2001-2006

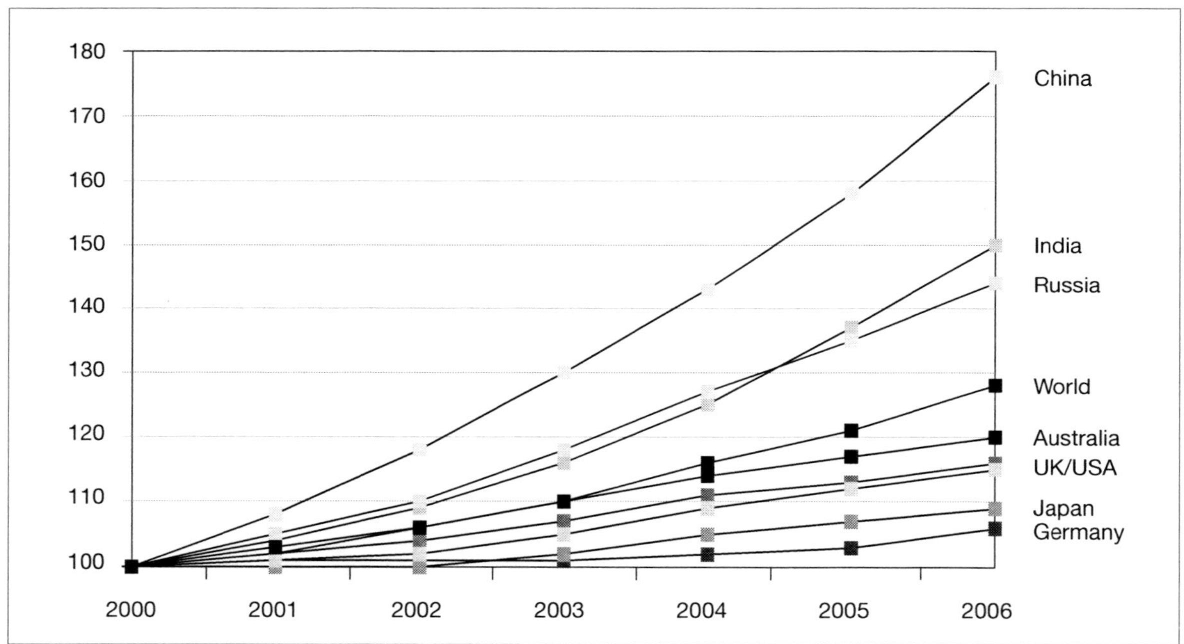

Source: Calculated from IMF, *World Economic Outlook*, October 2007.

Current forecasts from the International Monetary Fund (IMF), published in October 2007 in its *World Economic Outlook,* suggest that China's GDP growth will be 11.5% in 2007 (1.5 percentage points above its April 2007 projections) and will fall very slightly to 10% (half a point higher than the April forecast) in 2008. Projections for India and other developing economies have also been revised upwards, reinforcing the argument that global economic growth will continue to be led much for the foreseeable future by emerging markets.

Figure 2.4 Forecast GDP Growth for Selected Key Economies, 2007-2008 (%)

Selected key economies	2007	2008
World	5.2	4.8
United States of America	1.9	1.9
Japan	2.0	1.7
Germany	2.4	2.0
China	**11.5**	**10.0**
United Kingdom	3.1	2.3
Russian Federation	7.0	6.5
Australia	4.4	3.8
India	8.9	8.4

Source: IMF, *World Economic Outlook*, October 2007.

2.1.2 Regional Performance

Economic performance, unsurprisingly, varies geographically, and prosperity is generally concentrated in the eastern and southern coastal provinces. It is proving more difficult – but is a political priority – to generate growth in 'rural' areas, in the inland and western provinces, and in the north-east region, with its depleted oil and coal sectors and concentration of declining heavy industries.

Three major agglomerations form the backbone of the Chinese economy. They are the city groups of the Pearl River Delta around the main city of Guangzhou, the Changjiang River Delta and the different urban areas around Shanghai, and the Beijing-Tianjin-Hebei area around the Bohai Sea. They are also the three major tourism-generating areas of China.

Figure 2.5 The Three Major Economic Regions in China

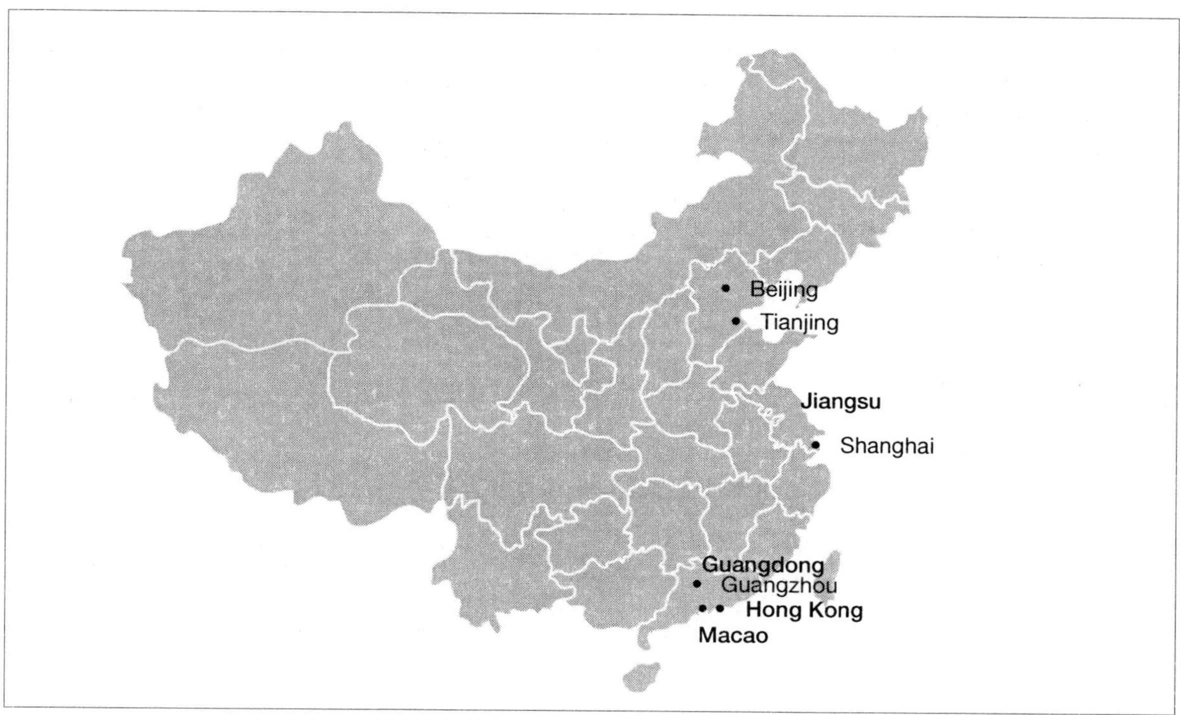

Source: ETOA.

Figure 2.6 The Economic Strength of China's Three Main City Groups, 2003

Indicators	Changjiang Delta		Pearl River Delta		Beijing-Tianjin-Hebei	
	Amount	Share (%)	Amount	Share (%)	Amount	Share (%)
Area (km^2)	100,000	1.0	22,000	0.2	217,000	2.3
Population (million)	75.34	5.9	26.25	2.0	79.63	6.1
Number of cities	15	-	9	-	3	-
GDP (Rmb billion)	2,278	19.5	1,145	10.0	655	6.0

Source: UNWTO, *China – The Asia and the Pacific Intra-regional Outbound Series*, 2006, from *The Economy Almanac of China.*

There are wide variations in the degree of economic development and in Chinese incomes. They are differences between town and country, between different economic units, and even within cities and the rural areas. In the sequence of per capita GDP figures (cf. figure 2.7), the population of the first ten provinces and municipalities combined is 36% of the nation's total, while their combined GDP is 65% of the total of the country.

The per capita GDP of the ten provinces and municipalities is over US$ 1,000. These ten provinces and municipalities are the Beijing-Tianjin area and Liaoning and Heilongjiang Provinces, East China with Shanghai as the centre (Shanghai, Zhejiang, Jiangsu and Shandong Provinces), and South China (Guangdong and Fujian Provinces). The tourism industry is better developed in these areas, with their inhabitants travelling more as a result of the relatively prosperous regional economies.

Figure 2.7 Ten Chinese Provinces and Municipalities with the Highest GDP per Capita, 2002

Area	Population (million)	GDP per capita		Consumption per capita		Disposable income per capita	
		US$	Rank	US$	Rank	US$	Rank
Shanghai	16.25	3,633	1	1,483	1	2,015	1
Beijing	14.23	2,464	2	934	2	1,889	2
Tianjin	10.07	2,223	3	826	3	1,385	5
Zhejiang	46.47	1,831	4	696	5	1,757	3
Guangdong	78.59	1,635	5	718	4	1,646	4
Jiangsu	73.81	1,558	6	597	8	1,266	7
Fujian	34.66	1,455	7	621	7	1,350	6
Liaoning	42.03	1,418	8	646	6	967	-
Shandong	90.82	1,268	9	500	10	1,140	8
Heilongjiang	38.13	1,096	10	549	9	902	-

Note: Disposable income figures are for 2004. Liaoning and Heilongjiang are not among the first ten provinces in terms of per capita disposable income. The population figures used in this analysis differ slightly from those shown elsewhere in this study.

Source: UNWTO, *China – The Asia and the Pacific Intra-regional Outbound Series*, 2006, from *China Economic Growth Report 2004.*

2.1.3 Performance of Key Sectors

Agricultural production, which had been rising by about 3% a year in 2001-2003, rose by 6.3% in 2004, 5.2% in 2005 and by 5.0% in 2006. Typically, output of grains was falling, while that of fruit and vegetables (often for export markets) was rising. However, in 2004-2005, in order to reverse the decline in grain production, the government offered direct subsidies to grain producers. (It estimated the total grain harvest at 484 million tons in 2005, compared with consumption requirements of 480 million tons). It also removed taxes designed to discourage production of fruit and vegetables and is trying to prevent the diversion of agricultural land to other uses.

The result was a sharp – and welcome – increase in rural incomes in 2004-2005. Although bird flu was widespread and 21 million birds were reportedly culled, commercial poultry production was not greatly affected. Cotton production, however, fell by 9.8% in 2005 to 6.8 million tons, requiring imports of 2.6 million tons. Poor rains in some areas constrained output of grains and some other crops in 2006 and, so far, in 2007.

Industrial production rose by 31% in 2004, 30% in 2005 and an estimated 23% in 2006. There have been huge increases in output of many products, including steel and aluminium products, motor vehicles and electrical and electronic equipment (China is now the world's third-largest market for cars). The government is taking steps (not always successful) to restrain over-investment in specific sectors, including steel, aluminium, cement and motor vehicles, and to boost that in others, including coal, oil, gas, railways and electricity generation (including nuclear power). However, many cities are being transformed by construction booms, and the preparations for the Olympic Games include the wholesale reconstruction of large areas of Beijing.

Simultaneously with this hectic development, state-owned enterprises (SOEs) are being reorganised. Many have been dissolved and, in 2003, the State Asset Management Commission was created to control 196 of the largest, many of which are treated as 'national champions'. Official figures suggest a dramatic reduction in SOE losses. The OECD published estimates suggesting that in 2003 SOEs accounted for 27% of business output, 'collective companies' for 8% and private companies, widely defined, for 63%.

The government's current priorities include 'harmonious society' (involving consultation, the rule of law, increased social spending and a focus on less developed regions and on environmental and quality of life issues), as well as on shifting economic growth away from investment towards consumption. It is eager to maintain social and political stability in the run-up to the 17th Party Congress in 2007 and the Summer Olympic Games in 2008.

2.1.4 Fiscal Policy

Until 2003, China's fiscal policy was expansionary and monetary policy loose, but the government has since tightened up on both. The lax attitude to credit led to a heavy burden of non-performing loans and the need to recapitalise the large state-owned banks repeatedly, in 1998, 1999 and 2003. Strenuous efforts are now being made to reform them, but there is a risk that over-investments will bring a new wave of bad loans as capacity outruns demand.

The government deficit has been reduced to around 1% of GDP and tax revenues were boosted from 11% of GDP in 1995 to 20% in 2004. The national debt is modest (around 22% of GDP in 2006) and China's foreign exchange reserves are the world's largest.

2.2 Financial Indicators

2.2.1 Inflation

Inflation has tended to be nil or negligible in China in recent years. After a brief upturn in 2004, it fell back to 1.8% in 2005 and 1.7% in 2006. However, it is likely to increase to about 3% a year in 2007-2008 because of rising food, fuel, utilities and housing prices, and (in urban areas) rising healthcare and education costs.

China's extraordinarily rapid growth is having a well-publicised effect on international commodity and oil prices. Chinese producers' raw materials prices were reported to be up about 12% in 2004, 8% in 2005 and 6% in 2006. However, these increases are not reflected in consumer prices for manufactured goods, which are broadly stable or even declining slightly. Manufacturers report that they cannot pass on production costs to consumers.

There has been much discussion about the likely effect of excess capacity in the Chinese steel industry within the next two or three years on international and domestic steel prices, and steel prices have recently shown signs of extraordinary volatility. This is clearly not the only sector where such fears are reasonable.

The government has been asking the banks to restrain the supply of credit (especially for property), and the central bank raised official interest rates and bank reserve requirements in both 2006 and 2007. In practice lending tends to be based on the relationships between companies, banks and local politicians rather than on interest rates, and the government has been seeking other means of restraining lending and reducing liquidity (including a more relaxed attitude to investments abroad and to a rising yuan/ renminbi).

Figure 2.8 Other Economic/Financial Indicators, 2001-2006

Indicators		2001	2002	2003	2004	2005	2006	AAGR[a] (%)
Population (million)		1,279	1,287	1,296	1,304	1,313	1,321	0.6
GDP per capita (US$)		1,030	1,130	1,270	1,485	1,735	1,990	14.1
Inflation (%)		0.5	-0.7	1.2	3.8	1.8	1.3	–
Exchange rates:	Rmb : US$	8.28	8.28	8.28	8.28	8.19	7.97	-0.8
	Rmb : €	7.41	7.79	9.34	10.28	10.19	10.08	6.3

a) AAGR = Average annual growth rate 2001-2006.

Sources: IMF; Economist Intelligence Unit (EIU), United Nations.

2.2.2 Exchange Rates

China's local currency, the yuan (or renminbi) was effectively pegged to the US dollar at Rmb 8.28 : US$ 1.00 for eleven years. In July 2005, after intense international pressure and speculation, the government announced that it was shifting to a 'managed floating exchange rate regime' based on a basket of currencies with daily revisions to the central parities. Daily variations would be permitted of up to 0.3% against the dollar and 1.5% (later revised to 3%) against other currencies.

The immediate revaluation against the US dollar, of 2.1% to Rmb 8.11, was very modest, and for a while it drifted upwards only very gradually. However, from September 2006 (when it was trading at around Rmb 7.95 to the US dollar) it began to rise more rapidly; it had risen to Rmb 7.82 by the end of the year (cf. figure 2.8 and 2.9) and has continued to rise in 2007.

Figure 2.9 Exchange rate Chinese yuan/renminbi vs US$ and €, 2002-2007

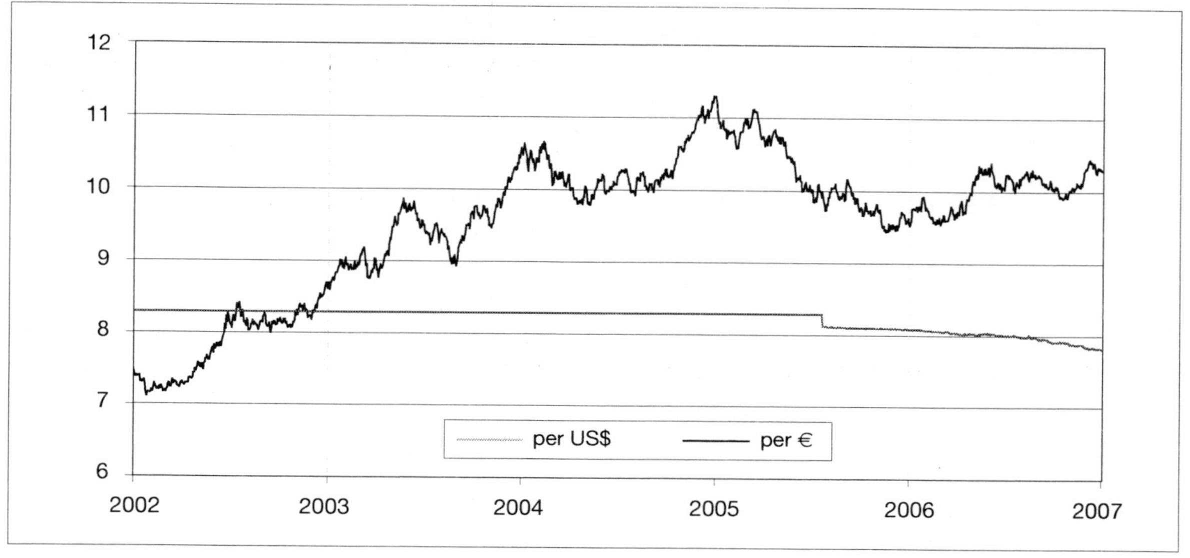

Source: UNWTO from De Nederlandse Bank.

Foreign exchange controls are being progressively relaxed by the Bank of China. Chinese citizens can take up to US$ 5,000 in foreign currency with them on their trips abroad of up to six months. For visits expected to last longer, they can convert the equivalent of US$ 8,000. Outbound travellers can also buy foreign currency themselves, rather than having to go through a travel agency.

2.2.3 Spending Power

GDP per capita in nominal US dollar terms was estimated at US$ 1,990 in 2006 (cf. figure 2.8 above). It has been rising by about 17% a year in US dollar terms (recently a little less in renminbi terms). Much of this increase is going into investment. It is estimated that private consumption increased in real terms by about 7% a year in 2004-2006. The government is trying to shift the focus of growth from investment towards consumption.

In 2003, it was estimated that average disposable incomes were still only around Rmb 4,500 (US$ 543) and that fewer than 100 million people had disposable incomes of over US$ 2,000. But, as already indicated, there are great disparities in incomes across the regions, which are causing the government concern. Incomes in rural areas have generally been growing more slowly than those in urban areas, but this trend may have been reversed by the increase in food prices since 2004.

In mid-2004, average incomes of official residents in urban areas were quoted to be Rmb 7,590, up about 15% in a year, compared with Rmb 2,110, up 17%, in rural areas. The real disparity in incomes is, however, much greater, because people in rural areas must pay for agricultural inputs and for numerous local fees and taxes, while those in urban areas receive greater benefits, including housing, education, health and electricity. In 2003 the National Bureau of Statistics reckoned the true ratio between rural and urban incomes might be 6:1, and that the average disposable income for consumer spending in rural areas was only Rmb 180 per person.

The government is raising subsidies for rural areas and instructing local governments to reduce their fees and agricultural taxes. In 2006 it rolled out a programme to phase out education fees in rural areas, and a programme to reduce the burden of healthcare is to follow.

The total labour force was officially put at 737 million in 2002. Of these, roughly 500 million are classified as 'rural'. This includes about 130 million people employed in township and village enterprises (TVEs) and over 150 million who have migrated 'illegally' to the cities in search of work. The formal urban labour force is around 200 million.

Official unemployment was 4.2% (8 million people) in mid-2005. Real unemployment is higher: the official figures essentially cover registered urban workers, and unemployment is much higher among migrants to urban areas and in rural areas. There is also a good deal of underemployment.

2.2.4 Monthly Incomes in Urban Areas

Despite China's gargantuan size, the number of extremely affluent households is very limited. Households with annual incomes of more than Rmb 160,000 (US$ 20,460) make up a mere 0.3% of China's total urban households, and only 30,000 households earn more than Rmb 400,000 (US$ 51,150) a year.

China nevertheless has a growing middle class. The nation is estimated to have 300 million households. More than 10% (involving say 150 million people) earn over US$ 3,000 a year. The incomes of urban households in the three major regions of Beijing, Shanghai and the whole of Guangdong Province for the month of September 2005 are shown in the following table.

Figure 2.10 Average Incomes of Urban Households, September 2005

	Number of households (× 1,000)	Total monthly income		Disposable monthly income	
		(Rmb)	(US$)	(Rmb)	(US$)
All China	54,494	944	117	875	108
Beijing	2,000	1,632	202	1,468	182
Shanghai	1,000	1,689	209	1,512	187
Guangdong	1,600	1,312	162	1,186	147

Source: National Bureau of Statistics (NBS).

2.3 Government's Role in Travel and Tourism

The China National Tourism Administration (CNTA) is the government body responsible for the tourism industry, and it plays a central role in regulating and overseeing China's travel and tourism. CNTA is directly regulated by the State Council and is responsible for developing, promoting and regulating China's inbound, domestic and outbound tourism industries. The Public Security Bureau (PSB) is in charge of monitoring and issuing passports to mainland Chinese nationals.

Although regulations are complex and difficult to deal with, it is fair to say that – as discussed in more detail in chapter 6 – rules regarding outbound travel, travel agency licensing and foreign tour operations, etc are being steadily relaxed, in line with the requirements of China's membership of the World Trade Organization (WTO).

As an example, CNTA announced in June 2007 that it would cancel the limit on foreign travel agencies' forming of branches in China from the following month. It said it would offer the same treatment to foreign travel agencies as to domestic travel agencies, as part of its commitments to the WTO. At the same time, CNTA is actively encouraging Chinese travel companies to run businesses in foreign destinations.

Another important step recently taken by the Chinese Government was to enact a new law "to create a sustainable travel industry", to quote CNTA. Known as the Chinese Citizens Outbound Travel Contract, it is an agreement that is to be signed between travel agencies and travellers and is applicable to Chinese mainland travel agencies and outbound travel groups, excluding FIT travellers.

The new law, according to the Chinese Government, is aimed at regulating the outbound travel environment and is to promote a healthy relationship between travel agents and consumers by protecting the interests of travel agents and consumers. More details of this law and its implications for foreign tour operators are provided in chapter 6.

2.4 Passports

Despite the progressive easing of regulations, China is still one of the few countries in the world where outbound travel restrictions are still a major factor. Three types of passport have basically been available to the Chinese:

- 'Private' passports, issued by the Ministry of Foreign Affairs.
- 'Public' passports, for official (i.e. government and business) travel – usually sponsored by foreign companies – obtained from the Ministry of Public Security.
- Passports for seamen, obtained from the Ministry of Communications.

Public passports have been, and continue to be, issued to a wide range of traveller categories, although it is mostly non-holiday travellers who use these passports. Private passports are issued to Chinese visiting friends and relatives (VFR) and some other leisure travellers. From 2005, ordinary private passports were – in theory, at least – available to "most citizens on production of an ID and a proof of residence", to quote CNTA. In early 2006, there were reportedly 6.2 million Chinese with private passports.

Business travellers can in practice travel abroad on either public or private passports. Since the late-1990s and the introduction of the ADS scheme, due to the rapid growth in demand for holiday travel, a new type of passport has also been available – 'tourism passports'. These are generally issued for one year and cover one exit and entry.

The validity of some other passports, meanwhile, has been extended to five years. Before this, they were also only valid for a single trip.

2.5 Approved Destination Status (ADS)

The first phase of China's outbound tourism started in 1983 with so-called 'family visits', first to Hong Kong, China, and Macao, China, and later to several South-East Asian countries, ostensibly paid for by the receiving side. This policy provided the opportunity for the development of outbound leisure tourism by offering a way of obtaining the necessary passports, foreign currency and visas. At the same time, the beginning of China's integration into the world economy resulted in a growing number of delegations travelling to the leading global players to attend fairs, business meetings, training programmes, technical visits, etc. Almost all these trips had some kind of 'tourism' element, and many were in fact simply leisure trips in disguise paid for by public or government money or, in some cases, arranged by foreign business partners.

The second phase started in 1997 with the official recognition of the existence of outbound leisure tourism (as opposed to family reunions and business trips) in the 'Provisional Regulation on the Management of Outbound Travel by Chinese Citizens at Their Own Expense'. This resulted in the development of the ADS scheme soon after, although group travel abroad was limited to neighbouring countries until 1999.

The ADS scheme is based on bilateral agreements, which permit Chinese travelling as part of a leisure tour group, and paying for their trip themselves, to travel to the specific destination with a special visa. Only ADS countries can openly be promoted as tourism destinations in China (cf. chapter 7). Some 132 destination countries now have ADS status (cf. annex I), although the scheme has not yet come into effect in all of them.

ADS is granted to countries that fulfil certain conditions to enable them to receive leisure tour groups from China. Destinations that do not have ADS can still receive visitors from China – but not leisure tour groups, which has been the fastest-growing sector of the market in recent years.

Australia was the first western destination to obtain ADS, in 1997 (it came into effect two years later), followed by New Zealand, and Germany was the first major West European country, in 2002. (There were a few smaller countries that beat Germany to it – Malta being one example). Most of the established

EU member countries finalised ADS negotiations en bloc in April 2004, welcoming their first Chinese leisure tour groups in September of the same year (cf. 'The Memorandum of Understanding' signed between the EU and China, available online at http://www.etc-intranet.org /DWL/mou_291003_en.pdf). The new EU member countries, who joined in May 2004 and January 2007 – and which did not already have ADS – were approved automatically on becoming EU members (cf. annex I).

ADS agreements are complex:

- They involve three government departments in China – the Ministries of Foreign Affairs and of Public Security, and CNTA, which is the national tourism administration, equivalent to a tourism ministry and NTO rolled into one. In the receiving country, the same – or similar – departments/ agencies are involved – Immigration, Foreign Affairs and the NTO. (This system excludes privatised NTOs and trade bodies such as the Travel Industry Association of America.)
- As already indicated, ADS covers only Chinese travelling as part of a leisure tour group out of China – with the added stipulation for most countries of a minimum five participants in each group. Business travel, government/official travel – 'public' travel – and some other types of travel, such as students going abroad for education, sports travel, or incentives, are not included.
- The ADS system was initially a means of restricting the number of Chinese travellers going abroad (for economic reasons) and of reducing the risk of travellers not returning to China and seeking immigration in the host country – legally or illegally. The economic concern has reduced as China has grown richer, but illegal emigration continues to be a critical factor.
- ADS specifies the number and names of travel agencies in China that can send leisure tour groups to other countries, and the number and names of inbound agencies in the receiving destinations. (An up-to-date list can be found at http://www.cnta.gov.cn/ziliao/other/oumeng22.asp). There may be other requirements, such as limiting destinations to receive travellers only from specific areas such as Beijing, Shanghai and/or Guangdong province.

The current thinking is that ADS will be phased out within one or two years. Meanwhile, requirements are expected to become looser and implementation less strict as the Chinese Government improves checks and controls on travellers applying for tourism passports and increasingly cooperates with foreign governments to limit the number of 'tourists' who overstay their visas. Leisure group travellers are also usually expected to deposit a sum of money with their travel agent to help ensure that they do come back to the country. This averages Rmb 30,000-50,000 (US$ 3,000-5,000) – and is invariably on the higher side for European destinations. But illegal emigration appears to be mainly prevalent among travellers from just a few regions of China, not the main tourism generating centres.

2.6 Visa Issues

2.6.1 General Regulations and Visa Fees

Although visa applications for Chinese leisure group travellers are the responsibility of their travel agents, the process of applying for and obtaining a visa can be arduous and lengthy, not to mention expensive. Some believe that it is a deterrent to tourism demand from markets such as China, especially for non-Schengen countries.

In theory, if not always in practice, Chinese citizens can travel with one visa across 15 Schengen countries – i.e. the five founding members of the Schengen Agreement and the ten which signed up in 1996 (cf. annex II) – for up to 90 days for leisure or business purposes. The ten new EU members that joined in May 2004 have also signed the Schengen Agreement and, with the exception of Cyprus, are set to implement the Treaty sometime in early 2008.

It is difficult to provide accurate information on visa fees for Schengen and non-Schengen countries, or even countries within Schengen, as average fees vary, and they usually involve additional charges for processing – e.g. for photocopying, translation, and sometimes despatch of passports to the country of the issuing government (not for ADS visas), etc.

The main differences in the visa situation from one country to another are cost and timeliness. The average cost of a Schengen visa was increased from € 35 to 60 in 2007, but this is still deemed reasonable compared with the current € 98 (£ 65) for a standard tourist visa for the United Kingdom. And visa fees for students have risen even more sharply. The initial fee is now € 54 (£ 36) but the cost of extensions runs into several hundred euros (as well as pounds sterling).

2.6.2 Absconding Tourists and Other Misdemeanours

However, there are a number of weaknesses with the Schengen visa system. Visas cannot be issued for stays of more than 90 days and they cannot be extended. In addition, while applications for Schengen visas to some Schengen member governments take only a few days, for others the processing time can be more than three weeks.

Since the ADS system in Europe is relatively new and there has been a high incidence of Chinese absconding while on holiday in the region, European governments are understandably more strict than usual in issuing visas. In fact, a number of European governments suspended visa issuance for Chinese tourists for different periods in 2005 and 2006 because of abuse of the system. But the problems to date are widely seen as teething problems and are expected to ease in due course.

The situation facing national tourism organizations (NTOs) is summed up neatly by VisitBritain, which admits that it suffers from an ambivalent position in China. On the one hand, the granting of visas is a sensitive political issue for the Home Office, which is very anxious to be seen to have illegal immigration under control; on the other, there is a strong commercial drive to extend tourism revenue from the Department of Culture, Media and Sport.

For group tours from China based on ADS visas, the travel agent takes care of the group application, as already indicated, so the process is more streamlined than in some countries. The travel agent is responsible for carrying out the first checks and recommending each traveller for a visa.

Travellers to most parts of Europe pay the Chinese travel agent a deposit of Rmb 50,000 (around € 5,000), which is only reimbursed at the end of the trip, i.e. when the traveller returns to China. Travel agents in China have been known to keep quiet about a traveller who has absconded on a trip and to have pocketed the deposit, but the punishment is very severe, so the practice is not widespread.

The length of the suspension for travel agents held responsible for misdemeanours seems to vary according to the misdemeanour. It is not just a matter of losing clients altogether, but also, for instance, failing to sift out a dodgy application in the first place, or changing the tour itinerary or a hotel without informing the authorities in advance – something that is often unavoidable for ground handlers in Europe.

2.6.3 The United Kingdom's Outsourcing of Visa Processing

In a drive to speed up visa processing in China and cut costs, the British Government – like some others – has outsourced visa processing to a network of Visa Application Centres (VACs) that are considered by the industry and the British Council to be very efficient.

Would-be Chinese travellers to the United Kingdom are reportedly put through rigorous inspection. First, the travel agent must screen the tour applicant and only passes on applications to the VACs that look genuine. Then the visa office of the Embassy and/or Consulate General in Beijing, Shanghai and Guangzhou also scrutinises the application.

2.6.4 Australia Case Study

Tourism Australia says that one of the main attractions of the ADS visa is that the whole process from application to granting of the visa (at least for Australia) involves a 3-4 day turnaround, while other visas require two weeks' processing. For this reason, Australian inbound operators and agents often use the ADS scheme simply to speed up visa processing for individual travellers (FITs).

Within the ADS-approved agency framework, Tourism Australia appoints and trains 'Aussie Specialists'. In early 2006, there were 75 travel companies in China specialised in selling Australia and 505 individual travel consultants with Aussie Specialist accreditation, as well as another 750 consultants undertaking accreditation training.

In addition, the Australian Department of Immigration, Multicultural and Indigenous Affairs (DIMIA) has trained and appointed Aussie Specialist companies to process and assist with the distribution of Australian tourist visas. This is a value-added service which, Tourism Australia believes, gives Australia a competitive edge over other destinations.

According to Tourism Australia, the ADS scheme has been extremely successful in providing an avenue for large numbers of Chinese tourists to visit Australia, while ensuring high levels of integrity and compliance with visa conditions. From the inception of the scheme in August 1999 to 30 June 2005, around 170,000 tourists travelled to Australia on ADS visas and the level of misdemeanours, including the number of Chinese absconding during their trip, has been extremely low.

The system of visa issuance developed by DIMIA, in conjunction with Tourism Australia, is reportedly operating well. The Aussie Specialist agents are designated through a three-tiered system according to ability, knowledge and track record. Level 1 agents have access to full electronic processing and issuance. Level 2 agents have access to electronic processing and manual visa issuance, while level 3 agents have visas processed and issued manually.

A special courier service ensures a secure collection and delivery service for passports between Aussie Specialist agents and the three issuing posts in China. Processing time for passports sent through Aussie Specialist agents is three days, whereas for other agents it averages 15 days.

Other avenues for issuing visas for travel to Australia include:

- reliable business partners;
- the Sponsored Family Visitor programme;
- the APEC (Asia Pacific Economic Co-operation) Business Travel Card;
- the Sponsored Business Visitor programme;
- Australia's International Event Coordinator Network;
- the Student Visa Programme.

Each has its own application processing system, and some visas are processed and issued electronically.

2.7 Holiday Entitlement

As China is predominantly an agrarian society involved with subsistence farming, paid holidays are not standard throughout the country. But for those not involved in agriculture, the amount of paid leave has been growing. In 1992, a week-long holiday was introduced for government employees and those working in larger companies. In 1994 the average week for these workers was reduced to 44 hours; in 1995 it was further reduced to 40 hours, establishing an effective five-day week. This has resulted in increased weekend trips – mainly to domestic destinations, but also to Hong Kong, China, Macao, China, the Republic of Korea and Thailand.

In 1999 the three so-called Golden Weeks were established, and these remain the principal holiday periods:

- Spring Festival – Lunar/Chinese New Year – is on the first day of the first month of the lunar calendar. Officially, Spring Festival lasts for three days but many people take a week off work.
- May Week, which includes International Labour Day (1 May) and National Youth Day (4 May).
- The National Holiday, which includes 1 October, National Day that marks the anniversary of the founding of the People's Republic of China.

According to a report by the dean of the tourism administration department at Beijing International Studies University, the Chinese Government is likely to shorten the Golden Week holidays and declare public holidays on dates of other traditional festivals by 2009. Speaking at a forum in Xiamen, Fujian Province, Zhang Hui revealed that the May Day and the National Day holidays may be shortened, while only the Lunar New Year Golden Week would be preserved. Traditional Chinese festivals like the Mid-Autumn Festival and the Lantern Festival may be chosen as public holidays to make up for lost holidays.

This decision comes in the light of feedback from domestic tourism experts that the current volume of domestic travel during the holidays is threatening many heritage sites and scenic spots, and there are increasing appeals to cancel the Golden Weeks to reduce congestion at these times.

A full list of official Chinese public holidays for 2007 is included in annex V.

Chapter 3

Aviation Overview

3.1 Background

3.1.1 The World's Second Largest Civil Aviation Market by 2020

No analysis of China's travel potential can ignore the contribution that aviation is making – and will increasingly make – to the market's growth. The country currently has 142 airports open to commercial aviation, with no less than 108 new airports either under construction or on the drawing board, for completion by 2020. Although only a few of these airports handle international flights, and most such flights are to neighbouring countries of North-East and South-East Asia, demand for international traffic is growing almost as fast as that for domestic traffic.

The forecasts for air transport to, from and within China over the next 20 or so years are staggering. US aircraft manufacturer Boeing believes China will be the world's second largest civil aviation market, after the United States of America, by 2019, accounting for 10% of the world's total passenger aircraft by that time.

European Airbus, meanwhile – whose forecasts for China are very similar to Boeing's – estimates that the Chinese mainland passenger fleet will more than triple in the 20 years from 2005 to 2025, from 760 to 2,700 passenger aircraft. The total value of the new and replacement planes required for the massive expansion is estimated at US$ 368 billion.

The drivers of China's aviation expansion include economic growth of at least 8% annually for the next decade, progressive liberalisation of the market, and fast growth in household spending on transport. Airbus predicts airlines will have a potential market of 650 million consumers by 2015, and this will combine with a big wave in Chinese outbound tourism and the nation's emergence as a major tourism and business destination.

Airbus is pinning its hopes on the country as a major market for its double-decker A380 super jumbo, predicting that more than 110 will be required to serve long-haul, intra-Asian and domestic trunk routes. But it also anticipates the opening of 110 long-haul routes to and from China requiring small to intermediate twin-aisle aircraft. The biggest explosion in terms of aircraft numbers will nevertheless be on domestic routes, which are expected to grow in terms of traffic demand by 11.3% per annum.

3.1.2 Reorganization of Civil Aviation

The Civil Aviation Administration of China (CAAC) was formed at the time of the creation of the People's Republic of China in 1949 to oversee all aspects of civil aviation in China, including operation of the country's airline. CAAC was therefore the China's supreme civil aviation body, with responsibilities unparalleled in the western world.

In 1984 a plan was announced to reorganise civil aviation. CAAC would cease to exist as an airline and, in its new role as the civil aviation body, it would "set up a number of airline companies operating separately on international and domestic air routes". The six new airlines (with the roles defined at the time) were:

- Air China – based in Beijing and operating mainly international and some domestic routes;
- China Eastern Airlines – based in Shanghai, operating mainly domestic routes, but also to Japan and Hong Kong, China;
- China Southern Airlines – based in Guangzhou, operating mainly domestic routes, but also to Hong Kong, China, and to some South-East Asian countries;
- China Southwest Airlines – based in Chengdu and operating mainly domestic routes and 'some' international routes (only Hong Kong, China, was named);
- China Northwest Airlines – based in Xian and operating domestic routes and to Hong Kong, China; and
- China Northern Airlines – based in Shenyang and operating mainly domestic routes and 'some' international routes (only Hong Kong, China, was named).

This set-up continued until 2000, when CAAC moved to a phase of consolidation and rationalisation of the country's air transport industry. It decided that the biggest (CAAC-owned) airlines would be combined – either through mergers or alliances – into just three airlines: Air China, China Eastern and China Southern. A report in 2001 clarified these plans:

- Beijing-based Air China would acquire China Southwest and CNAC (a holding company that owned a small share in Cathay Pacific and sizeable shares in Dragonair and Air Macau);
- Shanghai-based China Eastern would acquire China Northwest and Yunnan;
- Guangzhou-based China Southern would acquire China Northern and Xinjiang. (It already had a majority share of Xiamen Airlines.)

Those mergers took place in 2003 and, with the formal completion of the consolidation process in 2004, CAAC again began cautiously to issue new operating licenses. This so-called 'post-consolidation' phase follows extensive airline mergers and acquisitions in recent years. The new phase is also characterised by rapid traffic growth stimulated by liberalisation, deregulation and new airline entry. Domestic passenger numbers, for example, grew by 16.7% in the first half of 2007.

However, despite the strong underlying traffic growth, China's major carriers are still struggling to convert this into profitability. High fuel prices, increasing debt levels and rising operating costs (notably staffing costs, largely due to the difficulties of merging several airlines and keeping up with rapid growth) continue to damage earnings.

In August 2007, CAAC announced that it would not entertain any new airline applications until 2010, meaning there will be no new airlines in China until 2011 at the earliest.

3.2 The Air Transport Environment

Figure 3.1 Airports in China, 2006

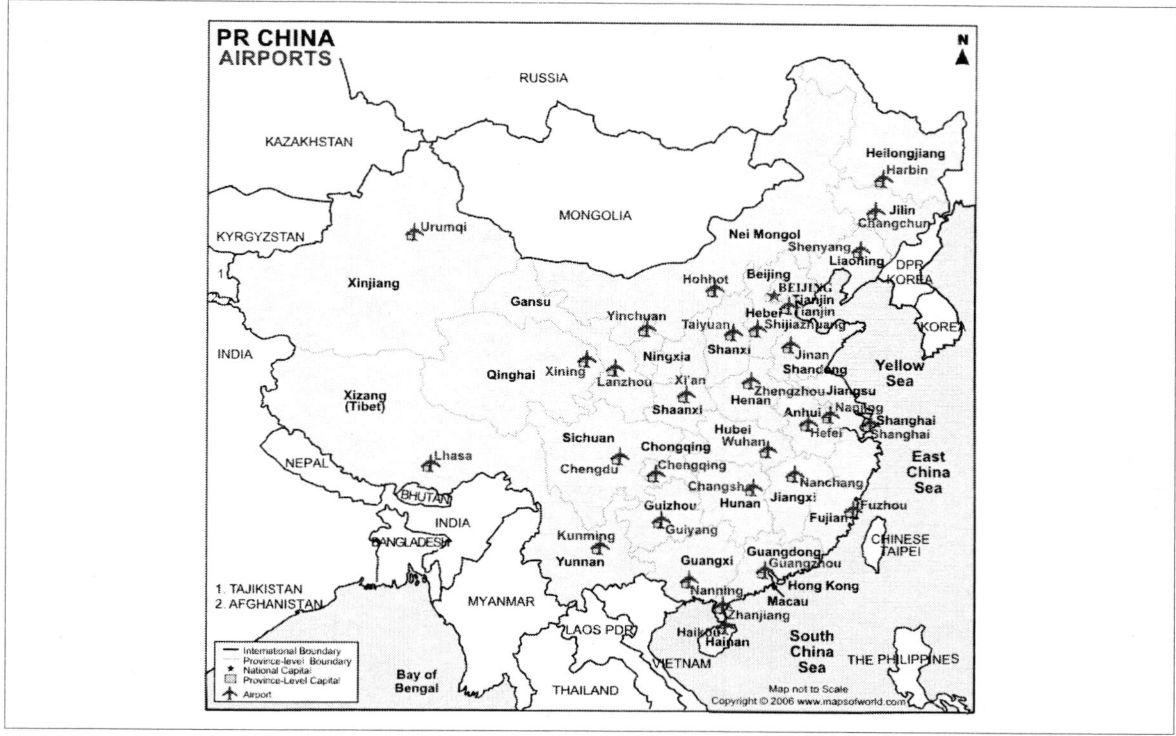

Source: Maps of the World (www.mapsofworld.com).

3.2.1 Airport Capacity Severely Strained

China's 142 airports (excluding those in the Chinese Special Administrative Regions of Hong Kong and Macao) handled 330 million passengers in 2006, up 16% on 2005. Domestic traffic strongly dominates, with a share of more than 90% of the total last year. Total airport passenger numbers are predicted to increase rapidly, on the back of the surging Chinese economy, to around 560 million passengers by the end of this decade. However, growth may well be stymied by airport congestion.

Airports throughout China are straining from a lack of infrastructure, but the impact is being felt most at major hubs. The number of flights at Beijing's Capital International Airport, China's busiest, are already being cut by 336 flights a day, with the reductions occurring in phases through October. Prior to the cuts, Capital Airport had more than 60 flight movements an hour at peak times, and over 1,000 per day.

Under China's 11th Five-Year Plan, US$ 17.5 billion is being spent on airport expansion and construction. While a portion of this will go to airport expansion in Beijing, Guangzhou and Shanghai, US$ 6.67 billion will go to airports in China's western regions. Flights to these new and upgraded airports are causing capacity and safety issues at major hubs where infrastructure has not kept up with the growing number of flights from China's hinterlands.

3.2.2 The 'Big Three' Dominate International Routes

China's consolidation strategy has resulted in the 'big three' airlines controlling some 65% of total seats offered in the domestic market today, as well as 90% of the international capacity operated by mainland Chinese airlines.

The largest, in terms of seats per week, is Guangzhou-based China Southern Airlines, which last year carried some 49 million passengers – three times more than neighbouring Cathay Pacific Airways. The carrier offers almost 1.3 million seats per week across its network. China Eastern is the second largest carrier in terms of seats, followed by Air China. However, China Southern comes third to Air China and China Eastern in terms of international passenger numbers (even though China Southern operates to more destinations outside China).

Figure 3.2 Leading Chinese Airlines, 2007[a]

Airline	Passengers (overall seat load factor) 2006	Fleet, March 2007	Number of destinations served, 2007 (international)	Main hubs	Airline alliance[b]
Air China	34.0 million (75.9%)	194 49 Airbus 135 Boeing	184 (42)	Beijing Chengdu Chongqing Hangzhou Tianjin	Star Alliance
China Eastern	35.0 million (71.3%)	207 111 Airbus 74 Boeing	103 (43)	Shanghai-Hongqiao Shanghai-Pudong Kunming Xian Nanjing Wuhan	OneWorld
China Southern	49.0 million (71.7%)	262 103 Airbus 150 Boeing	121 (58)	Guangzhou Beijing Dalian Shenzhen Shenyang Urumqi Wuhan	SkyTeam
Hainan Airlines	14.4 million (75.4%)	125 11 Airbus 73 Boeing 29 Dornier	90 (10)	Haikou Lingbo Beijing Sanya Taiyuan Tianjin Urumqi Xian	OneWorld *(aspiring to)*
Shandong Airlines	5.4 million (73.4%)[c]	32 22 Boeing 10 Bombardier	46 (2)	Jinan Quingdao Yantai	-
Shanghai Airlines	7.5 million (69.2%)	49 43 Boeing	66 (7)	Shanghai-Hongqiao Shanghai-Pudong Hangzhou Nanjing	Star Alliance

Airline	Passengers (overall seat load factor) 2006	Fleet, March 2007	Number of destinations served, 2007 (international)	Main hubs	Airline alliance[b]
Shenzhen Airlines	7.1 million (77.9%)[c]	45 9 Airbus 36 Boeing	60 (3)	Shenzhen Guangzhou Nanning Shenyang Wuxi Zhengzhou	-
Xiamen Airlines	> 7.0 million (79.6%)[c]	43 43 Boeing	54 (7)	Xiamen Fuzhou	

a) Airlines with at least a minimum of international services.

b) Actual or planned.

c) 2005 data.

Source: LC Associates, based on data provided by respective airlines, the Centre for Asia Pacific Aviation (CAPA) and *Air Transport World.*

3.2.3 The Leading Players

Air China enjoys a favourable (and favoured) position, with its main base in the capital city Beijing, and it has traditionally been the country's main flag carrier, with the bulk of China's international traffic rights. In 2006 it served an estimated 42 international destinations, including several in Europe (cf. annex III). Its passenger count was just under 34 million and it made an operating profit of € 257 million on a turnover of € 4.27 billion. Traffic is forecast to increase by 12.7% in 2007, with average seat load rising to 77%.

In May 2006 the airline signed a cooperation agreement with Lufthansa, opening the door to membership of Star Alliance, which it is expected to join in early 2008. The same year, following Hong Kong-based Cathay Pacific's acquisition of Dragonair (which finally gave it the right to operate to mainland China), Air China and Cathay Pacific signed a network co-operation agreement, which will probably result in an exchange of shares, as well as the creation of a joint freight subsidiary, based in Shanghai.

Air China's sister company, China National Aviation Corporation (CNAC), owns 11% of China Eastern – increased from 9.9% in September 2007 – and Air China is also the majority shareholder in Shandong Airlines, Air China Cargo and Air Macau.

It was also announced in September 2007 that a 24% stake in **China Eastern** was being sold to Singapore Airlines. Until a deal is concluded, China Eastern's ownership is split roughly 62% in the hands of the Chinese Government and 38% among private shareholders. The airline is due to become a member of the OneWorld alliance, although the decision may be changed if Singapore Airlines becomes a shareholder (the Singaporean carrier is a member of Star Alliance).

Founded in 1988 and based in Shanghai, China Eastern was the first airline in China to be listed on the stock exchange. It was Shanghai's rise as an international business hub that helped propel China Eastern to become the country's largest international airline, although its financial situation has been fairly precarious for some time. In 2006 it made an operating loss of € 266.5 million on a turnover of € 3.5 billion. This has nevertheless not stopped the carrier's expansion plans. In 2007 it is due to take delivery of more than 20 aircraft and is forecasting an increase of 22% in passengers carried over the year.

China Eastern handled just over 35 million passengers overall in 2007, up 44.3% over 2005, operating 423 routes – 299 domestic, 19 regional – to and from Hong Kong, China, and Macao, China – and 105 international.

China Southern, which is set to join the SkyTeam alliance, is based in Guangzhou. As already indicated, it is China's largest carrier – both in terms of passengers carried and number of flights. But international passenger traffic accounts for just 6.3% of its total weekly seats as against 13% for China Eastern and 12% for Air China. (The respective share is less than 5% for all other Chinese carriers, with the exception of Shanghai Airlines which, along with Air China, is preparing to join the Star Alliance.)

After three years of losses, China Southern made a profit of € 17.9 million in 2006 on a turnover of € 4.4 billion. The airline is expected to see a rise in profits in 2007, as well as in passenger traffic – forecast to increase to 60 million, up 22% over 2006 – thanks in no small part to an expansion of its fleet to 300 aircraft by the end of 2007, as well as significant route expansion.

Since the beginning of this year, China Southern has launched new services to Siem Reap, Vientiane, Rangoon and Phuket from Guangzhou, plus a second daily frequency to Ho Chi Minh City. New routes are also being opened to different countries of Central Asia.

A fourth pillar of Chinese aviation is rapidly emerging, according to the Sydney-based Centre for Asia Pacific Aviation (CAPA). **Grand China Airlines,** a company established in 2004 as the vehicle for merging the major aviation assets of Hainan Airlines, Xinhua Air, Changan Air and Shanxi Air, has cleared a major hurdle in receiving its operating licence from the CAAC. The move paves the way for Grand China Airlines to complete a planned listing in Hong Kong, China, possibly as early as the second half of 2007. The listing, which could raise up to US$ 500 million, would be a huge achievement for a carrier with roots in the resort island of Hainan in the South China Sea.

Hainan Airlines has been shedding its leisure routes and focusing on the main business centres, particularly Beijing and Tianjin. It also already operates a number of international routes – to Osaka, Seoul's Incheon, Bangkok, Brussels, Budapest and Novisibirsk, as well as St Petersburg and Geneva since summer 2007 – and clearly has greater aspirations on the world stage.

Xiamen Airlines, which is 60% owned by China Southern, is the fifth largest airline in China, followed by the carriers established in the 1990s by municipal and provincial governments: **Shenzhen Airlines** (based just over the border from Hong Kong, China), **Shanghai Airlines, Sichuan Airlines** (based in Chengdu in Western China) and **Shandong Airlines,** with bases at Qingdao and Jinan in the coastal region of Eastern China.

3.3 International Airline Services

3.3.1 Chinese Traffic Rights Currently Underutilised

Internationally, China's carriers still have some miles to travel, to quote the Centre for Asia Pacific Aviation (CAPA). Traffic rights in key markets like the United States of America are under-utilised by the Chinese airlines, due to their lack of brand recognition and their limitations to distribute their product effectively in foreign markets. In the short term, this increases the pressure for membership in a global alliance, to help enhance market presence.

The first airline group to make the international breakthrough – which will inevitably be Air China/Cathay Pacific – will then have the advantage of being able to generate much greater domestic hub operations. This joint power is substantial, even though the global alliance outcome (Cathay in OneWorld, and Air China in the Star Alliance) remains unclear. This makes 2007-2008 a critical period for China's aviation industry. It is impossible to underrate the importance of the 2008 Summer Olympics in the wider scheme. As Air China/Cathay Pacific positions itself effectively internationally, so Air China's ability to hub through the mainland will give it an enormous edge over its competitors in the domestic market.

3.3.2 Routes to Europe

Although cutbacks in airline frequencies have since been made by CAAC to ease congestion, as already indicated, it recently approved 27 new international routes to Europe and America, which are scheduled to open in the next two years. In addition, 206 more flights a week are planned on existing routes to Europe and America. The new routes will be operated by Air China, China Southern, China Eastern, Shanghai Airlines and Hainan Airlines.

In addition to Air China, China Eastern, Shanghai and Hainan Airlines, nearly 20 European carriers now operate direct scheduled services from China to Europe, including most of the region's national flag carriers. In August 2007, according to SRS Analyser, the total number of direct flights weekly was 289 – or 406 including flights from Hong Kong, China. Travel via Hong Kong, China, is a popular routing for Chinese heading to Europe. The number of weekly seats available on direct outbound flights to Europe, meanwhile (i.e. excluding flights via Hong Kong, China), was 81,681.

Air China operates the highest number of frequencies from mainland China (65 in August 2007), ahead of Lufthansa (38) Air France (29), China Eastern (21) and KLM (20). But a further five airlines (Finnair, British Airways, China Southern, SAS and Aeroflot) have ten flights or more weekly direct to a European point – from Beijing, Shanghai and/or Guangzhou.

The following tables show the total weekly capacity in the months of January and August over the four years 2003-2006. Services from Hong Kong, China, are also included. A more detailed breakdown, including the respective airlines on each route, is provided in annex III.

Figure 3.3 Direct Scheduled Flight Capacity from China to Europe, 2003-2006

Departures/ week	January				Growth 03/06 (%)	August				Growth 03/06 (%)
	2003	2004	2005	2006		2003	2004	2005	2006	
Shanghai	31	45	87	126	306	50	72	97	91	82
Beijing	76	76	90	105	38	72	105	120	158	119
Guangzhou	0	5	13	25	400[a]	0	11	18	20	82[a]
Hong Kong, China	96	99	106	122	27	90	107	119	147	63
Total	**203**	**225**	**296**	**378**	**86**	**212**	**295**	**354**	**416**	**96**

a) 2004-2006.

Sources: Pacific Asia Travel Association (PATA); SRS Analyser.

Figure 3.4 Direct Scheduled Airline Seat Capacity from China to Europe, 2003-2006

Seats/week	January				Growth 03/06 (%)	August				Growth 03/06 (%)
	2003	2004	2005	2006		2003	2004	2005	2006	
Shanghai	8,653	13,120	26,069	32,105	271	15,787	22,097	29,577	25,388	61
Beijing	22,558	22,967	26,061	30,969	27	20,952	32,303	35,399	44,825	114
Guangzhou	0	1,300	2,463	6,517	400[a]	0	3,053	5,403	5,901	93[a]
Hong Kong, China	30,937	31,691	34,038	38,587	25	30,182	34,458	38,459	46,510	54
Total	**62,148**	**69,078**	**86,631**	**108,178**	**74**	**66,921**	**91,911**	**108,838**	**122,624**	**83**

a) 2004-2006.

Sources: Pacific Asia Travel Association (PATA); SRS Analyser.

3.3.3 European Airline Marketing Initiatives

European airlines are increasingly taking initiatives to strengthen their competitive positions in the Chinese market. Although it has fewer services a week than many of its direct competitors (12 out of mainland China), British Airways has taken a lead in launching a Chinese-language website targeting Chinese domestic students. Apart from providing such basic information as flight timetables, air ticket promotion and air agents' demography, the website also offers a large variety of travel and life related information to help Chinese students living in the United Kingdom. It is also providing Chinese-language services on the ground.

Air France's live broadcast of CCTV (mainland Chinese) news programmes on its flights caters for Chinese passengers' requirements. It also provides an interpreter on board for each flight operating to/from China, as well as Chinese-speaking staff at the airport to help Chinese tourists go through the various formalities. This is in addition to offering Chinese-language newspapers, magazines, films, and authentic Chinese food on board.

SAS also launched a Chinese-language website to enable Chinese passengers to know about the airline and book air tickets. The company is reportedly recruiting 34 Chinese-speaking hostesses to offer a hand in case of need. They will also provide Chinese-language publications on board. Finnair began to offer Chinese-language ground services at Helsinki Airport as early as two years ago, and the airline has also set up Chinese signs at the airport for the convenience of passengers from China.

Other examples of airlines catering to Chinese travelling to Europe include Austrian Airlines and Lufthansa, which publicise the fact that they provide Chinese food and newspapers inflight, and Lufthansa claims to have appointed a Chinese chef to prepare food for its passengers.

3.3.4 Outlook for European Airlines in China

The last few years have seen significant growth on airline routes into and out of China, not least to Europe – for which the increase in airline seat capacity between China and Europe has been staggering, up to 60% a year between 2003 and 2006. This compares with a relatively modest 10-15% rise in available seat capacity on routes to/from other parts of Asia over the past three years.

Several European airlines have increased frequencies or entered the market for the first time, and others are looking at inaugurating services. Nevertheless, despite the continuous growth in demand for travel to/from Europe and other intercontinental points, long-haul access to China will probably be restricted as long as China's flag carriers are unable to compete more effectively for foreign inbound travellers. And this situation will continue as long as their branding and offshore distribution problems remain unresolved – likely provoking the need for innovative foreign partnerships.

Chapter 4

The Outbound Travel Market

4.1 Overview of Trends and Forecasts

4.1.1 A Fast-Growing Market

China is one of the fastest growing outbound travel markets in the world. Its annual growth in outbound trip volume has averaged 22% since 2000 and just under 15.5% since 1995 (comparisons with earlier years are not reliable as the methodology for data collection was changed in 1995). In 2002, it overtook Japan as Asia's leading source market (in volume of trips abroad), and it extended its lead in 2003 despite the dampening effect of SARS, with a 22% increase in foreign trip volume, followed by a staggering 43% rise in 2004.

Perhaps unsurprisingly, the last two years have seen a slowdown in growth, but the annual increase has still been well above the regional and world averages. Moreover, in 2006, the market's outbound count of 34.5 million was almost double that generated by the Japanese (17.5 million), placing China among the top world travel source markets in terms of trip volume.[1] Preliminary estimates also suggest that China's outbound travel market will achieve another record year in 2007, exceeding 40 million trips.

Figure 4.1 Outbound Travel from China, 1990-2006 (million)

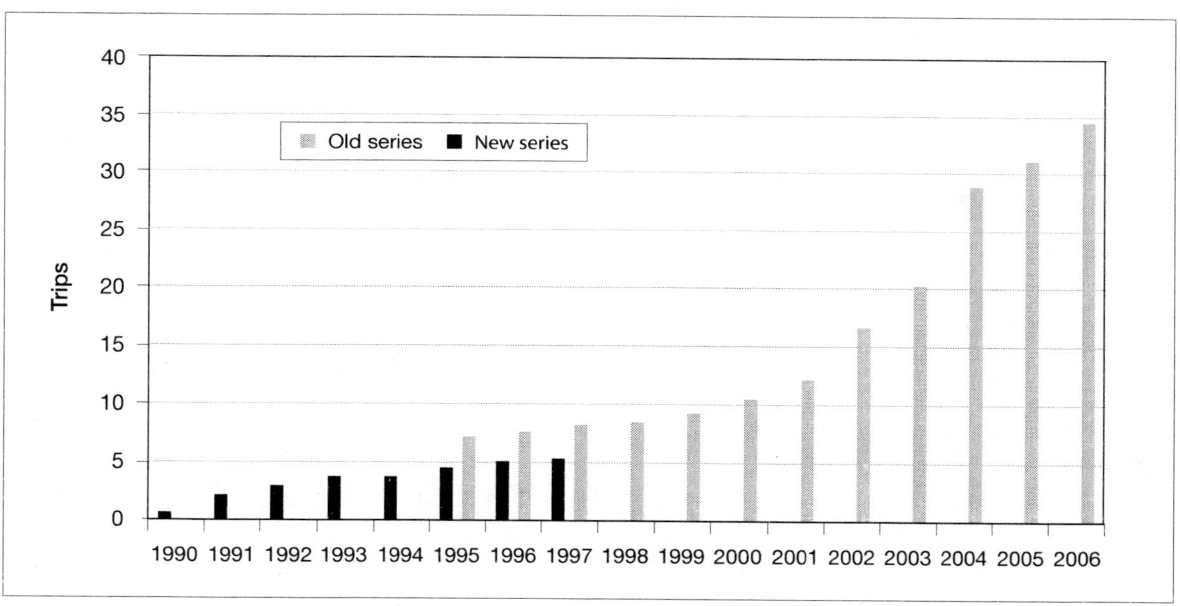

Note: See text for explanation of 'old' and 'new' series.

Source: China National Tourism Administration (CNTA).

1 Caution needs to be taken in comparing countries in terms of outbound trip volume, since many markets do not specify if the number of trips also includes same-day visits or just overnight (tourist) trips.

Despite China's impressive growth, the outbound statistics need to be interpreted with caution since more than 70% of the 34.5 million trips 'abroad' in 2006 were for the Chinese Special Administrative Regions (SARs) of Hong Kong and Macao. Moreover, the two SARs have attracted the strongest growth of all destinations in recent years. This must be taken into consideration when looking at trends and perhaps explains why so many long-haul destinations, not least NTOs in Europe, have been somewhat disappointed with the market's short-term growth performance.

Figure 4.2 Breakdown of Main Destination Regions Visited by Chinese – Number of Trips Abroad, 2005 (%)

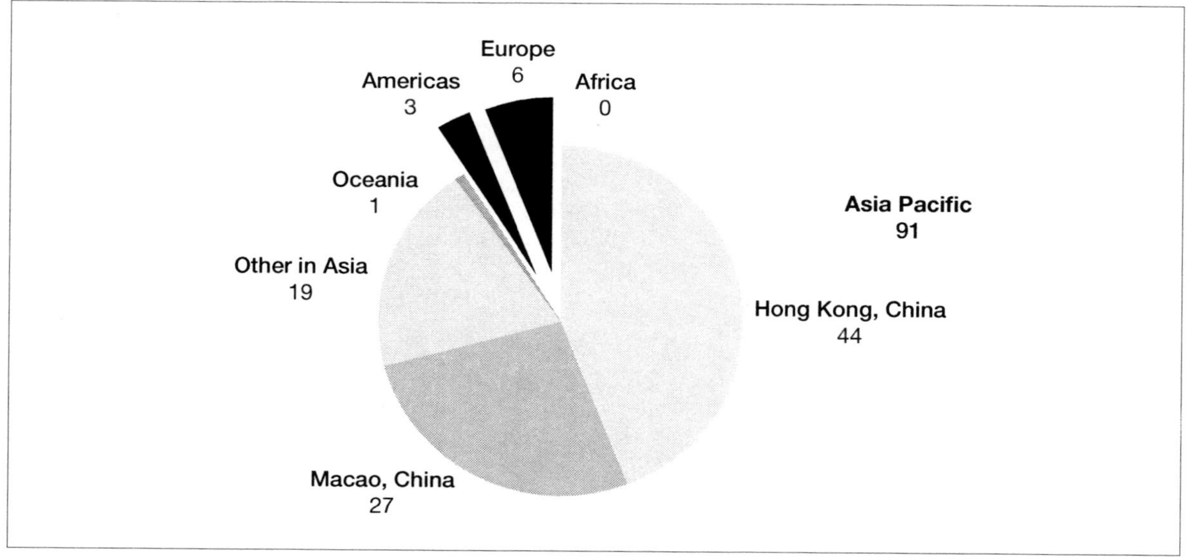

Source: CNTA.

In terms of international tourism expenditure, data gathered by the World Tourism Organization (UNWTO) – and translated into US dollars to facilitate comparative analysis – puts China in sixth position in the world ranking, behind Germany, the United States of America, the United Kingdom, France and Japan. While spend per trip has been falling as foreign travel opens up to a broader economic segment of China's population, some private surveys of Chinese outbound travel (e.g. ACNielsen – see below) suggest that the market is one of the world's biggest spenders per trip.

Figure 4.3 Top Ten Markets in Terms of International Tourism Expenditure, 1995-2006 (US$ billion)

Market	1995	2000	2004	2005	2006
Germany	60.2	53.0	71.6	74.4	74.8
United States of America	44.9	64.7	65.8	69.0	72.0
United Kingdom	24.9	38.4	56.5	59.6	63.1
France	16.3	17.8	28.8	31.2	32.2
Japan[a]	36.8	31.9	38.2	27.3	26.9
China	3.7	13.1	19.1	21.8	24.3
Italy	14.8	15.7	20.5	22.4	23.1
Canada	10.3	12.4	15.9	18.2	20.5
Russian Federation	11.6	8.8	15.7	17.8	18.8
Republic of Korea	6.3	7.1	12.4	15.4	18.2
World	**405.0**	**474.0**	**629.0**	**676.0**	**733.0**

a) Japan changed its methodology for calculating international tourism expenditure twice between 2000 and 2005, so annual growth trends are not reliable.

Source: World Tourism Organization (UNWTO).

4.1.2 Set to Exceed UNWTO Growth Forecasts

According to UNWTO forecasts *(Tourism 2020 Vision)* China's outbound market will be the world's fourth largest by 2020, behind Germany, Japan and the United States of America – reaching 100 million trips abroad that year. However, these forecasts – which were developed in 1996 with 1995 as the base year – projected 'only' 12.8% annual growth over the 25 years to 2020. And this growth has been comfortably exceeded until now, so the 100 million count (which of course includes travel to Hong Kong, China, and Macao, China) may be reached well before 2020.

Figure 4.4 World's Leading Outbound Markets, 1995 and 2020

Destination	Base year 1995 (million)	Forecast 2020 (million)	AAGR[a] 1995-2020 (%)	Market share 1995 (%)	Market share 2020 (%)
Germany[b]	75	153	2.9	13.3	9.8
Japan[b]	23	142	7.5	4.1	9.1
United States of America[b]	63	123	2.7	11.1	7.9
China[c]	5	100	12.8	0.9	6.4
United Kingdom[b]	42	95	3.3	7.4	6.1
France[c]	21	55	3.9	3.7	3.5
Netherlands[b]	22	46	3.0	3.8	2.9
Italy[b]	16	35	3.1	2.9	2.3
Canada[c]	19	31	2.0	3.4	2.0
Russian Federation[c]	12	31	4.0	2.1	1.0

a) AAGR = Average annual growth rate.

b) 1996 base year.

c) Absolute numbers for 1995 estimated based on inbound tourism data from destination countries.

Source: UNWTO.

4.2 Domestic Travel

4.2.1 Tomorrow's Outbound Travellers

No report on China outbound travel can afford to ignore domestic travel demand. China has the world's largest population and it is estimated that about 70% of Chinese citizens travelled within the country at least once in 2006. Today's domestic travellers are tomorrow's outbound travellers.

Domestic trip volume has risen by around 6.9% a year since 1995, the year the current data series was established. The number of trips exceeded 1 billion for the first time in 2004, reaching 1.3 billion in 2006, resulting in expenditure of Rmb 582 billion (US$ 73 billion or € 58 billion). Although the ratio of domestic to international trips has dropped sharply as more Chinese opt for foreign destinations, it is still at 38:1, reflecting the huge potential for growth in outbound travel demand.

Figure 4.5 Domestic versus International Travel, 1990, 1995 and 2000-2006

Year	Domestic trips (× 1,000)	International trips (× 1,000)	Ratio domestic : international
1990[a]	280,000	620	452 : 1
1995[a]	629,000	4,521	139 : 1
2000	744,000	10,473	71 : 1
2001	784,000	12,133	65 : 1
2002	878,000	16,602	53 : 1
2003	870,000	20,222	43 : 1
2004	1,102,000	28,853	38 : 1
2005	1,200,000	31,026	39 : 1
2006	1,310,000	34,520	38 : 1
AAGR[b] 2000-2006 (%)	9.9	22.0	–

a) 'Old series': data not strictly comparable with later years – see text for further information.

b) AAGR = Average annual growth rate.

Source: CNTA.

China National Tourism Administration's (CNTA's) five-year plan suggests that domestic travel will grow by around 8% per annum over the coming four years, reaching 1.8 billion trips by 2010 – and generating 50% higher expenditure than in 2006.

4.3 Outbound Travel

4.3.1 Main Drivers of Growth

The Chinese Government's relaxation of controls on outbound travel has clearly been one of the most important factors driving demand for outbound travel over the past ten years or more. Concerns that future governments might change their minds and try to reduce currency losses through a clampdown on outbound travel – as has happened in the past in the Republic of Korea – now seem ill-founded as the country increasingly opens up to the outside world, following its membership of the World Trade Organization, boosting trade and personal contacts.

There are a number of other positive factors that have already boosted both business and leisure travel, and which augur well for continued growth in demand. As already indicated, and as discussed in more detailed in chapter 5, Chinese citizens have more and more leisure time, and disposable income is growing. The National Bureau of Statistics says that household savings in urban and rural China have now far exceeded Rmb 10 trillion (US$ 1.25 trillion). GDP per capita is around US$ 1,990 – twice the level at which travel was expected to become a 'lifestyle essential', according to earlier forecasts by CNTA.

Foreign exchange controls have also been relaxed and more Chinese travel agencies are being allowed to operate outbound tours – 672 in 2005 as against only 67 in 2000 (cf. chapter 6).

4.3.2 Annual Growth Trends

In 1990, the number of outbound trips totalled just 620,000 (see figures 4.1 and 4.5 above). Over the next five years, outbound trip volume increased by as much as 630%, or 49% per annum. CNTA changed its methodology for calculating outbound trip volume in the mid-1990s, which complicates long-term analysis of trends. In addition, it is further complicated by the fact that some annual counts have been restated more than once. But the last 15 years have seen substantial growth of close to 20% per annum, culminating in 34.5 million trips in 2006 (cf. figures 4.1 and 4.5).

Moreover, the changing destination breakdown from the late 1990s, after the market was significantly opened up, reflect the increasing liberalisation of travel and choice of destinations available to the Chinese. Nevertheless, the two Chinese SARs of Hong Kong and Macao continue to dominate the destination profile.

4.3.3 Geographical Sources of Chinese Outbound Travel

The main tourism generating areas in China are the three most economically developed regions of Beijing, Shanghai and Guangdong Province. Taking holidays is still a relatively recent phenomenon and is limited to urban populations whose disposable incomes are increasing. For the foreseeable future, there will still only be a very modest share of China's population who are in a financial position to be able to experience the luxury of foreign travel – although, in terms of absolute volume of trips, this will still be a significant number.

The top ten provinces and municipalities by outbound traveller volume are Guangdong, Beijing, Shanghai, Fujian, Heilongjiang, Inner Mongolia, Liaoning, Shandong, Yunnan and Xinjiang and, according to the latest data from CNTA (published in 2006), these contribute more than 90% of total outbound trip volume.

Detailed statistics on geographical sources are scarce but the number of outbound tourists from Shanghai rose from 27,500 in 1996 to 140,200 in 2000. In the same year, 137,106 citizens travelled from Beijing, although 52.5% of them went to the SARs of Hong Kong or Macao. However, outbound travel in China started from Guangdong (due to its proximity to Hong Kong, China, and Macao, China) and the number of outbound from this region exceeded 1.2 million in 2000 – with the vast majority travelling to the two SARs.

There are over 200 ports of exit for travellers from China – of which 33 are international airports – but most departures are still through the main land borders (close to 80%), reflecting the dominance of travel to Hong Kong, China, and Macao, China, in the total trip volume. Airports account for around 15% of departures, and the balance are through seaports.

4.4 Expenditure on Travel Abroad

4.4.1 The World's Biggest Spenders

There are a number of different and, in some cases, conflicting sources of data on Chinese expenditure on travel abroad. According to official figures compiled by UNWTO – from China's balance of payments' data and the International Monetary Fund – Chinese spent an estimated US$ 24.3 billion in 2006. This was 85% more than in 2000 and represented an annual increase of 10.8% per annum over the six years from 2000 (as measured in US$ terms).

A decline was registered in only one of those years, 2003 – due no doubt to the impact of SARS on foreign travel demand – and annual growth has since returned to double-digit figures.

Figure 4.6 Expenditure by Chinese Tourists Abroad, 2000-2006

Year	International tourism expenditure (US$ million)	Annual change (%)	Expenditure per trip (US$)
2000	13,114	20.7	1,252
2001	13,909	6.1	1,146
2002	15,398	10.7	927
2003	15,187	-1.4	751
2004	19,149	26.1	664
2005	21,759	13.6	701
2006	24,300	11.7	704

Source: UNWTO.

4.4.2 Spending per Trip

Not surprisingly, UNWTO data shows that spending per trip by Chinese has fallen quite sharply over the past six years – from US$ 1,252 to US$ 704 – as the market for foreign travel has opened up to Chinese citizens with lower incomes, who travel abroad for shorter periods and/or to destinations closer to home, leading to a surge in the volume of trips. However, since this average includes spending on trips to Hong Kong, China, and Macao, China, it does not give a clear picture of trends in Chinese spending to other destinations.

To illustrate the point, in August 2006, CNTA stated that the average spend per Chinese tourist on a holiday to Europe was € 3,000, broken down as follows: 34% for shopping, 17% airfare, 18% accommodation, 9% entertainment and 3% travel agency services. IPK International's World Travel Monitor – which measures total spending related to a trip, including spending in one's own country before a trip – also points to much higher than average spending by Chinese on trips to destinations outside Greater China – i.e. excluding trips to Hong Kong, China, Macao, China, and Taiwan, Province of China.

Clearly, there are big differences in spending per trip, depending on destination. Another survey by Ctrip, the Chinese internet-based travel agency – which also sells by telephone and in retail outlets in key Chinese cities – indicates spending of over US$ 4,000 by 5% of Chinese on a trip to Europe. However, the majority of Chinese travellers to Europe spend between US$ 1,200 and US$ 4,000. By way of comparison, Ctrip says, the majority of travellers to Australia spend between US$ 1,200 and US$ 2,500 and a trip to South-East Asia would cost US$ 400-600, or even less.

4.4.3 Price-conscious, except for Shopping

It might seem incongruous to talk of the high spending by Chinese travellers abroad – especially to inbound tour operators who handle the Chinese group tour market, not to mention outbound tour operators/travel agents in China organising tours to ADS destinations. As the travel trade and consumer research for this study revealed, Chinese on ADS group tours tend to look for the lowest possible package prices and they are reportedly ready to switch from one operator to another to make even modest savings.

Yet once the Chinese finally reach their destinations, they appear to stop worrying about how much they can afford. A breakdown of Ctrip's sales data (excluding air fares) shows that shopping accounts for a much higher share of total Chinese spending abroad than for any other market – 30% of the total trip price, excluding air fares, or the same percentage as for accommodation.

These findings are corroborated by the latest ACNielsen China Omnibus survey, conducted in February 2007, which suggests that Chinese spend an average of US$ 928 per person when abroad – and US$ 1,408 in Europe (2006 data). This excludes spending on the package holiday itself, which is pre-paid. Moreover, ACNielsen says that the Chinese have become the world's biggest spenders on shopping during foreign trips.

Expenditure data from Visa Asia Pacific also supports the Ctrip and ACNielsen findings. In quarter 2 2006, Chinese travellers abroad spent some US$ 80 million using their Visa cards on retail goods alone – 53% more than on accommodation, twice as much as on transport, and 185% more than on restaurants, food and beverages.

4.5 Destinations

4.5.1 Asia Remains Favourite

Further to figure 4.2, the following table shows the destination breakdown of Chinese outbound trips for the five years from 2001 to 2005. (Detailed data for 2006 is not yet available.) As in the majority of source markets in the world, intra-regional travel dominates. In the case of China, Asia and the Pacific accounted for 91% of trips in 2006 (including travel to Hong Kong, China, and Macao, China) and attracted 72% more trips over the period. This compares with overall growth of 56% and growth of only 54% for Europe and 36.5% for the Americas. The results demonstrate the importance of other intra-regional destinations for the still relatively immature Chinese outbound travellers.

Figure 4.7 Chinese Trips Abroad by Main Destination Regions,[a] 2001-2005 (× 1,000)

Destination	2001	2002	2003	2004	2005
Asia Pacific	10,345	14,484	18,248	26,182	28,162
Hong Kong, China	5,320	7,771	9,310	13,002	13,525
Macao, China	1,800	2,783	4,791	7,490	8,479
Other Asia	3,015	3,665	3,882	5,329	5,749
Oceania	210	265	265	361	409
Americas	585	618	531	680	799
Europe	1,177	1,398	1,351	1,807	1,810
Africa	13	51	46	115	144
Unidentified	13	51	46	68	111
Total	**12,133**	**16,602**	**20,222**	**28,853**	**31,026**
Annual average growth rate (%)	**15.9**	**36.8**	**21.8**	**42.7**	**7.5**

a) Destination counts refer to first country visited.

Source: CNTA.

It should be noted that the destination breakdown of Chinese citizens provided by CNTA is based on the traveller's first port of call, so it is not necessarily the main destination of each trip. This may partly explain why, in figures 4.8 and 4.9, Europe and the Americas appear to have lost significant share over the 2001-2005 period in favour of Asia, despite an increase in absolute volumes.

Figure 4.8 Trends in Chinese Outbound Trip Volume by Main Destination Regions, 2001-2005

Destination	2001	2002	2003	2004	2005
Passengers (× 1,000)					
Total	**12,132**	**16,602**	**20,201**	**28,852**	**31,026**
Asia	10,090	14,195	17,840	25,820	27,753
Oceania	209	265	265	360	409
Americas	585	618	530	680	798
Europe	1,177	1,397	1,351	1,807	1,810
Africa	58	74	89	115	143
Annual growth (%)					
Total	**13.9**	**36.8**	**21.7**	**42.8**	**7.5**
Asia	14.1	40.7	25.8	44.7	7.5
Oceania	39.6	26.5	0.0	36.2	13.5
Americas	11.9	5.7	-14.2	28.2	17.4
Europe	9.1	18.7	-3.3	33.8	0.2
Africa	24.1	26.8	19.6	29.7	24.5
Share (%)					
Total	**100.0**	**100.0**	**100.0**	**100.0**	**100.0**
Asia	83.2	85.5	88.3	89.5	89.5
Oceania	1.7	1.6	1.3	1.3	1.3
Americas	4.8	3.7	2.6	2.4	2.6
Europe	9.7	8.4	6.7	6.3	5.8
Africa	0.5	0.5	0.4	0.4	0.5

Source: UNWTO, *China – The Asia and the Pacific Intra-regional Outbound Series*, 2006, from CNTA China Tourism Statistics Almanac.

Figure 4.9 Europe's Share of Chinese Outbound Trips, 2001-2005 (%)

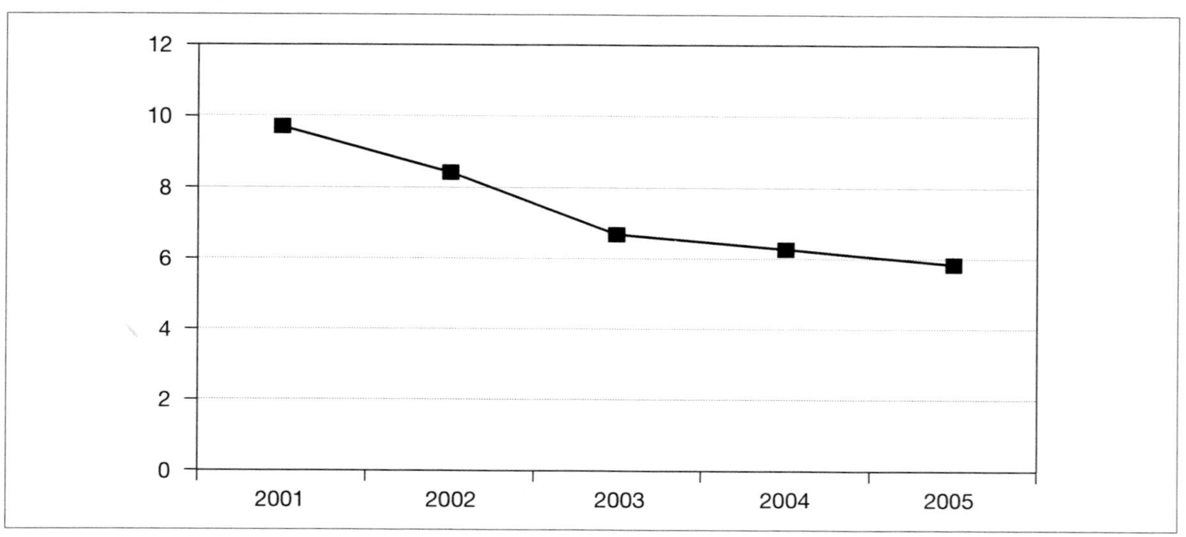

Notes: Derived from figure 4.8. CNTA's destination counts refer to first country visited, and therefore do not accurately reflect Europe's actual market share. Outbound trips include those to Hong Kong, China, and Macao, China.

Source: CNTA.

4.5.2 Hong Kong, China, and Macao, China

As already indicated, Hong Kong, China, and Macao, China, accounted for 70% of all Chinese outbound trips in 2005, and preliminary estimates suggest there was no significant change in 2006. In fact, it is surprising in many ways that the share has not increased more over the last few years, since the Chinese Government has extended its 'Individual Visit Scheme' for the two SARs so that a growing number of mainland China residents can travel independently to Hong Kong, China, and Macao, China. The scheme now covers the entire Guangdong Province and a growing number of cities in Fujian, Jiangsu and Zhejiang Provinces.

According to data compiled by the Hong Kong Tourism Board (HKTB), these individual tourists are not just visiting friends and relatives, or travelling on shoe-string budgets, either. In fact, the Chinese are Hong Kong's highest spending visitors, contributing HK$ 6,018 (US$ 772) per trip to the SAR's economy in 2005, as against the foreign tourist average of HK$ 5,502 (US$ 705). And over half the spend goes on shopping.

Although a significant share of Chinese visitors to Hong Kong, China, and Macao, China, are same-day travellers – usually termed 'border-hoppers' – more than 55% of all Hong Kong's arrivals and 57% of Macao's come from China, showing just how heavily the two SARs depend on the market.

4.5.3 Other Destinations in Asia and the Pacific

Data gaps

Figure 4.10 shows the major destinations visited by Chinese, measured by their arrivals in the different destinations. Some leading destinations, notably Taiwan, Province of China, are missing from the table due to a lack of data, but rankings are estimated for countries where only 2006 data is missing. Arrivals cannot be strictly compared, of course, as different measures are used by different destinations. As an example, some count arrivals at frontiers while others measure arrivals in different forms of accommodation. In addition, some destinations count arrivals by nationality rather than residence, which also distorts the overall picture.

After Hong Kong, China, and Macao, China, the most important destinations for Chinese outbound travellers are Singapore, the Republic of Korea, Japan and Thailand. The mix in terms of purpose of trip clearly varies for each destination, with Thailand, for example, attracting a large majority of leisure tourists, while Japan and Korea are important business destinations. While the Russian Federation is considered the most important European destination, the main traffic from China to Russia comprises cross-border flows into Russia's Far East region – essentially for trading and similar activities – which makes it more of a short-haul destination.

Figure 4.10 Top 20 International Destinations for Chinese Outbound Tourists According to Reported Arrivals at Destination Countries,[a] 2000-2006 (× 1,000 arrivals)

Destination	Series[b]	2000	2001	2002	2003	2004	2005	2006[c]	AAGR (%)[d]
Hong Kong, China	TF	2,707	3,066	4,757	5,693	7,794	8,030	8,434	21
Macao, China	TF	1,038	1,076	1,451	1,431	2,191	2,370	2,627	17
Singapore	VF	434	497	670	569	880	858	1,037	16
Republic of Korea	VF	443	482	539	513	627	710	894	12
Japan	TF	352	391	452	449	616	653	812	15
Thailand	TF	704	695	763	624	779	762	na	2
Russian Federation	VF	494	461	726	680	813	799	765	8

Destination	Series[b]	2000	2001	2002	2003	2004	2005	2006[c]	AAGR (%)[d]
Vietnam	VF	626	673	724	693	778	753	516	-3
Germany	TCE	215	237	270	268	387	418	441	13
Malaysia	TF	425	453	558	351	550	352	439	1
United States of America	TF	249	232	226	157	203	270	320	4
Australia	VF	120	158	190	176	251	285	308	17
Mongolia	TF	49	57	89	90	139	170	179	24
Austria	TCE	na	na	na	na	172	177	177	na
Canada	TF	73	81	96	76	102	117	145	12
Philippines	TF	15	19	28	32	40	107	134	44
Switzerland	THS	49	69	69	63	na	110	133	18
Indonesia	TF	29	32	37	41	30	112	na	31
Italy	TF	109	89	162	126	96	95	117	1
Belgium	TCE	55	62	113	107	114	109	107	12
New Zealand	VF	34	53	77	66	84	88	107	21
United Kingdom	VF	41	58	64	68	95	95	107	17

a) Ranked by 2006 arrivals, with ranking estimated for countries with no data.

b) Series (UNWTO): TF = tourist arrivals at frontiers;
THS = tourist arrivals at hotel and similar establishments;
VF = visitor arrivals at frontiers;
TCE = tourist arrivals at all forms of commercial accommodation.

c) Preliminary estimates.

d) AAGR = Average annual growth rate 2000-2006 (2000-2005 for Thailand and Indonesia).

Note: Some leading destinations – e.g. Taiwan, Province of China, and France – are missing from the list due to a lack of data as these do not report arrivals from China individually but rather include them in categories such as Asia or other Asia.

Source: UNWTO.

Although both the absolute data and the annual trends need to be interpreted with caution, given the – still existing – degree of incomparability of official statistics, the above table suggests that the fastest growing destinations out of China in the six years from 2000 to 2006 were intra-regional – the Philippines, Indonesia, Mongolia and New Zealand. However, a number of other destinations also recorded double-digit annual growth, including several non-Asia Pacific destinations, such as Switzerland, the United Kingdom, Germany, Canada and Belgium.

Australia: a maturing destination

Australia was the first non-Asian country to be granted ADS in 1999. As such, it is the best example of a maturing destination for Chinese leisure visitors. Over the past six years, it has also been one of the strongest growth destinations for Chinese outbound travel (+17% average annual growth from 2000-2006), and China has become the fastest growing market for Australia's tourism – in terms of both arrivals and visitor spending. In 2006, arrivals in Australia from China exceeded 300,000 for the first time – up from 120,000 in 2000 – and trends so far in 2007 suggest there will be a 20% increase this year. The Australian Tourism Forecasting Council, meanwhile, is projecting annual growth in arrivals from China of nearly 13% between now and 2016.

One reason for Australia's popularity with Chinese is the fact that it is in the southern hemisphere and has opposite seasons to those in China, providing a welcome escape from the Chinese winter. Travel to Australia is especially popular during the Spring Festival/Chinese New Year period. Tourism Australia is also considered a 'best practice' case study on how to ensure successful management of ADS group tour business.

Far fewer Chinese have absconded during trips to Australia in the 17 years since 1999 than from Europe over the past three years. In large part as a result of this, the Chinese Government has eased the rules governing ADS travel to Australia, so that tour groups are now obliged to have a minimum of only two participants, and they can come from almost anywhere in China.

Extension of ADS

In August 2006, ADS for Australia was extended to include the whole of China. ADS allows all Chinese nationals to travel to Australia on private passports for leisure tourism purposes. While ADS arrivals currently make up a large proportion of holiday visitors to Australia, there are also government and business tours as well as incentive and study groups that travel on non-ADS visas on largely leisure-focused itineraries.

Not surprisingly, travellers to Australia tend to be more experienced outbound travellers than those to South-East Asia, with a higher socio-economic level and greater social disposable incomes. Australia's International Visitor Survey shows that around 45% of Chinese visitors are unaccompanied travellers, but they include a significant share of Chinese visiting friends and relatives (VFR) and students. This partly explains why as many as 43% are repeat visitors. Average length of stay is over 40 nights – skewed by the number of students and VFR travellers.

Like Australia, New Zealand has become more and more popular among Chinese, with arrivals from China increasing by 160% over the six years to 2006.

4.5.4 Inter-regional Travel

Apart from Russia, there are eight countries outside Asia Pacific within the top 20 Chinese outbound destinations (for which data is available), with the United States of America attracting the highest number. It should nevertheless be noted that most Chinese travel to the United States of America was up to recently composed of students or business or technical trips – i.e. either paid for by the traveller's company or the Chinese Government, or sponsored by a foreign partner/associate. Most of these trips usually involve some kind of leisure content, but group tours are only permitted since late 2007 when the US and Chinese governments signed an ADS agreement after many years of negotiation.

Delay in granting ADS to the United States of America appears to have been the result of stalling tactics on the part of the US Government, which understandably sees the ADS negotiation as part of a wider trade issue. Canada, in turn, has been unable to conclude an ADS agreement with China up to date since there were concerns that Chinese tourists, once in Canada, might try to cross the border illegally into the United States of America. And this would have a negative impact on Canada-United States of America relations. Despite not enjoying ADS status, Canada attracted 145,000 arrivals in 2006.

4.5.5 Chinese Travel to Europe

According to CNTA data on trips abroad, or departures, the three favourite European countries for Chinese (excluding Russia) are Germany, France and the United Kingdom. As already indicated, however, numbers need to be interpreted with caution, since only the first destination visited is officially recorded among CNTA's outbound departures. Germany of course benefits from having the highest number of direct flights ex-China, which often makes it a first stop on a multi-destination tour of Europe. And it is also an important business destination for Chinese.

There is no firm arrivals data for France, but estimates put the total number of arrivals in the country at around 300,000. Arrivals data for the other leading destinations, meanwhile, suggests that Austria, Switzerland and Italy also attracted more Chinese tourists in 2006 than the United Kingdom.

Figure 4.11 Chinese Arrivals in Selected European Destinations,[a] 2000-2006 (× 1,000)

Destination	Series[b]	2000	2001	2002	2003	2004	2005	2006[c]	AAGR (%)[d]
Russian Federation	VF	494	461	726	680	813	799	765	8
Germany	TCE	215	237	270	268	387	418	441	13
Austria	TCE	na	na	na	na	172	177	177	na
Switzerland	THS	49	69	69	63	na	110	133	18
Italy	TF	109	89	162	126	96	95	117	1
Belgium	TCE	55	62	113	107	114	109	107	12
United Kingdom	VF	41	58	64	68	95	95	107	17
Turkey	TF	21	24	32	27	35	43	55	17
Finland	TCE	14	25	45	41	49	37	49	23
Czech Republic	TCE	na	na	na	na	na	18	30	na
Hungary	TF	na	na	na	na	11	17	na	na
Poland	TF	5	5	6	5	8	11	15	20
Ukraine	TF	5	4	8	8	11	13	14	19
Romania	VF	9	8	8	7	9	10	11	3
Iceland	TCE	na	na	na	na	na	6	8	na
Bulgaria	VF	4	3	4	3	4	4	5	4

a) Destinations attracting a minimum of 4,000 Chinese in 2005.

b) Series (UNWTO): TF = tourist arrivals at frontiers;
THS = tourist arrivals at hotel and similar establishments;
VF = visitor arrivals at frontiers;
TCE = tourist arrivals at all forms of commercial accommodation.

c) Preliminary data.

d) AAGR = Average annual growth rate 2000-2006.

Note: Some leading destinations, e.g. France, are excluded from the list due to a lack of data.

Source: UNWTO; data filed by European NTOs on TourMIS.

Like other countries that are not signatories to the Schengen Agreement (cf. annex II), the United Kingdom is at a disadvantage with regard to attracting leisure tour groups from China. Chinese leisure group tourists like visiting two or more destinations in one trip, and it is cheaper and simpler if they ensure that all these destinations are part of Schengen as they require an additional visa for the United Kingdom or other non-Schengen countries. Nevertheless, the United Kingdom is seen as a desirable destination for both study and business travel from China.

Arrivals data

Only about eight countries in Europe attract more than 100,000 Chinese arrivals a year, and there is a big gap between Belgium and the United Kingdom (at 107,000 arrivals in 2006) and the next on the list – Turkey and Finland at 55,000 and 49,000, respectively. Based on quantitative and qualitative trends identified by European NTOs – members of the European Travel Commission – estimated arrivals for 2006 in European countries are very roughly on the following scale:

International arrivals from China	Countries
500,000-1,000,000	Russian Federation
250,000-500,000	France, Germany
100,000-250,000	Austria, Belgium, Italy, Switzerland, United Kingdom
50,000-100,000	Netherlands, Turkey
25,000-50,000	Czech Republic, Denmark, Finland, Greece, Norway, Spain, Sweden
10,000-25,000	Hungary, Poland, Portugal, Romania, Ukraine
5,000-10,000	Bulgaria, Croatia, Iceland, Montenegro
< 5,000	Albania, Armenia, Azerbaijan, Belarus, Bosnia and Herzegovina, Cyprus, Estonia, Georgia, Ireland, Israel, Latvia, Liechtenstein, Lithuania, Luxembourg, Macedonia, Malta, Monaco, Serbia, Slovakia, Slovenia, Ukraine

However, despite the low numbers, growth in percentage terms was quite impressive in 2006, with eleven countries attracting double-digit increases in arrivals from China. Italy and the Czech Republic appear to have recorded the best growth – of around 70% – followed by Slovakia and Slovenia (around 50%), Estonia (43%), Poland and Turkey (about 34%), Lithuania and Switzerland (over 20%).

Overnight data

Statistics on Chinese overnights in selected European destinations indicate that the United Kingdom, Italy, France and Germany attract the highest counts, with Austria (in fifth place) well below the leaders. In the case of the United Kingdom, the much longer than average length of stay is due to its higher share of students and VFR tourists.

Italy also attracts a long average stay, while France's (estimated by Maison de la France at 3.0 nights) and Germany's (2.1 nights) are in line with the estimated 2-night European average. This is of course explained by the trend – at least among first-time Chinese visitors to Europe – for travel to two or more destinations in one trip, on an average holiday trip of 7-10 days. And most of these trips cover only capital and other leading cities.

Figure 4.12 Chinese Overnights in Selected European Destinations,[a] 2004-2006 (× 1,000)

Country	Series[b]	2004	2005	2006[c]
United Kingdom	NAA	2,157	1,650	1,376
Italy	NCE	1,291	1,220	na
France	NHS	na	863	na
Germany	NCE	789	853	925
Austria	NCE	237	249	217
Switzerland	NHS	na	226	258
Netherlands	NCE	134	150	173
Belgium	NCE	146	142	147
Finland	NCE	87	73	94
Sweden	NCE	23	70	70
Turkey	NCE	61	na	na
Denmark	NCE	na	58	63
Norway	NCE	47	54	67

Country	Series[b]	2004	2005	2006[c]
Czech Republic	NCE	35	39	66
Hungary	NCE	28	35	46
Portugal	NCE	32	35	37
Poland	NCE	22	30	na
Iceland	NCE	na	10	na
Romania	NCE	11	10	10
Monaco	NCE	3	5	6
Slovakia	NCE	2	4	5
Slovenia	NCE	na	4	5
Cyprus	NCE	na	3	3
Estonia	NCE	na	2	5
Lithuania	NCE	2	2	3

a) Destinations are ranked according to overnight volume in 2005.

b) Series (UNWTO) (except for NAA = nights in all forms of accommodation):
NCE = nights in all forms of commercial accommodation;
NHS = nights in hotels and similar establishments.

c) Preliminary estimates (in some cases, 2006 estimates are based on rounded figures for 2005, which may cause some distortion).

Source: TourMIS; respective NTOs/ETC members

Figure 4.13 Average Length of Stay by Chinese Tourists in Selected European Countries,[a] 2004-2006 (nights)

Country	2004	2005	2006[b]
United Kingdom	22.7	17.9	12.9
Italy	13.4	12.8	na
Poland	2.8	2.7	na
Czech Republic	na	2.2	2.2
Switzerland	na	2.1	1.9
Germany	2.0	2.0	2.1
Finland	1.8	1.7	1.9
Turkey	1.7	na	na
Iceland	na	1.7	na
Austria	1.4	1.4	1.2
Belgium	1.3	1.3	1.4
Romania	1.2	1.0	1.0

a) Countries are ranked according to 2005 length of stay – which relate to the measures for arrivals and overnights specified in figures 4.11 and 4.12.

b) Preliminary estimates.

Source: Calculations based on data from UNWTO, TourMIS and respective NTOs/ETC members.

Destination preferences

First-time Chinese ADS group tour visitors to Europe are most likely to opt for a combination of destinations, such as France and Germany; France, Germany and Italy and/or Austria; France, Germany and Switzerland; or even France and Spain and/or Italy. Tourists to central and eastern Europe or the Nordic countries are much more likely to be on their second or third trip to Europe, and single-destination trips are very uncommon for tour groups, according to the research carried out by the European Tour Operators Association (ETOA) for the purposes of this report.

4.6 Seasonality and Purpose of Trip

4.6.1 Seasonality

At present, the peak periods for outbound, as well as for domestic travel, are the three 'Golden Weeks', which fall at Chinese New Year, in the first week of May and in the first week of October (cf. annex V). Many Chinese, especially whole families, prefer to travel during these holiday periods, so the demand for outbound, as well as domestic travel, is very heavy during these times. As a result, some Chinese are unable to travel where they want to because airlines or tours are fully booked.

There are reportedly plans to institutionalise holiday pay for workers in the near future. For the time being, only government officials and some employees of other official or semi-official organizations have access to paid holidays. But it is expected that ordinary workers will also soon have paid annual holidays averaging around two weeks a year. Those with less than three years of service are expected to receive a lower entitlement, but those with 3-5 years' service will probably get ten days, and those with 5-10 years' service 14 days. Chinese workers with more than ten years' service will likely have one more day for each year of service up to a ceiling of 30 days.

This means that, apart from public holidays, Chinese citizens will have additional holidays at their disposal, which will help to spread holiday travel more evenly through the year. Chinese will also be able to extend their holidays from one week to two weeks or even longer. Thus outbound tourists will have the opportunity of travelling further afield and staying longer at their destinations. At the moment, the 'holiday economy' is based on the fact that people rush to travel within a few days. In the future, it will gradually develop into a more balanced holiday pattern, which can only be good news for destinations in Europe.

Seasonal preferences clearly vary from one destination to another, and especially between regions. In Europe, May through September appears to be the most popular period for visits by Chinese, according to data and anecdotal evidence supplied by some ETC members, although Austria attracts Chinese mainly from July to September.

4.6.2 Private/Leisure Travel Gains Share at the Expense of Public/Business Trips

The share of public trips (i.e. trips for business or official travel) has declined sharply over the past decade – from 55% in 1995 to 19% in 2005 – as restrictions on outbound leisure travel, and especially group travel, have eased. Private, or leisure trips, meanwhile, have increased from 45% to 81% of total trip volume over the ten years and appear to be gaining further share.

Figure 4.14 Outbound Travel from China by Purpose/Type of Trip,[a] 1995, 2000 and 2005

	1995	2000	2005
Trips (× 1,000)			
Public	2,467	4,843	5,886
Private	2,054	5,631	25,140
Total	**4,521**	**10,473**	**31,026**
Annual change (%)			
Public	4.2[b]	14.4[c]	0.2
Private	18.4[b]	22.3[c]	9.4
Total	**9.9[b]**	**18.3[c]**	**7.5**
Share (%)			
Public	54.6	46.2	19.0
Private	45.4	53.8	81.0
Total	**100.0**	**100.0**	**100.0**

a) See text for further clarification regarding the type of trip. Passports for 'public', or official and/or business, travel are issued to a wide range of categories, but mostly non-holiday travellers. 'Private' passports are issued to VFR and some leisure travellers. In effect, business travellers could travel abroad on either type of passport, although they are more likely to have 'public' passports.

b) Average 1993-1995.

c) Average 1995-2000.

Source: CNTA.

4.6.3 Public/Business Travel

Still a growing market

Despite the drop in share, the absolute volume of public (business/official) trips and organised technical tours continues to grow. And, according to the Shanghai Business International Travel Service, growing Chinese contacts with foreign countries is certain to boost demand for this type of travel further. Visa applications for business travellers are also being streamlined, and the amount of money that can be taken out of the country has been raised from US$ 2,000 (or equivalent in yuan/renminbi) to US$ 5,000. These measures can be expected to further fuel demand.

Shanghai is the main source

Official/business tours abroad are taken by people in government ministries, institutions and state enterprises, as well as foreign-owned and Chinese commercial companies. Interestingly, Shanghai – rather than Beijing – is the primary source of outbound business/official travel. Emerging as China's commercial hub, it has established 'friendship city' relationships with several countries and cities. It is home to many consulates, about 300 foreign financial institutions, more than 20 foreign bank branches and the offices of several thousand multinational and foreign corporations.

Recent data is not available but, in 2002, more than 15,000 official outbound tour groups were authorised by the Foreign Affairs Ministry of the Shanghai Municipal Government. Another 150 commercial exhibition tours were organised by the Municipal Trade Promotion Organization. Other authorised companies sent many more. Even during the SARS crisis, in July 2003, the Shanghai Government organised more than 20 business travel groups for sales promotions and communication.

The 2008 Beijing Olympic Games and 2010 Shanghai World Expo will create new opportunities for business/official overseas travel. One Shanghai consultancy group has designed more than 20 professional training programmes to Australia for the Beijing Olympic Games Committee. And the German Meisha Conference Corporation of Shanghai has prepared several overseas training programmes for the Shanghai World Fair Committee.

More profitable than leisure tourism

While business/official trips/tours mainly comprise small groups of six or seven people, conference, training and commercial exhibition groups can include hundreds of participants. The expenses involved are far higher than for leisure tours, largely because they are paid for by organizations and require higher levels of customisation. For the travel agency, organising a business/official tour is more profitable per person than organising a private/leisure holiday trip.

Nevertheless, it is important to point out that government policy has an unusually strong impact on business/official travel. In 1994, for example, the number of official outbound travellers declined when the Chinese Government placed tighter controls on spending to clamp down on corruption.

Services for business/official overseas tours are provided by five entities:

- the state-owned service centre or representative office;
- the commercial consultative corporation dealing with business/official outbound tour business;
- companies handling personal overseas tours;
- travel agencies; and
- offices of foreign travel agencies in China.

Travel agencies have little involvement in business/official travel

Travel agencies handle only a small share of the business/official travel market. The main reasons are that travel agency business is more or less limited to countries that have ADS. The administrative department in charge of travel agencies has punished agencies that have organised self-sponsored group travel to non-ADS countries. Many government units do not accept the invoices of travel agencies because they do not fully understand what agencies do. Government units also believe that if agencies handle official tours, the units will also be suspected of organising them at public expense.

Another reason why travel agencies are not often involved in official/business tours is that, while they usually have excellent contacts with airlines, hotels and places of interest in the destinations, they may not have adequate resources to manage trips that require other types of official contacts. Business/official tours also need to have an invitation letter from the institutions to be visited. If agencies do not have proper contacts, they have to decline the business.

4.6.4 Private/Leisure Travel

Holidays generate the highest share of demand

While the official data is not strictly comparable with that from other sources such as IPK International's World Travel Monitor or the China Outbound Monitor from ACNielsen and the Pacific Asia Travel Association (because of the different methodologies used to compile the data), most other surveys confirm that private/leisure travel accounts for the bulk of all trips abroad by Chinese, with visits to friends and relatives (VFR) generating about 15%.

Cities attract the highest share of holidaymakers (around 50%) – usually trips involving several capital cities. But demand for sun and beach and other types of holidays is growing, and this trend looks set to continue as Chinese visit more and more resort destinations in Asia. But urban attractions are likely to remain the main draw for Chinese tourists in Europe.

Purpose of trip varies from one destination to another

As might be expected, there is a big difference in the breakdown of purpose of trip from one destination to another – even within Europe. Unfortunately, not many destinations provide this kind of breakdown, so comparisons are difficult. However, it is interesting to compare some examples. Holidays and other types of leisure account for just 25% of all arrivals in the Nordic countries, according to research carried out by the Scandinavian Tourist Board. In contrast, some other European destinations, such as Italy or Belgium, attract as much as 70-80% leisure tourism in their overall count, with the balance coming from conferences and meetings business.

One interesting case is the United Kingdom, which probably attracts a higher share of business travellers from China than any other European country except Germany. The United Kingdom is also much more important than average for study trips, notably for English-language courses. Since 1999, according to VisitBritain, despite rises in fees for students and visa costs, the number of Chinese students in the United Kingdom has increased 14-fold.

As can be seen from the following table, holiday visits accounted for an average of only 19% of visits, 6% of nights and 9% of spending by Chinese in the United Kingdom over the six years 2000-2005. (An average for the six years is shown as samples are small and the data is not considered to be statistically robust on an annual basis.)

Figure 4.15 Purpose of Chinese Travel to the United Kingdom, 2000-2005[a] (share, %)

Purpose	Visits	Nights	Spend
Holiday	19	6	9
Business	45	26	38
VFR	18	13	10
Study	14	51	40
Miscellaneous	5	3	3
Total	**100**	**100**	**100**

a) Averages for the six years.

Note: Totals might pass 100% due to roundings.

Source: United Kingdom International Passenger Survey (IPS).

Chapter 5

Profile of the Chinese Outbound Traveller

5.1 Key Characteristics

In an apparently homogenous country there is an understandable tendency to treat China as one market and one area of operation. Yet, while it is one nation, geographical and cultural differences can create huge variations in demand profiles. Other factors, such as the operating environment, also have a significant influence on demand. It is therefore difficult to identify general characteristics of outbound travellers, especially as demographic and lifestyle groups also vary sharply depending on the destinations visited.

Nevertheless, the following provides a brief summary of the main characteristics of today's Chinese outbound travellers. The list of trends is gleaned from various reports issued by the China National Tourism Administration (CNTA), as well as different privately run surveys conducted by organizations such as ACNielsen and Visa International. The profile excludes travellers to Hong Kong, China, and Macao, China.

- The proportion of male to female travellers is now quite balanced, with females outnumbering males by 53:47. But Europe attracts almost 50% more males than females (60:40), largely because of the higher than average share of business trips.
- Around 50% of outbound travellers are aged between 25 and 44 years, which is widely considered the age segment with the best growth potential. But a higher share of Chinese in the 45-plus age group travel to long-haul destinations, including Europe and Australia, and this age group is set to increase sharply in numbers.
- At least 70% of outbound travellers are travelling for leisure purposes, but a majority of those going to North Asia and some destinations in Europe (e.g. the United Kingdom and the Nordic countries) are business travellers.
- The major urban centres of Beijing, Shanghai, Guangzhou and Shenzhen account for most of the outbound travel demand among Chinese, but demand from smaller cities and towns is now also growing fast.
- The great majority of outbound travellers from China (over 85%) – excluding those travelling to Hong Kong, China, and Macao, China – arrive at their destinations by air.
- The share travelling in groups is still high (60% overall and 80% for first-timers), but it is falling.
- In each destination, average length of stay is usually close to the average for all tourists to that destination; a trip to Europe averages 8-15 days.
- The share staying in paid accommodation is generally high – at least 70%.
- Repeat travel is growing – to some destinations over 30% of Chinese are repeat visitors.
- As far as Europe is concerned, Chinese would prefer an indepth tour covering a maximum of three countries, rather than a whistle-stop tour of 5-6.

5.2 Disposable Incomes and Propensity to Travel

There is no real consensus of opinion as to the size of the middle class in China and official statistics are not available. However, it seems to be generally accepted that the criterion for defining the middle class is a monthly household income of Rmb 5,000 (US$ 665 or € 475 as at mid-September 2007).

According to the *Annual Report of China Outbound Tourism Development 2004* by researchers from four leading universities, published in 2005 and cited in the World Tourism Organization's (UNWTO's) *China – The Asia and the Pacific Intra-regional Outbound Series,* 2006, two thirds of all outbound travel from China (including cross-border trips to Hong Kong, China, and Macao, China) is by people from households earning more than Rmb 5,000 a month (US$ 604 or € 486 in 2004). The report covers the urban centres of Beijing, Shanghai, Guangdong and Chongqing, which are the major sources of outbound travel from China.

Families with monthly incomes of Rmb 5,000-10,000 make up 31% of all outbound travellers from China, according to the report's findings; households earning Rmb 10,000-20,000 account for 17%; 8% come from households generating income of Rmb 20,000-30,000; and 10% are from families earning over Rmb 30,000. This means that two thirds of all travellers are from households earning more than Rmb 5,000 monthly while one third earn less than Rmb 5,000.

Figure 5.1 Chinese Outbound Travellers by Income Groups, 2004

Family Income (Rmb)	Family Income (US$)	Income Structure (%)
< 5,000	< 604	34
5,001-10,000	604-1,208	31
10,001-20,000	1,209-2,416	17
20,001-30,000	2,417-3,625	8
> 30,000	> 3,625	10

Note: Exchange rate in 2004: US$ 1 = Rmb 8.28; € 1 = Rmb 10.28. (See chapter 2 for further details on exchange rates).

Source: Dujiang and Daibin (2005), *Annual Report of China Outbound.*
Tourism Development 2004, cited in the World Tourism Organization's (UNWTO).
China – The Asia and the Pacific Intra-regional Outbound Series, 2006.

Although one third of all Chinese outbound trips are said to be made by people from households earning less than Rmb 5,000 a month, very few of these trips would be for long-haul destinations. In fact, most would be simply for Hong Kong, China, and Macao, China, and group tours to popular holiday destinations in South-East Asia, such as Thailand and Singapore. Nevertheless, even among the lower income groups – and particularly young people – an amazing 53% of disposable income – after all essentials are paid for – is reportedly spent on travel, according to research conducted in early 2007 by ACNielsen.

5.3 Changing Lifestyles and Shifting Demographics

5.3.1 Travel by Age Group

The breakdown of foreign travel from China by age group reported by different sources varies significantly, depending on the survey sample and the different criteria for measurement. The use of different age segments does not facilitate analysis. Official statistics, which include travel to Hong Kong, China, and Macao, China, suggest that Chinese aged 26-55 years make up 69% of all trips, while young people aged 18-25 account for 15% and those over 55 years old for 10%.

Figure 5.2 Age Profile of Outbound Travellers from China, 2005 (%)

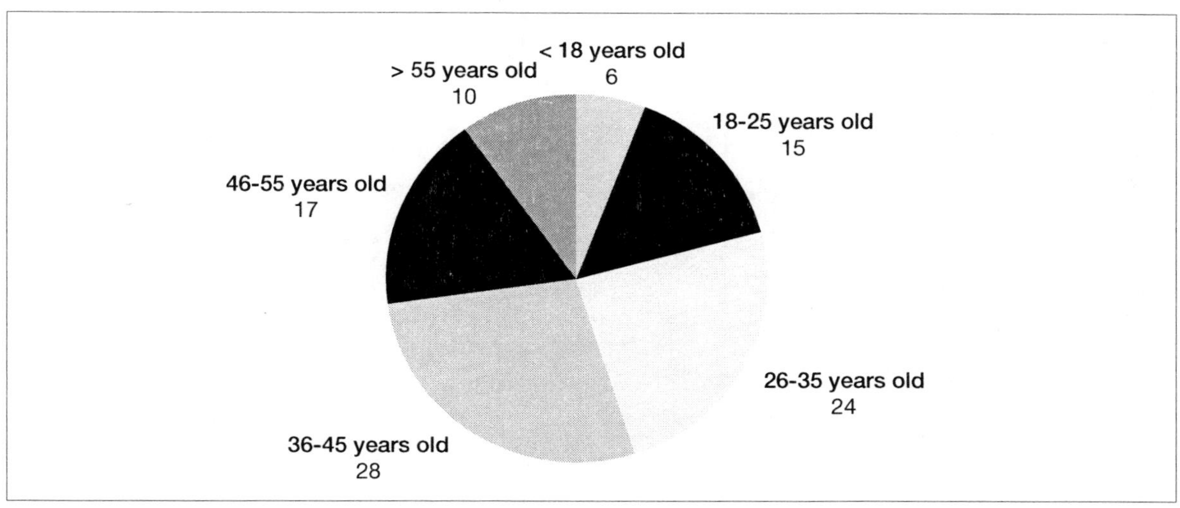

Source: Dujiang and Daibin (2005), *Annual Report of China Outbound Tourism Development 2004*, cited in UNWTO, *China – The Asia and the Pacific Intra-regional Outbound Series*, 2006.

However, as the following chart and table confirm, different destinations appeal to different age groups, and longer-haul destinations – which inevitably cost more to visit – attract primarily the older segments. Student travel is of course one exception to the rule, and the two countries shown as examples below – Australia and the United Kingdom – both attract a higher than normal share of students from China. Data from other European countries surveyed for this report tends to confirm the predominance of older travellers in ADS tour groups.

Figure 5.3 Chinese Visitors to Australia by Age, 2005 (%)

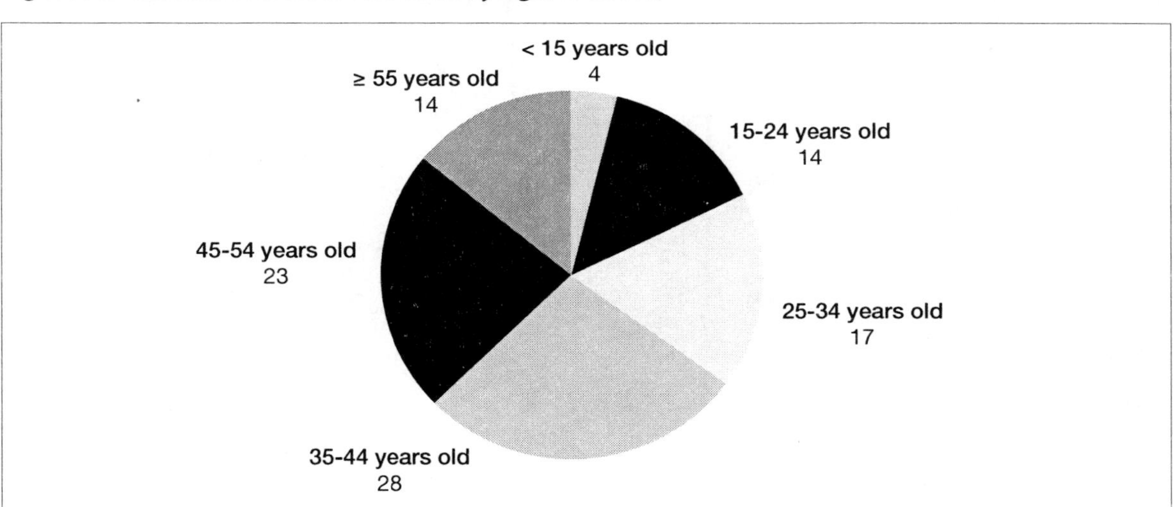

Source: Tourism Australia, 2005.

Figure 5.4 Profile of Chinese Travellers to the United Kingdom, 2001-2005[a] (share, %)

	Arrivals	Spending
Gender		
Female	34	35
Male	66	65
Age		
0-15	6	8
16-24	11	32
25-34	29	24
35-44	30	22
45-54	18	10
55-64	6	2
≥ 65	2	1

a) Averages for the five years. Given the small survey sample, the data is not considered to be statistically robust.

Source: IPS.

5.3.2 Research by Visa International

Research by Visa International among its Chinese cardholders highlights the different profile of Chinese travelling in different countries abroad. Clearly, the results must be interpreted with caution since they only apply to Chinese affluent enough to be able to obtain an international Visa card. But the findings are nonetheless interesting.

As an example, the predominance of business travel to North Asia means that it attracts more males than females (60:40) from a broad age range, the 21-50 year-old segment. By contrast, the profile of Chinese tourists to South-East Asia – the main destination for ADS tour groups in the 1990s – is younger (25-44 year-olds). The region is now starting to attract incentive groups from China, as well as education-related travel and VFR.

Australia and New Zealand are most popular among the 30-50 year-olds, according to Visa International's research, with family travel also growing strongly. Finally, Europe and other long-haul destinations attract primarily business travellers – often accompanied by associates, spouses, or adult family and friends – with 60% of Chinese Visa cardholders in Europe aged between 25 and 44. Female travel is nonetheless growing more strongly than male travel.

5.3.3 Age and Income Groups with the Main Growth Potential

In the mid-1990s, the Chinese population was young – 56% of the population was under 30 years old. But the Chinese Government's 'one child per family' policy has had a significant impact on the ageing of the population. The highest growth segment of the last 10-15 years was the 'householder' – the 30-59-year age group. And the main growth segment of the next ten years will be the more mature householder – the 40-69-year age group. All other age groups will decline in size and their segment value will therefore not increase in real terms over the next decade.

The age/lifecycle segment considered to offer the greatest travel growth potential over the next 20 years is the 25-44 year-old group, and particularly the younger Chinese in this group. ACNielsen says that these are the Chinese spending the highest share of their disposable incomes on travel and they are reportedly prepared to borrow money to ensure they have the means to do so.

However, another important age segment are the working-age 'empty-nesters' – those whose children are probably more than 20 years old and are economically independent. According to Global Demographics, they already have most of the home 'durables' they need, are experiencing rapidly increasing discretionary funds, and are the first wave of educated adults in China. Significantly, for travel and tourism, the Chinese mature householder is developing new interests and is now often looking for experiences rather than things. This group is projected to increase in size by 8.6% per annum to 2008 and by 6% every year thereafter to 2024. In value, it is growing at over 10% per year.

Figure 5.5 Size and Spending Power of the Chinese 'Working-age Empty-nester' Group, 2004-2024

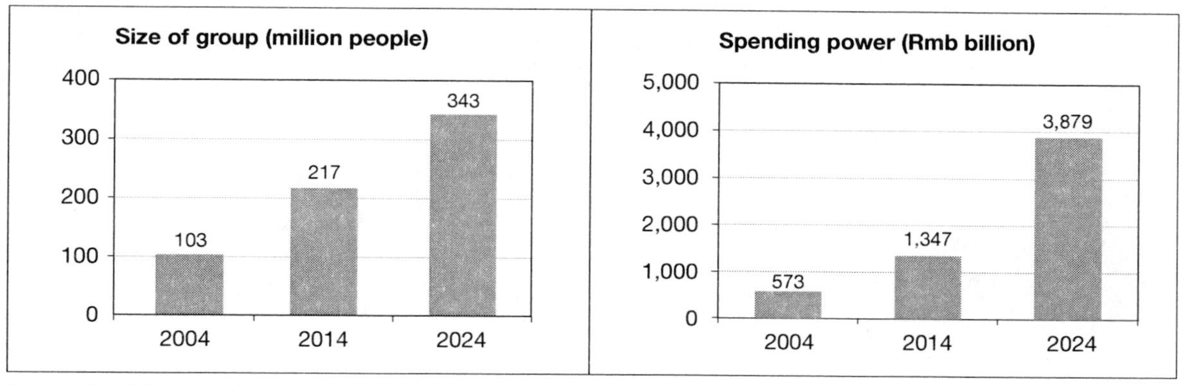

Source: Global Demographics.

While the size of the 'working-age, empty-nester' group will grow by 111% from 2004 to 2014 and by 233% from 2004 to 2024, reaching 343 million, the group's spending power will increase more sharply over the respective periods – by 135% and by 577%.

The new labour force also offers an opportunity. The population engaged in white-collar (office and service) occupations is projected to increase from 320 million now to 383 million in 2024. In value, this segment is expected to grow by 5.5% per annum to 2014. Its perceived value is all the more important since China's labour force is expected to stop growing by 2008. So this is one of the few segments whose potential will really increase.

Finally, the upper middle-class household is an extremely important high-growth segment for European suppliers. Between 2004 and 2014, the number of urban households earning Rmb 40,000-80,000 is forecast to grow by 10% per year; and those earning Rmb 80,000 or more will rise by 16% annually, according to Global Demographics.

5.3.4 Education Levels

More than 70% of all Chinese outbound travellers reportedly have either a university education or college training. This helps to explain why university lecturers, teachers, government employees, company managers and Chinese in the liberal professions tend to dominate tour groups. But, as far as travel to Europe is concerned, retirees are also important.

Figure 5.6 Level of Education of Chinese Outbound Travellers, 2005 (%)

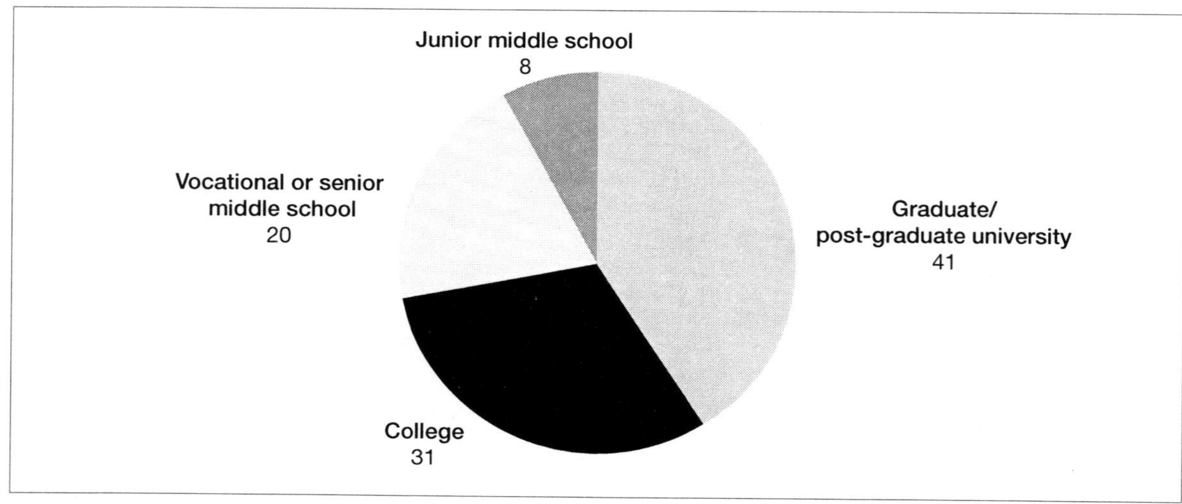

Source: Dujiang and Daibin (2005), *Annual Report of China Outbound Tourism Development 2004*, cited in UNWTO's *China – The Asia and the Pacific Intra-regional Outbound Series*, 2006.

5.3.5 Travelling Companions

According to the *Annual Report of China Outbound Tourism Development 2004* – cited in the World Tourism Organization's (UNWTO's) *China – The Asia and the Pacific Intra-regional Outbound Series*, 2006 – 38% of Chinese outbound tourists travel with some members of their family, and 20% are entire families travelling together. Another 20% travel with friends and 6% without travelling companions. Some 15% of travellers are participants in groups organised by their work units/companies – with most of this type of trip for technical tours, incentives and study.

Regarding travel with family members, families of three people (usually parents and one child) make up 57% of the total typical family structure among outbound travellers from the urban areas of China. Two generations (15% of travellers) imply parents who live with their grown-up children; while three generations include grandparents (10%).

Figure 5.7 Structure of Outbound Traveller Groups, 2004 (%)

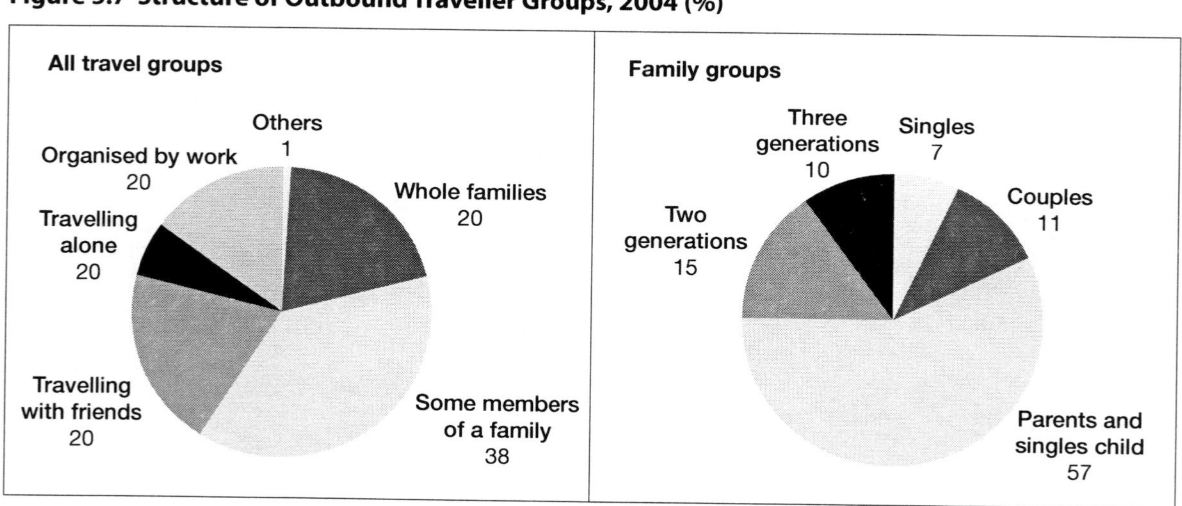

Source: Dujiang and Daibin (2005), *Annual Report of China Outbound Tourism Development 2004*, cited in UNWTO's *China – The Asia and the Pacific Intra-regional Outbound Series*, 2006.

5.4 Regional Variations

Although the research is now more than five years old, a survey commissioned by Tourism Australia (under its former name, the Australian Tourist Commission) still provides some valuable insights into the regional differences of Chinese mid- to long-haul travellers from the three major centres of Beijing, Shanghai and Guangzhou. The survey, which was conducted by Burak Jacobsen and Millward Brown, was of course intended to assess the potential of travel to Australia. But since Australia considers its competitors in the China market to be Europe and, to a lesser extent, the United States of America, the results are of value for these destinations.

The research shows that there are some marked differences in the demographic profiles of potential travellers in each city. Those from Beijing (30% of the overall sample surveyed) tend to be younger, with a slight skew towards women. They are more likely to be single and therefore less likely to have children. They tend to have achieved a higher education level and also claim a greater ability with the English language than their compatriots from Shanghai and Guangzhou.

Shanghai's potential travellers (45% of the sample) are older and therefore more likely to be married with children. In Guangzhou (25%), men are over-represented among potential travellers – perhaps because a higher share of business travel is generated there – and they are less likely to have received a tertiary education. Their claimed levels of facility with the English language are lower than in other cities.

Around 19% of the survey sample – comprising potential mid- to long-haul Chinese outbound travellers – said they had already travelled outside China, with 17% already having visited other parts of Asia. As far as individual destinations were concerned, Hong Kong, China, was the most visited destination, followed by Thailand, Singapore and the United States of America.

The following summarises the different characteristics in potential mid- to long-haul travellers from one city to another:

Beijing:

- Women, younger people and white-collar households were over-represented in Beijing relative to the other cities. They also tended to have a higher level of education and a greater facility with the English language. Their use of the internet was also greater.
- Although their experience of overseas travel was relatively low compared with residents of Guangzhou, they were more likely than others to profess a desire for independent rather than group holiday travel.
- Unlike travellers from Guangzhou, their interest in overseas destinations focused on Europe.
- They found Australia more appealing and were more interested in a visit there than Chinese from the other cities. They anticipated fewer cost or time difficulties associated with a trip to Australia and were less concerned about getting a visa to travel there.

Guangzhou:

- They were better travelled than residents of Beijing or Shanghai.
- Their travel experience was most likely to have been in other Asian countries and they also focused on this region when considering future holiday travel. Europe held less appeal for them. Their familiarity with and interest in Asian competitive set countries was stronger than for other destinations.
- Despite their travel experience, they appeared relatively unsophisticated in their travel behaviour, favouring group travel and being concerned about language barriers. This may result from the fact that they were relatively less well educated than others, and professed lesser ability with the English language.

Shanghai:

- They tended to be older than their counterparts in other cities and were more likely to have children. They were less well educated than residents of Beijing.
- Their experience of overseas travel was limited, like those surveyed in Beijing, but unlike them they did not tend to have an 'independent' traveller mindset.
- They were more likely to include Europe in the destinations they were seriously considering visiting – or simply dreamed of visiting – than their counterparts in Guangzhou, but showed more interest in Asian countries than those from Beijing.
- Australia held less appeal for them than for the residents of the other cities and their interest in a visit was consequently lower.

Chapter 6

Organization of Chinese Outbound Travel

6.1 Travel Distribution

6.1.1 Increasing Competition as the Market Expands

China's travel services market is expanding every year, as tourism demand becomes more personalised and government administration is strengthened. The increasingly open market and growth of internet technology are also placing more competitive pressures on existing providers.

In 1997, there were 67 travel agencies licensed for outbound travel. The number rose to 528 in 2002 and to 672 in 2005 – the latest year for which detailed information is available. By August 2005, 44% of all travel agencies involved in international travel business in China were licensed for outbound travel business as well as inbound.

Figure 6.1 Licensed Travel Agencies in China, 1997-2005

Year	Inbound and outbound	Inbound and domestic	Domestic only
1997	67	991	3,995
1998	67	1,312	4,910
1999	67	1,256	6,070
2000	67	1,268	7,725
2001	67	1,310	9,222
2002	528	1,349	10,203
2003	528	1,364	11,997
2004	529	1,319	na
2005	672	1,472	13,867

Source: Arlt, W. G. from *Chinas Outbound Tourism*, with data from CNTA, 1997-2003, and Hu and Graff, 2004-2005.

Outbound travel agencies are spread out across the country. In 2005, 69 were in Beijing, 111 in Guangdong Province, 35 in Shanghai, 36 in Jiangsu and 29 in Zhejiang. There were at least 3-4 agencies per province in the rest of the country.

As Beijing, Shanghai and Guangzhou have better access to information – whether international flight data, or information on visas and other formalities from foreign embassies and consulates – they continue to dominate the market. Many have set up business relationships with their counterparts in countries with Approved Destination Status (ADS). A number of travel agencies in the three major cities have also become outbound travel wholesalers, with licensed outbound travel agencies in other provinces becoming the retailers of the established wholesalers/travel agencies in the three main cities. The retailers receive local bookings and then ask the leading agencies in the three main cities to take them over and handle all the formalities such as visa applications. As agents, their profits are higher than they would be if they operated independently, so this system suits them, and it clearly suits the major agencies/wholesalers as they retain control.

Outbound travel business in the three big cities is relatively concentrated in the hands of a few established travel companies. As an example, in the Beijing area, 60% of passengers to South-East Asia are handled by just 3-4 travel agencies. In 2005, some 70,000 Chinese participated in organised tours to Europe and, of these, 15,000 were handled by the biggest travel agency, China Travel Service, and the first four travel agencies combined handled 40,000 passengers, leaving just 15,000 to smaller agents. The most important travel agencies are listed in the following table. More information on them is available in annex IV.

Figure 6.2 The Largest Outbound Travel Agencies in China, by Major Source City

Beijing	Shanghai	Guangdong
China Travel Service (CTS) HQ	JinJiang Tours Ltd.	GZL International Travel Service
China Comfort Travel Co.	HuaTing Overseas Tourist Company	CTS Guangdong
China Youth Travel Service (CYTS)	CTS Shanghai	China International Travel Service (CITS) Guangdong
Spring Travel		Shantou Tourism General Company

Source: Scandinavian Tourist Board (STB), 2004.

China Travel Service (CTS) is the largest, generating a 7% share of total outbound sales in 2004, according to the China National Tourism Administration (CNTA), and it has offices in all the major cities, as do China International Travel Service (CITS) (6%) and China Youth Travel Service (CYTS) (4%). These top three are all state-owned.

The established travel companies plan their products and advertise them in the media, marketing them to individual passengers through their retail shops all over the main cities, or increasingly over the internet. Many of those involved in business travel – and, in particular, in the meetings industry segment – have specialised departments for handling such outbound travel business.

Figure 6.3 China Travel Agencies' Share of the Chinese Travel Market, 2004 (%)

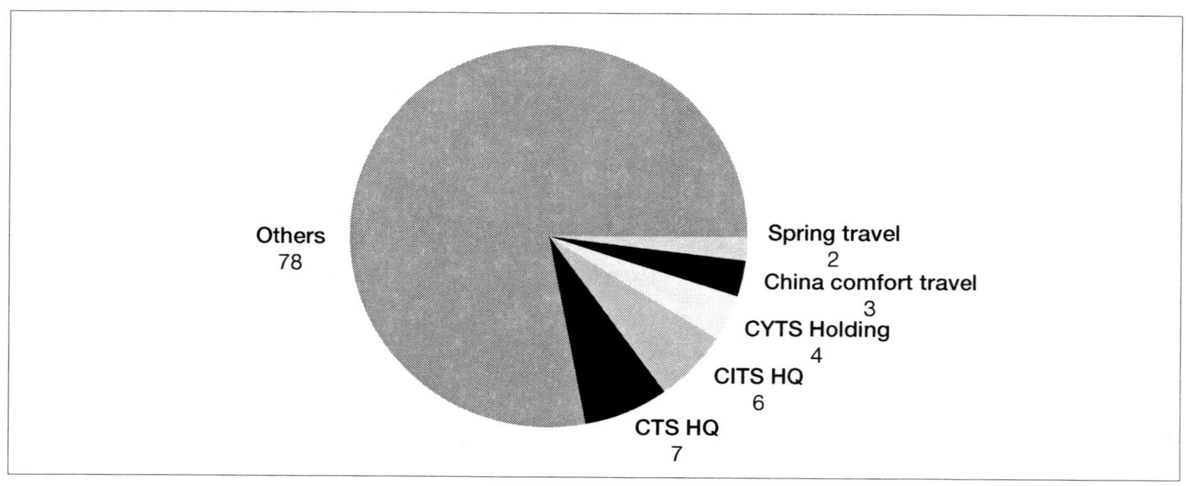

Source: CNTA, 2005.

6.1.2 Joint Ventures with Foreign Companies

Over the last few years, there have also been a growing number of joint ventures. Since the beginning of 2003, in line with the General Agreement on Trade in Services (GATS) signed by China on its accession to the World Trade Organization (WTO), foreign-owned travel agencies have been allowed a controlling stake in joint ventures.

Under the terms of GATS, agencies/operators were even allowed to be fully owned by foreigners from 2005. Among the best known are Gullivers Travel Associates (part of Travelport since April 2005), Jalpak International (China) Co Ltd, Japan-based All Nippon and Singapore-based Star Cruises. Such groups need to have a worldwide turnover of at least US$ 40 million and are, in theory, not yet allowed to conduct outbound travel business.

As far as existing joint ventures are concerned, most business is inbound but the foreign partners are also generally responsible for handling the Chinese outbound business in their destination countries. Among the different joint ventures set up to date, the following should be mentioned:

- CITS and American Express Travel Services formed a joint-venture travel company in December 2002, headquartered in Beijing. (China Comfort Travel and Rosenbluth also formed a joint-venture partnership, but this fell apart when Rosenbluth and Amex themselves merged in 2003.)
- CTS Hong Kong and Synergi partnered to form CTI Sunshine Business Travel Management Company in November 2003.
- TUI China Travel Company, formally launched in September 2003, was the first Sino-foreign tourism joint venture controlled by foreign partners. The launch of the joint venture, which involves 75% foreign capital, followed the signing of an initial cooperation agreement, in November 2002, between CTS, TUI and Martin Büse (a TUI subsidiary). All three companies are signatories to the joint venture.
- GCTS and TUI China Travel Company Ltd signed a cooperative venture in April 2004 to cover cooperation in all sectors of tourism, including outbound leisure and business travel.
- Kuoni Travel strengthened its position in China in 2004 by acquiring full control of Hong Kong-based tour operator P&O Travel Hong Kong. The Switzerland-based group already held 50% of the company which has now been fully integrated into the Kuoni Group. P&O is established in China.
- United Kingdom-based Business Travel International (BTI), the world's leading corporate travel management company, launched a joint venture with Shanghai Jin Jiang International (Group) Ltd in August 2004.
- Flight Centre Ltd, the largest travel agency group in Australia, established a joint venture, Flight Centre Comfort Business Travel Service, with China Comfort Travel in August 2004.
- Gullivers Travel Associates (GTA), which launched its China subsidiary in August 2004, is operating inbound and domestic travel services, although it also handles Chinese inbound business in Europe and other destinations on behalf of Chinese tour operators/agencies. GTA has set up two companies and three representative offices in Beijing, Shanghai, Chengdu and Hong Kong, China.
- Cendant Travel Distribution Services (now Travelport) signed an agreement for a joint venture in August 2004 with CYTS Tours Holding. As part of the joint venture, Cendant TDS contributed the assets of its Beijing-based subsidiary, Si Hai Tong Jie Reservation Service Co Ltd, a leading hotel consolidator and online booking engine acquired by the company in June 2004.

6.1.3 Tour Groups versus Fully Independent Travellers (FITs)

The majority of Chinese outbound leisure passengers are obliged to join tour groups of minimum five participants organised by licensed travel agencies. (For Australia, the minimum size of an approved tour group is now two, as already discussed.) They have to stay with the same group for the whole of the trip and all travel activities during the tour are the responsibility of a tour manager. Official figures cited in the UNWTO report *China – The Asia and the Pacific Intra-regional Outbound Series,* 2006 show that, in 1993, travel agencies in China organised 730,000 outbound passenger trips. The number increased eight-fold over the following eleven years, reaching 5.6 million in 2004 (including trips to Hong Kong, China, and Macao, China).

If domestic tours and tours to Hong Kong, China, and Macao, China, are included in the count, there was a decline from 2000 to 2004 in the share of tours organised by travel agencies – from 40% to 20% overall – although absolute volume rose by 44% over the four years. But as far as tours to foreign countries are concerned (i.e. excluding trips to Hong Kong, China, and Macao, China), the respective share rose steadily from 28% to 47% over the four-year period, as the following table shows.

Figure 6.4 Travel Agencies Share of the Chinese Outbound Tourism Market, 2000-2004

	Total	To foreign countries[a]	
	Passengers (× 1,000)	Passengers (× 1,000)	Share (%)
2000	4,302	1,193	27.7
2001	3,695	1,520	41.1
2002	4,598	1,838	49.4
2003	4,403	1,726	44.6
2004	6,479	2,639	47.2
AAGR[b] (%)	10.8	22.0	–

a) Excludes Hong Kong, China, Macao, China, and border areas.

b) AAGR = Average annual growth rate 2000-2004.

Source: UNWTO's *China – The Asia and the Pacific Intra-regional Outbound Series*, 2006, from CNTA's *China Tourism Statistics Almanac.*

6.1.4 Simplifying and Clarifying Rules Governing Travel Agencies

As already discussed briefly in chapter 2, CNTA and the State Administration for Industry and Commerce have announced a new standard contract for outbound travel, known as the Chinese Citizens Outbound Travel Contract. This is the basic agreement between travellers and their travel agencies. Until now, too many travel agents have been operating according to non-standard contracts, which causes problems in dealing with infringements.

The new agreement, which was due to be implemented in 2007, should make it possible for travel agencies to transfer a tour group to a third-party travel agency provided that it can guarantee the same service standards and get approval from the tour participants before departure. The new contract also encourages tourists to protect their own rights and to take measures to minimise losses when an infringement occurs.

In addition, it is reported that CNTA will promote the construction of a long-term travel credit system. This is designed to compile information on travel agencies who break travel-related rules in China, as well as to provide information to consumers about trustworthy travel companies. As the Chinese outbound travel market has grown, the number of disputes has also risen. These arise mainly from unregulated travel contracts in cases in which tour guides do not bring their tour group members to promised locations or force travellers to buy souvenirs at selected shops. The new legislation will hopefully minimise these problems.

6.2 Online Travel

6.2.1 Growing Importance of the Internet

There appear to be as many different estimates of the number of internet users in China as there are sources of information, and the main problem would seem to be that the growth in internet usage is constantly greater and faster than predicted. So statistics are usually out of date. In 2006, a report in *eMarketer,* quoted in the European Travel Commission's ETC's *New Media Review,* estimated the number of users at 127 million, or 9.4% of the total population, forecasting that it would rise to 184 million by 2010 (13.6% market penetration).

Figure 6.5 Internet Users in China, 2004-2010

Year	Users (million)	Share of the population (%)
2004	94	7.2
2005	111	8.4
2006	127	9.4
2007	143	10.8
2008	158	11.9
2009	171	12.8
2010	184	13.6

Source: *eMarketer,* 2006.

The 2006 estimate has now been superseded by the latest data from the China Internet Network Center (CNNIC) – probably the most reliable source – which put the total at 137 million in December 2006, and which shows that, by the middle of 2007, the number of internet users in China was as high as 162 million, representing 12.3% of the country's population. So the *eMarketer* forecast for 2010 looks certain to be too low.

While the overall internet penetration level is still small compared with that in many other countries around the world, in absolute volume, China ranks second only to the United States of America in the total number of users online. In fact, many analysts feel that the number of internet users in China will surpass the number of US users within two years. At the current rate of growth it is forecast that Chinese internet users will exceed today's 210 million US users by 2009 and, by 2011, according to forecasts from the International Telecommunication Union, the total should reach 250 million, 19.2% of the population.

Figure 6.6 Growth of Internet Usage in China, 2000-2006

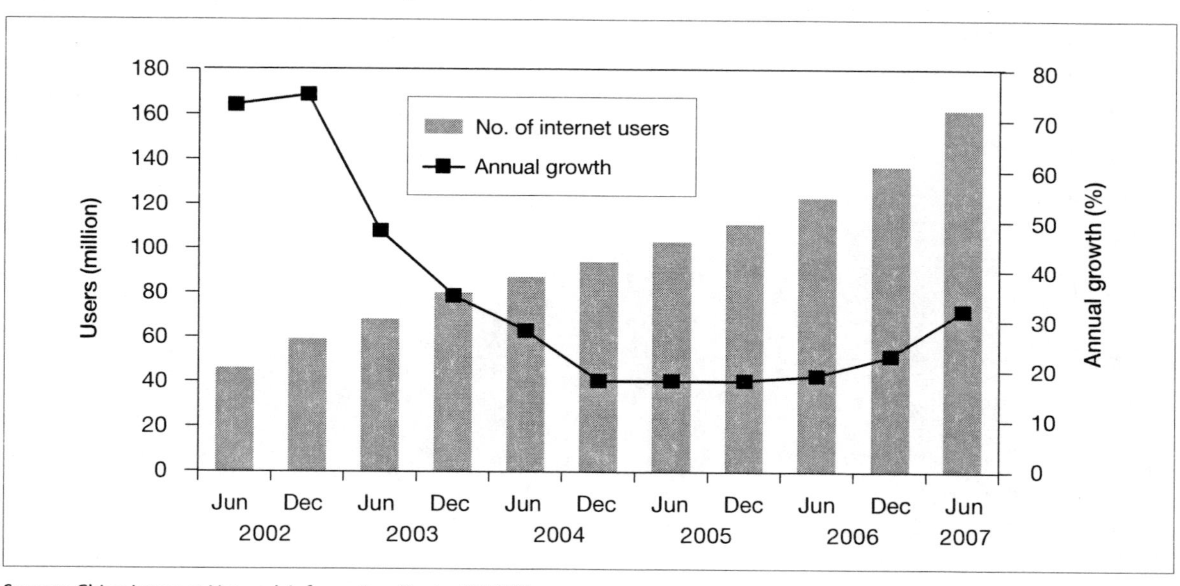

Source: China Internet Network Information Centre (CNNIC).

Figure 6.7 Top Ten Internet Countries, 2006[a]

Country	Internet users (million)	Population (million)	Internet penetration (%)	Share of world users (%)
United States of America	209	299	69	19
China	123	1,306	9	11
Japan	86	128	67	8
Germany	51	83	61	5
India	40	1,112	4	4
United Kingdom	37	60	63	4
Republic of Korea	34	51	67	3
Italy	31	59	52	3
France	29	61	48	3
Brazil	26	184	14	3

a) Ranked by absolute number of users.

Source: Internet World Stats, 2006.

ACNielsen's February 2007 Omnibus research suggests that, in the major cities – and even in some so-called second-tier cities – internet penetration is as high as 60-70% of the 18-40 year age segment. And among Chinese with university and college education, the online population accounts for a share of more than 90%.

It is, however, important to note that there are still only about 70 million connected computers in China, so 50% or more Chinese users connect on shared-access points, such as internet cafes and school labs, or by hand-held mobile devices. Access aside, the CNNIC figures show that Chinese internet users closely resemble users around the world, although the user population does include more male (58.3%) than female (41.7%) users.

The age of internet users in China (as a % of the total) was estimated in 2006 by the CNNIC at:

- < 18 years old: 17.2%
- 18-24: 35.2%
- 25-30: 19.7%
- 31-40: 18.6%
- 41-60: 8.4%
- > 60: 0.9%

6.2.2 E-commerce in China

E-commerce in China is in its infancy, according to *eMarketer*. The country lacks an online payment system for handling credit card transactions in a safe, efficient manner. Poor logistic and distribution networks restrict how far apart sellers and buyers can be. In addition, internet retailers offer limited product selection, and quality is often suspect. These obstacles have not curbed the desire of foreign internet retailers to establish operations in China, despite the high costs involved. However, it will be a long time before China comes close to the United States of America in retail e-commerce sales.

Analysys International projects that retail e-commerce sales in China in 2007 will reach US$ 955.1 million, compared with *eMarketer's* projection for retail e-commerce in the United States of America for 2007 of US$ 125.1 billion. In November 2005, less than 20% of internet users claimed to shop online even only "sometimes", according to CNNIC.

The internet is chiefly used for communication and information gathering. During the SARS epidemic in 2003, online shopping reportedly gained an important boost from the fact that people did not want to go outside to shop for fear of 'catching' the disease, but statistical evidence does not bear this out. It remains an undeveloped market and purchases are overwhelmingly concentrated on books, audiovisual material and communications equipment.

Figure 6.8 Internet Transactions in China, 1998-2005 (× 1,000)

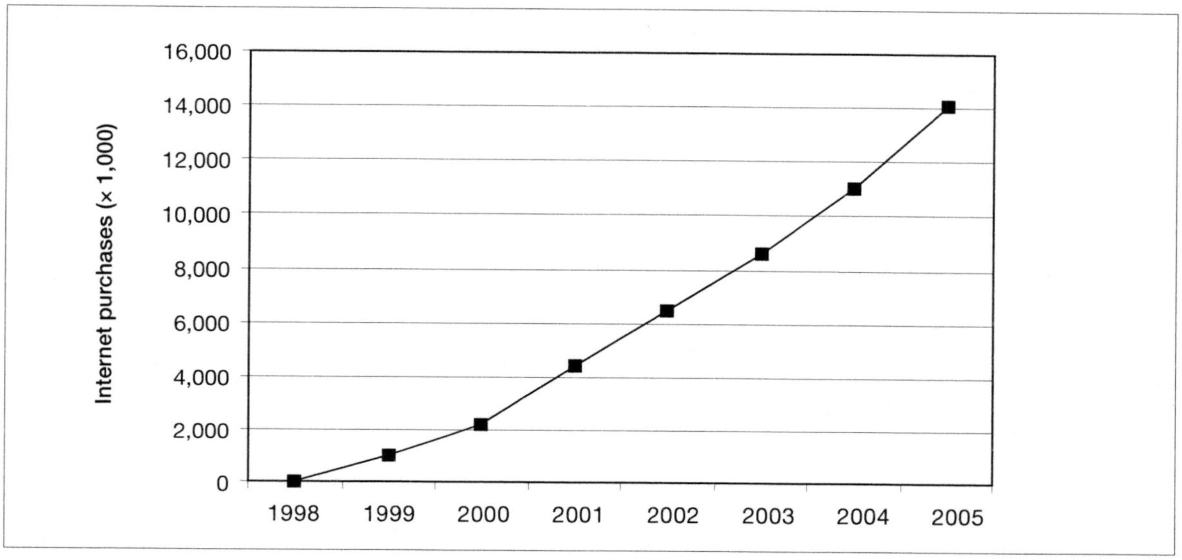

Source: ICT Group, http://www.ictgroup.com.

In terms of online business, of the 8.3 million small and medium-sized enterprises (SMEs) registered in China, nearly half have a web presence of some kind, but only one in ten conduct electronic transactions. By comparison, 80% of SMEs in the United States of America use the internet to conduct commercial transactions. China was rated only 27th in the analysis of 28 countries' 'informationalisation' level conducted by China's National Bureau of Statistics in 2004, although it almost certainly ranks higher three years later.

6.2.3 Online Travel 'Looking' and 'Booking'

The internet is the preferred method of obtaining travel information amongst internet users in China in 2005, according to CNNIC:

- Internet: 82%
- Travel agency: 54%
- Word of mouth: 46%
- Travel books/magazines: 34%
- Government advice: 30%
- Media: 21%

However, although the number of internet users is rising steadily, it is primarily used as a research tool, and not for actual purchasing. A 2004 survey of consumers in Shanghai and Guangzhou showed that only 1% of travel customers purchased travel and tourism services on the internet. The majority of Chinese do not have credit cards, making online bookings difficult. Many also still prefer to pick up the phone and speak to a voice they recognise, as well as try to bargain for a better deal.

In November 2005, 50.6% of internet users claimed to have searched and arranged travel online at some point, according to CNNIC. The frequency of searching and arranging travel online among internet users in China in 2005 (as a % of respondents) was as follows, according to CNNIC statistics quoted by *eMarketer:*

- Never: 49.4%
- Seldom: 27.2%
- Sometimes: 15.3%
- Often: 7.0%
- Always: 0.9%

China's online travel services market reached Rmb 254 million (US$ 31.6 million) in the fourth quarter of 2005, split between airline ticketing at Rmb 77 million (US$ 9.6 million), hotel reservations at Rmb 165 million (US$ 20.4 million) and travel agency services (including packaged tours) at Rmb 12 million (US$ 1.49 million). The bulk of sales were for domestic travel.

China World Trade Corporation says that 75% of its air ticket sales are completed through electronic ticketing but most consumers are still paying offline, partly because of the deficient electronic payment system in China.

Nevertheless, the potential for online travel business should not be underestimated. According to the International Air Transport Association (IATA), China was the first country in the world to report 100% e-ticketing last year. This is music to the ears of the world airline body, which is pushing for 100% e-ticketing globally by the end of this year.

Moreover, there is a fast-growing number of online travel companies, including travel agencies, and the reportedly modest 1% demand from Chinese travellers for online travel is still a substantial figure. The purchasing habits of Chinese online travellers are similar to those anywhere in the world – motivated by price and rich content, such as maps, photographs and extensive information.

6.2.4 NTOs' Use of the Internet for Marketing

Throughout China potential holiday destinations are increasingly being researched on the internet. A survey by Tourism Australia of Chinese visitors to the country found that the most commonly used source of information for first-time travellers was the internet, which was used by 31% of visitors planning their trip, closely followed by travel agents.

As far as travel to Europe is concerned, VisitBritain's research suggests that the majority (90%) of potential travellers would consult the internet if planning a trip to the United Kingdom or the rest of Europe. But, due to visa requirements and the problems that have been encountered with expanding the process of electronic payment, there are some concerns among NTOs that online booking will not develop as a key factor in the market in the short term.

Nevertheless, a number of major NTOs are developing, or have already created, their own simplified Chinese websites to cater to the mainland market. Traditional Chinese characters are used for the Hong Kong and Taiwanese markets, while mainland Chinese and Singaporean Chinese read simplified Chinese characters.

Figure 6.9 European NTOs Offering Websites in Simplified Chinese, 2006

Austria	Ireland
Czech Republic	Luxembourg
Finland	Netherlands
France	Spain
Germany	United Kingdom
Hungary	

Note: The Scandinavia Tourist Board (STB) has a website in simplified Chinese for Chinese interested in Scandinavia.
Source: ETC, *Benchmarking Study on NTO Budgets*, 2006.

6.2.5 Online Travel Agencies

The online travel market is heavily dominated by the two leading players, Ctrip and eLong. In 2004, Ctrip accounted for a 61% share of online travel agencies in China. However, the vast majority of bookings are still made through traditional offline agencies.

Figure 6.10 Market Share of the Online Travel Agencies/Distributors in China, 2004 (%)

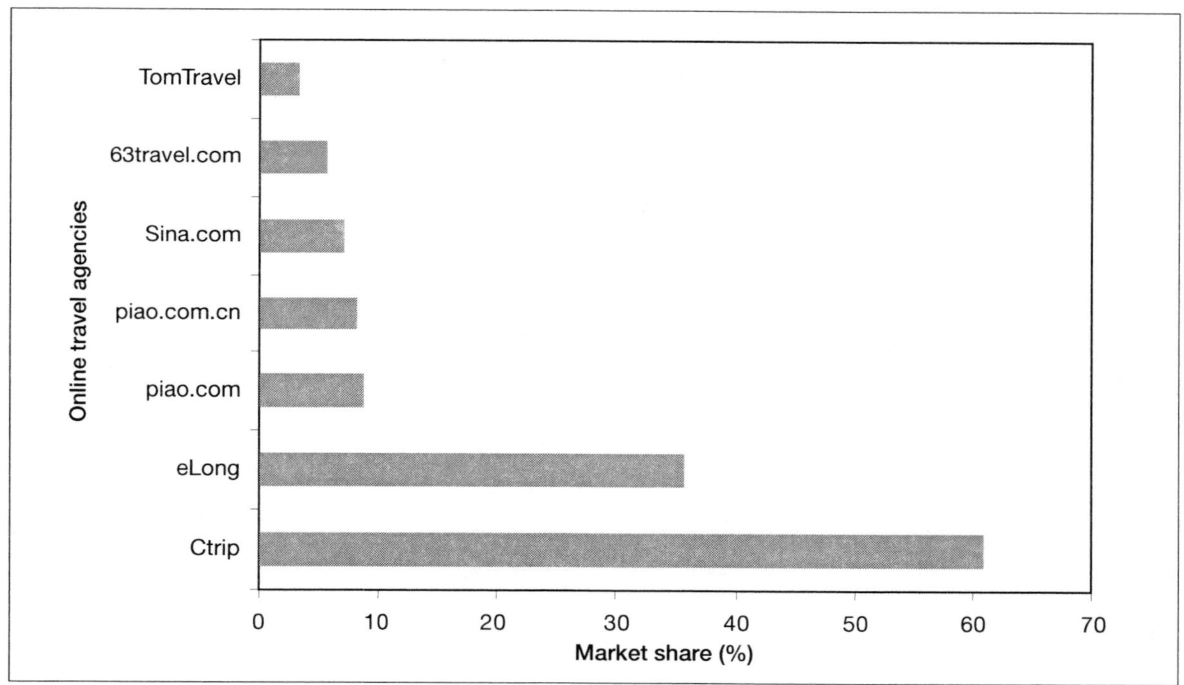

Source: CNTA, 2005.

Ctrip.com says that 70% of its business customers book offline through call centres while 70% of independent travellers (FITs) book online. But FIT customers are still few and far between. Both Ctrip and eLong agree that there is a growing trend among the higher social demographic sector away from the conventional packaged tours, and towards independent travel.

6.2.6 Prospects for Online Travel

There is no doubt that China's online travel industry is going to undergo rapid transformation over the next few years. The appetite for the internet in China, together with the market's brisk enthusiasm for reducing costs, is certain to increase the proportion of those who book online.

Driving this process forward will be the expansion of low-cost airlines, the increased use of credit cards, and the growth of the internet and of the Chinese economy. But it will not all be plain sailing for European suppliers since progress is likely to be inhibited by the continued requirement for visas from most ADS countries, restrictions on the ability of many Chinese to travel and the tradition of relying on cash transactions.

Chapter 7

Market Realities

7.1 European NTOs in China

7.1.1 An Essential Presence

Fewer than 30 foreign NTOs are established in China, although there are a handful of regional and city tourist offices, mainly from the United States of America. In fact, opening an office may be a difficult process. This is why many NTOs that do have a presence tend to be represented through their embassies, consulates, or national airlines.

Switzerland was the first European country to open an office in China, in 1998, and it has since been joined by 16 others. There are nine countries with full offices in Beijing headed by an expatriate director (five of these also have offices in Shanghai). In addition, Sweden, Norway and Denmark have a joint operation in Beijing and Shanghai under the banner of the Scandinavian Tourist Board (STB). Turismo de Portugal, the Portuguese tourism board, is represented abroad by ICEP, the Portuguese Agency for Foreign Trade and Investment. Two other countries (Germany and Ireland) have local marketing representatives (Ireland's is in Shanghai rather than Beijing). Hungary is represented by its embassy, and Italy by the Italian Chamber of Commerce.

Figure 7.1 European NTOs in China by Location and Type of Office,[a] 2006

Country/NTO	Beijing	Shanghai
Austria	1	1
Czech Republic	1	-
Denmark[b]	2	2
Finland	1	1
France	1	-
Germany	3	-
Greece	1	1
Hungary	4	-
Ireland	-	3
Italy	4	-
Netherlands	1	-
Norway[b]	2	2
Portugal	4	4
Spain	1	-
Sweden[b]	2	2

Country/NTO	Beijing	Shanghai
Switzerland	1	1
United Kingdom	1	1

a) 1 = Own NTO office;
2 = Joint NTO office;
3 = marketing representative/agency;
4 = c/o Embassy, Chamber of Commerce, etc..

b) Represented in China by the Scandinavian Tourist Board (STB), which is owned jointly by VisitSweden, VisitDenmark and Innovation Norway.

Source: Respective NTOs; ETC, *Benchmarking Study on NTO Budgets*, 2006.

It is expensive for foreign companies of any kind to operate in China and a number of NTOs – not necessarily those from Europe – have learned to their cost that it might have been wiser not to take funding away from established markets to invest in China, since inadequate budgets are often less effective than no budgets at all. But some have had very positive experiences, after making significant investments in the Chinese market.

In 2005, the STB's office had a shared operating budget that represented 17-20% of the three countries' total marketing budgets for Asia. This highlights the significant investment that the Scandinavian countries have been prepared to make in the Chinese market and their confidence of good returns on their investment.

All leading Asian destinations are established in China, including Australia. Canada also has an office, whose main role seems to be negotiation of Approved Destination Status (ADS) – its other functions are unclear as no country without ADS is officially allowed to undertake tourism promotions in the Chinese market. The United States of America does not have an office. However, the US state of Nevada was given permission to open an office in China in 2004 (Chinese are avid gamblers) – although it is prohibited from promoting gambling/gaming – and the state of Hawaii is also represented, as are the cities of San Francisco and Los Angeles.

New York City tourism officials have recently reached a deal with the Chinese Government on establishing a presence in the country, in Shanghai, in the hope of capitalising on increased interest in tourism to the United States of America among the Chinese. One third of all Chinese travellers to the United States of America make a stop in New York. Under the agreement, the city will not be able to advertise directly to Chinese citizens, but will hire representatives to work with local travel agencies and other providers.

While still fairly modest overall, NTO marketing activity in China is increasingly being boosted by activities on the part of local and foreign tour operators and travel agencies, as well as international hotel groups. In addition, some countries wisely link their tourism promotions with activities by trade missions in an attempt to stretch what are often meagre promotional budgets of NTOs.

7.1.2 Not an Easy Return on Investment

Although a presence in China is critical if NTOs are to ensure they capture their share of the market's growth, the excessive hype surrounding the Chinese market means that many countries have overly optimistic expectations as to growth prospects in the short term.

The experience of the first couple of years of ADS operation in Europe – i.e. handling leisure group tour business – has been disappointing, even for Europe's leading tourism destinations. Numbers have been lower than expected, yields are economically not viable and, despite fairly stringent checks, a significant number of Chinese have absconded during their trips, resulting in tour operators losing their right to handle the business, if only on a temporary basis.

Despite these early teething problems, China clearly has huge growth potential for the medium term and has become one of the most hotly contested markets in the world. But, for the foreseeable future, the principal players in Europe, in terms of ADS business, will continue to be the leading Schengen destinations, and especially France, Italy and Germany. Switzerland is also seen as a strong competitor – largely because Switzerland Tourism has the support of more than 50 Swiss tourism and non-tourism companies established in China, contributing to raising the image of the destination and sharing in the funding of joint promotions. And non-European competitors, such as Australia, New Zealand and South-East Asia, should not be disregarded.

The United Kingdom will continue to attract a significant share of business tourism and students from China – as long as visas do not become prohibitively expensive. But the difficulty of organising multi-destination tours including countries in the Schengen area and the United Kingdom, when a separate United Kingdom visa is required, makes them an unattractive proposition. (Switzerland's solution to the problem has been to grant visas automatically to anyone who has already secured a Schengen visa.)

7.2 Doing Business with the Chinese

There are a number of rules for NTOs and inbound European tour operators and suppliers to remember when trying to do business with Chinese tour operators and travel agencies. To summarise the most important: it helps to have some kind of representation in China; Mandarin-speaking staff and tour guides should be appointed (or Cantonese-speaking staff in Guangdong Province); a Chinese website is essential (cf. chapter 6); sales training and familiarisation trips need to be provided; suppliers should ensure detailed, itemised quotes and add value for FIT groups; and everyone should be conscious of price constraints, but should not sacrifice quality.

Suppliers who are prepared to work Chinese hours are also likely to benefit from increased business. Chinese expect their requests for quotes to be responded to on a 24/7 basis. They do not care what the official working hours are in destination countries. In addition, even if some requests seem strange, it is important to try to accommodate them. It is common to be asked to include tips in the package price, for example. Chinese travelling on government or company money do not want to put their hands in their pockets to pay tips. And even leisure tour group participants prefer to have a fully inclusive package price, so they know how much they have for shopping and other extras.

7.3 The Chinese Media

7.3.1 Advertising: An Expensive Proposition

According to Danwei.org, there appear to be well over 25,000 newspapers and magazines in China, as well as some 12,000 television and radio stations attracting a domestic television audience of over 1.1 billion. (Danwei.org is a website about media, advertising and urban life in China. The website is produced in Hong Kong, China, and hosted in the United States of America, and the latest information is dated 7 August 2007).

Deciding on where – even whether – to spend one's valuable, and often meagre, promotion budgets can be difficult. Advertising space is often very costly. Promotional activities, such as familiarisation trips for the media and 'in kind' support for TV and radio programmes, are often a much more attractive proposition in terms of return on investment. Nevertheless, travel and tourism advertising, while still modest, is growing in China, particularly on the internet.

7.3.2 Chinese Media Guide

The following media listing is by no means comprehensive, but it is recommended by Danwei – one of the most important media groups – and highlights the most relevant media as far as potential advertisers in the tourism sector are concerned. The list is updated periodically and can be found on www.Danwei.org.

National newspapers

People's Daily Group:

- *People's Daily* – national voice of the Party, also available in English.
- *Beijing Times* – part of People's Daily group but edited and managed like commercial newspapers such as the Beijing Youth Daily. It borrows its design from Southern Metropolis Daily, and aspires to be a working-class paper.

Southern Media Group:

- Southern Metropolitan Daily.
- Southern Weekly.

Beijing Daily Group:

- *Beijing Daily.*
- *Beijing Morning Post.*
- *Beijing Evening News.*
- *Beijing Daily Messenger* – also known as *Star Daily*, it has a large entertainment section.

Other important newspapers:

- *China Youth Daily* – published since 1951 and distributed nationwide, it has always had a large reader base because universities and high schools were strained to subscribe. It is a good and well-respected Chinese newspaper. According to its website, *China Youth Daily* sells about half a million copies every day.
- *Beijing Youth Daily.*
- *Legal Mirror.*
- *The First* – new paper launched in late 2004 and aligned somehow with the Beijing Olympic movement. It is a joint venture between the Beijing Daily Group, Beijing Youth Daily, and the Shanghai Media Group. It boasts a large quantity of photos and sports news.

Regional newspapers:

- *The Beijing News* – it is a Southern Media Group and Guangming Daily joint venture, on a quest to become the *New York Times* of China.
- *Xinmin Evening News.*
- *Oriental Morning Post.*
- *Jiefang Daily* – press organ of the Shanghai Party.
- *Chongqing Evening News.*
- *Yangcheng Evening News* (Guangzhou).

Business papers:

- *National Business Daily* – Shangai based joint venture between Jiefang Daily and Chengdu Daily newspaper groups; publishes eight pages apiece on domestic and international business news.
- *China Business News* – first Chinese business daily, aims "to be the most influential, authoritative and respected financial daily newspaper in China, matching the future of Chinese economic development, and equivalent to world-class papers like the *Wall Street Journal* and *Financial Times*."
- *The Economic Observer* – business weekly.
- *China Business* – business weekly published by the Chinese Academy of Social Sciences, which gives it access to lots of data and research.

Portals/websites:

- Xinhuanet – Xinhua's English service is at ChinView.
- Baidu (Baidu News, Baidu News Ticker).
- Sina (various news entities).
- Sohu (various news entities).
- Eastday.

Magazines:

- According to the World Tourism Organization's report *China – The Asia Pacific Intra-regional Outbound Series,* there are more and more travel magazines for the public in China, such as *Traveler* and *Tourist*. As travel has become an essential part of life of many families, it also has become an important subject in many newspapers and magazines – and not just confined to high-end magazines.
- As an example, white collars in Beijing like to read *Trend Magazine,* and travel is an important trend among Chinese. From *Trend Magazine* a new magazine has been born, *Trend Travel*. Similarly, the Gootrip media group has also developed new travel and tourism publications, born out of their general media – e.g. *The Player Magazine* spawned *Player's Travel*.
- *Global Travel* is a weekly publication which aims to "introduce foreign countries to the Chinese, as well as introduce China to, and make the country popular among, foreigners". Distribution is 200,000+ for each weekly issue across 604 tourism cities in China. Other key consumer publications include *National Geographic* (www.huaxia-ng.com) and *Chinese National Geography* (www.cng.com.cn).
- The most important of the travel trade magazines include *TTG China* (www.ttgasiamedia.com/ttgchinashtml), a leading Chinese-language monthly, targeting travel agencies and other travel professionals in the Greater China Region. It has a monthly distribution of 78,000 to travel trade readers.
- Meanwhile, *TTN China* (www.ttnmedia.com) has 17 years experience in the Chinese market. Published monthly, it is distributed throughout China, with a circulation in excess of 65,000 to travel and tourism professionals.
- *China Travel Agent* (www.lxsmedia.com), which is geared almost exclusively to the travel trade, is published monthly and has a circulation of 32,000 travel agents, plus an electronic distribution of 50,000 professionals.
- *Tong Ye Travel Message Weekly* (www.ctty.cn) is distributed to more than 18,000 Chinese travel agents weekly.

- Other travel trade publications include *China Travel & Tourism Press* (www.cttp.net.cn) and *TTG-BT MICE China* (www.ttgasiamedia.com/BTNC.shtml).

7.3.3 Marketing and Promotions

Many magazines now include articles about tourism. High-end magazines have more personalised information about tourism. They give tips on places few people have been to rather than just talking about the traditional scenic spots. Trekking, boating, driving tours, etc. have their adepts among readers. Even a magazine like *China Collection* advises readers "not to forget you are a collector when you travel in the spring". The magazine gives advice on how to visit museums, how to explore folklore and how to appreciate the costumes of ethnic groups.

On board planes, in VIP lounges or deluxe restaurants, hotels and banks, many magazines are on display. Travel, and outbound travel in particular, is an important topic in these magazines. Such magazines also carry advertisements and information about ADS, airlines and international hotel chains. In short, articles and advertisements in these magazines are full of promotions, giving vivid images to the reader that have lasting effects.

Travel agency advertisements focus on the short term. Their aim is to attract clients. These ads are small in size, giving information about travel routes, prices and dates. Such advertisements are placed in daily papers or weeklies. As an example, the *Exquisite Shopping Guide* is a weekly for middle-class wage earners. On 26 January 2006, the weekly carried ads about travel to Asia Pacific, which included: a six-day Valentine tour to Bali for Rmb 4,890 per person (US$ 614 or € 485); a five-day tour to the Maldives at Rmb 9,200 per person for a minimum two people; and a six-day Star Cruise at Rmb 6,980 each for two people minimum.

Daily newspapers carry a large number of advertisements from travel agencies.

A sample survey in Beijing, Shanghai and Guangzhou showed that during the whole of September 2005, in five newspapers in the three leading tourism source cities (*Beijing Evening News* and *Life Style* in Beijing; *Xinmin Evening Paper* and *Zhenjiang Service Guide* in Shanghai; and the *Guangzhou Daily* in Guangzhou), there were ads on outbound travel from 51 travel agencies (38.6% of the 132 outbound travel agencies in the three cities). The ads usually appear on Tuesdays and Thursdays.

7.3.4 Radio

In recent years, a traditional but fast-growing media has been the radio. One of the latest surveys shows that some 64% of the Chinese population listens to the radio and the proportion is 72% among the urban population – a total of 700 million or so.

Since 2002, radio advertising has grown overall by over 20%, with Beijing recording 40% growth.

The increasing popularity of cars has also increased use of the radio. While driving their cars, people enjoy listening to the radio and, since there is a lot of traffic congestion in Beijing, Shanghai and Guangzhou, which often leads to traffic jams, listening to the radio can make it easier to pass the time. So radio advertising is a good marketing tool – white-collar workers in Beijing drive their own cars, so they control the radio stations. They like music, culture and art stations. In contrast, white-collar workers in Shanghai usually take taxis (or several people share a taxi), so it is the driver who decides which radio stations they listen to. This makes it more difficult to target the appropriate market segment.

7.3.5 Television

With more than 1.1 billion viewers – most of the population has access to a television set – television is a primary means of distributing information. China is reportedly a major market for pay-TV – at the end of 2004 it had 115 million subscribers and the reported figures are set to beat predictions of growth significantly. The merging of cable and broadband combined with huge production potential is one of the most exciting commercial phenomena in China. The control of cable channels has been described as 'bottom up'. The 1,300 'approved' stations are licensed by local governments and, in addition, 2,000 counties, 600 townships and 1,400 work units run their own cable stations.

The availability of non-domestic TV is limited. Agreements are in place for AOL Time Warner, News Corp and the Hong Kong-based Phoenix TV to transmit via cable in Guangdong province. But there is evidence that the progress of cable is not as straightforward as anticipated. In Guangdong province the city of Foshan started promoting digital cable, with overseas TV programmes being the major attraction. Only 6,000 subscribers signed up in the city. In order to get people to opt for digital TV, the city decided to give subscribers free decoders. Hundreds of people now reportedly line up every day to get the free decoder in Foshan, and the number of digital cable users has at least quadrupled.

7.3.6 Internet

With more than 82% of China's internet users declaring the internet as their main travel information channel, according to CNNIC's *Annual Statistical Survey Report on Internet Development in China,* the advertising potential of the Chinese internet has never been better, according to Nielsen/NetRatings. Over the period May to July 2006, China's online space saw a strong and steady growth of online advertising activity. According to the AdRelevance report, 587 online display advertisers ran nearly 1,500 campaigns consisting of over 3,700 banners in May 2006. By July, the number of advertisers had grown by 39% to 817, while the number of campaigns and banners had increased respectively by 34% and 55% to 2,276 and 5,785.

The AdRelevance service estimates China's total online display advertising expenditure between May and July 2006 at Rmb 1.5 billion (US$ 190 million). This number is close to China's magazine advertising expenditure, which is projected at Rmb 1.9 billion for the same period by Nielsen Media Research. The big online advertising spenders are in the automotive, computer and electronics and fast moving consumer goods (FMCG) industries, jointly responsible for almost 60% of the quarter's advertising spend (Nielsen/Netratings, September 2006).

7.4 Other Tools for Promotion

7.4.1 Travel Fairs

There are a number of annual travel trade fairs in China and Hong Kong, China – a list of the most important is provided in annex VI. Travel trade fairs are seen as a good way for destinations to advertise their services within the country. The most important – if only because it has the support of the China National Tourism Administration (CNTA) – is the China International Travel Market (CITM), which alternates between Shanghai and Kunming every year in the month of November. But at least 75% of the fair is given over to inbound and domestic tourism and the Kunming event (which took place in November 2007) is not as well attended as the Shanghai fair.

A more dedicated outbound tourism event is the China Outbound Travel and Tourism Market (COTTM) in Beijing, last organised in May 2007. It has only been running for a few years and is therefore still small, but the quality of the buyers is reported to be high, according to China specialist, ChinaContact.

7.4.2 Credit Card Companies and Banks

The Bank Association of China announced that 10.8 million credit cards had been issued in the country in 2004 – an increase of 100% over the previous year, and six times more than in 2002. If debit cards are included, there are 815 million bank-issued cards in operation – roughly one each for 60% of the population (although some Chinese, of course, have several cards).

This new group of cardholders, emerging in the three major economic areas, have a selection of credit cards, mileage cards issued by airlines, cards for beauty saloons and cards for gymnasiums. Chinese credit cards are also linked with international credit cards. As an example, China Union Pay cards can be used as Visa cards and MasterCards. Various commercial institutions offer all kinds of preferential treatment to gold and silver cardholders, among which travel is an important item. Banks have issued dual-currency cards or debit cards that can be used abroad. Communications Bank, for example, had a promotion under the heading: 'Use your CUP cards to enjoy the Ice and Snow Festival in Korea'.

In the VIP room for gold or silver cardholders, *Player's Travel, Trend Magazine* and other travel magazines are on display. The Singapore Tourism Board cooperates with Visa International to issue multiple-entry visas valid for two years to Chinese platinum and gold Visa cardholders, since they are seen as being financially independent, creditworthy and (because they generate high travel demand) with high-yield potential.

Around 1 million Chinese have so far qualified for the multiple-entry visas. Cardholders simply have to go to one of the 12 appointed Chinese travel agencies to show their credit cards, pay Rmb 100 plus a small service charge, and they receive multiple visas for themselves and their spouses and children. According to the Singapore Tourism Board, Chinese Visa cardholders spent US$ 13 million in Singapore in 2004, a growth of 87% over 2002's level, and the total increased by more than 50% in 2005.

Debit cards in yuan/renminbi can currently be used in Hong Kong, China, Macao, China, the Republic of Korea and Thailand. Airlines have also moved into the market. Air China has issued a 'companion card', which is both a membership card of Air China and a credit card of the China Merchants Bank. By using the card for shopping or obtaining cash, Chinese can accumulate mileage. The card can be used in more than 200 countries worldwide, and when a cardholder spends money abroad in foreign currency, he can pay the bank back in Chinese yuan/renminbi. Air China promotes the 'world tourism supermarket' to its cardholders, who can buy tours to many places in the world with a combination of accumulated mileage and some Chinese currency.

Chapter 8

Current Propects

8.1 An Increasingly Sophisticated Market

8.1.1 Dynamic Growth Set to Continue

International trip volume expressed as a share of China's population is still very modest, although it has grown rapidly over the past 15 years – from around 0.2% in the early 1990s to nearly 1% in 2000, and to more than 2.6% in 2006. Even at this level, the Chinese propensity to travel abroad remains well below that of its Japanese neighbours (13%), reflecting the huge untapped potential of the market. When/if the Chinese reach the Japanese level of foreign trip taking, the market will be approaching 170 million trips a year.

Moreover, socio-economic forecasts augur well for continued dynamic growth in demand for travel and tourism. Annual GDP growth is expected to continue in double digits for the foreseeable future, and disposable income for many sectors of the population is growing rapidly. This is being boosted by the appreciating yuan/renminbi, rising levels of education and the strengthening of vocational training.

8.1.2 The Main Drivers of Growth

In addition to the positive socio-economic environment, a number of other important factors are expected to .drive growth in China's outbound travel market over the next few years. Among the most significant:

- the changing demographic profile of China – e.g. the young, affluent middle class that is emerging – from 175 million people now to around 500 million by 2025;
- the rapid urbanisation of the population – by 2015 almost half of China's population will live in major urban centres, and by 2030 that figure is expected to reach over 60%;
- increased leisure time – e.g. paid holiday time outside the three 'Golden Weeks';
- the rise of secondary and tertiary cities – both as population centres and as generators of tourism;
- a growing ability and desire to spend money on leisure, including tourism – as well as greater willingness to use credit cards or to borrow money to do so;
- increased demand for authentic, high-quality goods – and Chinese are prepared to travel to buy an authentic Gucci handbag or Burberry raincoat;
- increased online travel – for booking as well as 'looking';
- increased airline capacity from China to popular short- and long-haul destinations;
- increasing liberalisation/deregulation of China's travel and tourism industry.

8.1.3 Caveats

If all the projections look remarkably optimistic, some words of caution are nevertheless in order. The Chinese travellers' growing sophistication is already leading to stronger demands, not just for a quality experience, but also for fair and just treatment. Today's Chinese tourist no more enjoys being 'ripped off' than anyone else, so it is important to protect them from different forms of exploitation, prevalent mainly in Asia countries, such as the so-called 'zero-tours' – when local tour guides are dependent on commissions from shopping to make their money and are, therefore, extremely aggressive in trying to persuade their Chinese clients to shop where they want to take them.

Although not likely to dampen the Chinese enthusiasm for travel abroad, other concerns still need to be taken on board by hotels, inbound operators, ground-handling agents, etc in destinations chosen by Chinese. This is particularly important in Europe, where suppliers still have relatively little experience of handling Chinese tourism business. Suppliers must remain vigilant to the need to manage the cultural differences between Chinese and nationals of the host countries they visit and ensure they provide good service.

In addition, unwelcome as it may sound, the increased demand among Chinese for quality does not mean that they will become less price-conscious. There will likely be a continuing determination among group tourists to destinations with Approved Destination Status (ADS) to spend as little as possible on transport, food and accommodation. Most importantly, pricing will need to be totally transparent.

Other possible barriers to further Chinese outbound travel include:

- Fluctuations in the Chinese economy. Although unlikely, the national economy may overheat, or the yuan/renminbi may depreciate, compromising the purchasing power of Chinese travellers.
- Renewed terrorism, natural disasters, diseases or political unrest – Chinese are nervous about possible threats to their safety and security.
- The increased availability of lower-priced goods within China when the government fulfils its commitment to the World Trade Organization to reduce tariffs. This might make people feel they do not have to travel abroad to purchase branded goods.

8.2 Prospects for Europe

8.2.1 Focus on the Medium to Longer Term

Although the volume of Chinese travel to Europe will remain fairly modest for the foreseeable future, the medium- to longer-term prospects are excellent if the results of recent surveys offer an accurate picture of current Chinese thinking.

A survey conducted by Tourism Australia in 2006 to discover the awareness of, and intention for, foreign travel of 500 Chinese residents of Beijing and Shanghai found that Europe, and particularly France, hold a strong position in both Chinese cities.

Australia is a strong competitor for Europe in Beijing but it is weaker with residents in Shanghai. Interestingly, awareness of the United States of America as a destination is not strong and neither does the United States of America appear to be a direct competitor to Europe.

Many of the destinations considered in the Tourism Australia survey in Beijing and Shanghai were known to residents (see figures 8.1 and 8.2). For Europe, 11% of Beijing's and 13% of Shanghai's potential travellers had recently heard something about the destination.

Figure 8.1 Awareness among Beijing Residents of Foreign Destinations (%)

Australia	Singapore	Thailand	Europe	France	Japan
15	14	14	11	11	11

Source: Research by Tourism Australia, 2006.

Figure 8.2 Awareness among Shanghai Residents of Foreign Destinations (%)

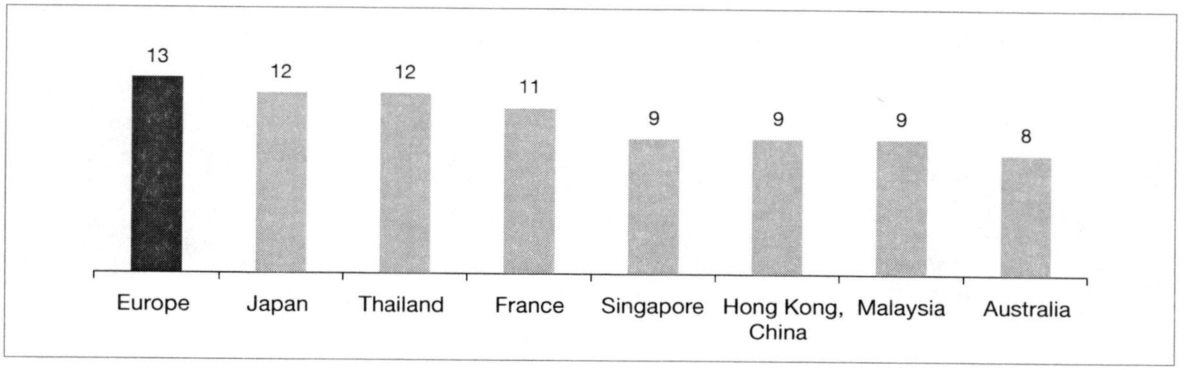

Source: Tourism Australia, 2006.

More significantly, Chinese in both Shanghai and Beijing rank Europe at the top of their lists of foreign destinations they realistically intend to visit – some day. Around 28% of survey respondents in both cities cited Europe as the destination they felt they would be most likely to visit, and 20% in Beijing and 17% in Shanghai also mentioned France separately – as a favourite destination second only to Australia in the case of Beijing residents, and second to Japan in the case of residents of Shanghai. No other European destination was identified individually by respondents.

Figure 8.3 Beijing Residents' Realistic Travel Intentions (%)

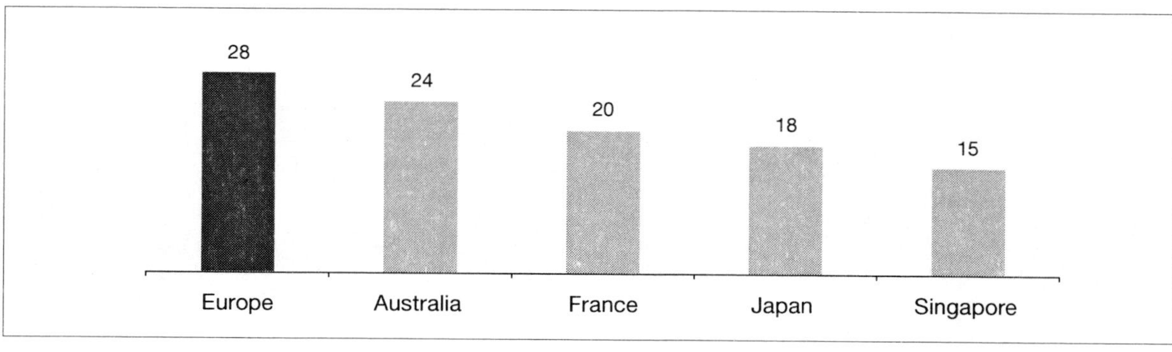

Source: Tourism Australia, 2006.

Figure 8.4 Shanghai Residents' Realistic Travel Intentions (%)

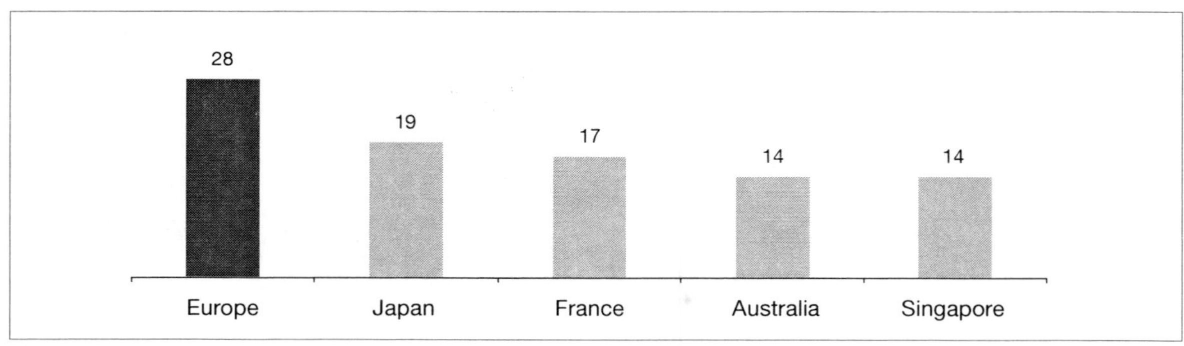

Source: Tourism Australia, 2006.

8.2.2 Europe High Up the 'Wish List' of Chinese Travellers

Interestingly, Tourism Australia's findings correlate well with research undertaken by both TNS (former Taylor Nelson Sofrès) and ACNielsen. A survey conducted by TNS in early 2007 asked Chinese which were their "most aspired to" destinations, with the question: "If you could go anywhere in the world, regardless of cost, where would you go?"

France came top of the list of (multiple-choice) responses, cited by 62% of respondents, followed by Switzerland (58%), Greece (56%), Italy (55%), Australia (53%) and the Caribbean (48%). The next most highly rated destinations among the top 15 were (in order of ranking): the United Kingdom, United States of America, New Zealand, Germany, Iceland, Antarctica, Brazil, South Africa and Monaco.

Finally, ACNielsen's February 2007 Online Omnibus shows that Europe continues to remain top of mind for Chinese. Almost one third (32%) of respondents – a representative sample of Chinese consumers in the first- and second tier cities in China – rated Europe as the "most desired dream destination". Lagging well behind was "somewhere in China" with 23%, and Australia/New Zealand and Hong Kong, China/Macao, China/Taiwan, Province of China, each with 13%. Canada and the United States of America together attracted only 6% of responses.

Chapter 9

Working with the Chines Market

9.1 Introduction

9.1.1 Background

This chapter includes details of the interviews and focus groups carried out by the European Tour Operators' Association (ETOA) and its partners with the travel trade, hotels and consumers. Partners included Amber Industry Insights in China, Consumerdata and key members of ETOA in Europe. The structure and methodology used for the interviews were in line with the specifications for the study laid down in the Invitation to Tender from the European Travel Commission (ETC) and the World Tourism Organization (UNWTO).

The purpose of this part of the study was to explore the perceptions of Chinese consumers and of the Chinese travel trade about Europe as a tourism destination, as well as their particular experiences in travelling to the region.

The surveys covered six main interest groups:

The travel trade:

- Travel agents in China who organise outbound tours to Europe.
- Tour guides from China, who have experience of leading groups around Europe.
- Inbound tour operators and hoteliers in Europe who handle/work with Chinese groups.

Consumers:

- Previous Chinese visitors to Europe.
- Potential Chinese visitors to Europe.
- Chinese travellers on tour in Europe.

Information is provided in each section as to the methodology used for conducting the surveys and the selection of the interview sample. Full details of the questionnaires used, as well as the responses from coach travellers, can be found in annexes VII-XII.

9.1.2 Structure of this Chapter

This chapter looks at each of the groups in turn, highlighting and analysing the results from the respective surveys. Where direct comparisons of the results for the different interest groups are relevant and possible – i.e. in the case of the different travel trade interviews – these are included in a separate section (9.6).

9.1.3 Language

The interviews in China, and also those with clients on tour in Europe, which were conducted in Mandarin Chinese and Cantonese, were developed in English and translated into Chinese. But the questionnaires and the responses were then translated back into English for the purposes of analysis and reporting. It is clear that some nuances may have been lost in translation and the accuracy of some of the responses must be considered questionable, particularly in the sections regarding image and perception. However, the impact of this on the overall survey results is deemed minimal.

9.1.4 Research Locations

The following map identifies the locations used for the interviews conducted in China for this report.

Figure 9.1 Research locations in China

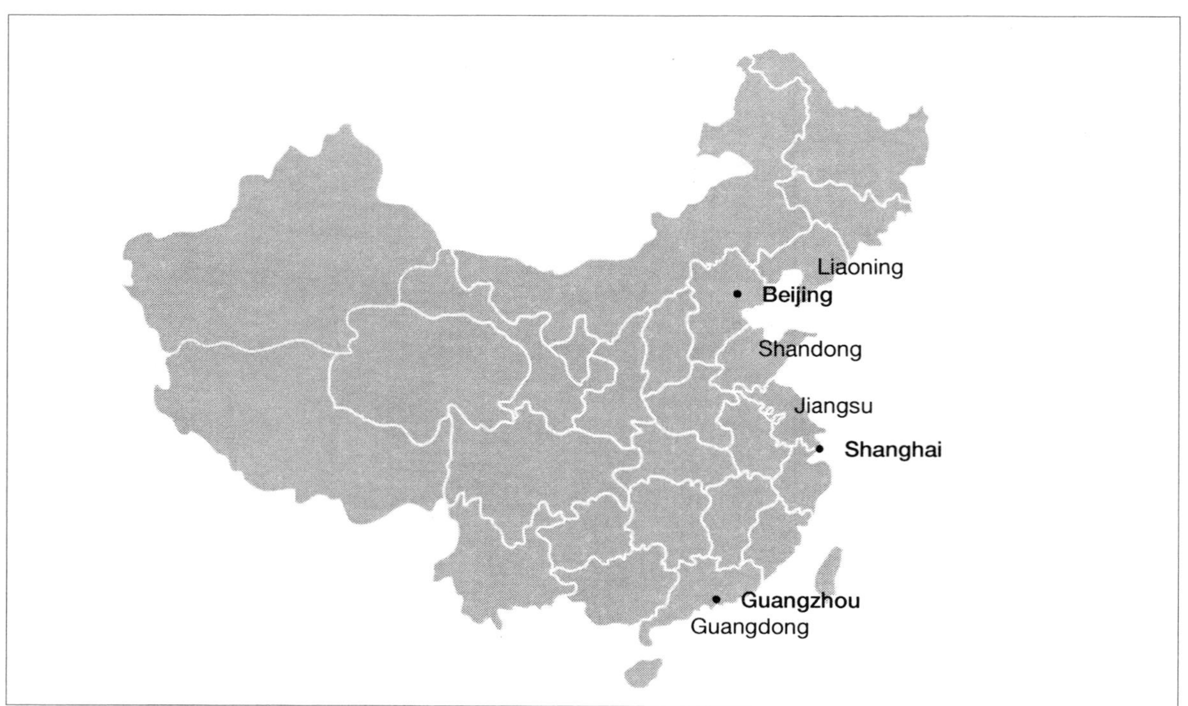

Source: ETOA.

9.2 Interviews with the Travel Trade

9.2.1 The Travel Trade's Role in China's Travel Industry

The responsibility for the distribution of outbound travel products in China essentially lies with travel agents, who effectively act in principal. This means that, rather than simply selling pre-packaged products, they gather together groups and identify the most suitable product for them from a range of different wholesale tour operators. They are thus responsible for choosing the operator with whom they work, as well as for supplying the tour guide to accompany the group.

Travel agencies were set up in the main Chinese cities comparatively recently, and are still almost non-existent in rural areas. The majority continue to rely on traditional ways of doing business, i.e. bookings are mainly manual, with some agencies having no electronic systems at all. This is despite the fact that most brochures are – by western standards – poorly printed and contain limited information.

The agency staff is unlikely to have any experience of Europe, or to be educated to university level. Travel is still an expensive luxury, which explains why, while some clients make enquiries by telephone or research products on the internet, bookings are invariably made in person.

For group leisure travel, based on the Approved Destination Status (ADS) scheme (see chapter 2), the agency is also responsible for processing the visa applications, which reinforces their central role. Even if the ADS system is one day replaced, the personal nature of the contract will ensure that the travel agency will remain central to the booking process.

9.2.2 Methodology

Travel agent interviews were conducted with representatives of four travel agencies in each of China's three main cities: Beijing, Shanghai and Guangzhou (12 interviews in total).

The starting point for their selection was a list of travel agencies provided by the China National Tourism Administration (CNTA). Selected agencies were then contacted by telephone to confirm their suitability as interviewees. Among the criteria used for selection, individual agents had to have:

- Experience at handling outbound tours to Europe.
- A city-centre location.
- More than two years' experience working in the travel industry.

One member of staff from each of the 12 travel agencies was interviewed. A detailed list of the questions posed in the interviews, which lasted between 30 and 40 minutes each, can be found in annex VII. All except one of the agents had personal experience of travel to Europe – most were higher-level managers of European departments – and had been to many ADS countries. The more junior customer-facing staff had not been to Europe.

9.2.3 Destinations Offered

In addition to Europe, all agencies interviewed offered a number of other destinations, most importantly: South-East Asia, Japan, the Republic of Korea and Australia. Six of the agencies said they also offered Africa, South America and New Zealand. A handful also offered the United States of America for business trips.

The 12 agents offered all ADS-approved countries in Europe. Some focused mainly on western Europe and a couple specialise in Scandinavia. The total list of countries offered includes: Austria, Belgium, the Czech Republic, Denmark, Finland, France, Germany, Greece, Hungary, Italy, Luxembourg, Monaco, the Netherlands, Norway, Portugal, the Russian Federation, Spain, Sweden, Switzerland and the United Kingdom.

Number of countries offered per tour

The average number of countries offered per tour appears to be decreasing steadily. Previously, the opportunities to travel outside China were limited, so people took advantage to visit as many countries as possible within their average two-week tours. The number of countries offered per visit ranged from 1-15.

The past two to three years have seen a significant change in preferences, with clients opting to spend longer in each country to ensure a more in-depth visit. The average number of countries visited is now seven and agents expect this to fall to four shortly.

Many Chinese travellers are now better able to identify the European countries in which they have a particular interest. This is partly due to increased exposure to the west through the media, which has generally improved the Chinese understanding of Europe. It is also partly attributable to the inevitable growth in repeat visitors. Demand for more specialised tours taking in fewer destinations is growing in line with the growth in numbers of repeat visitors to Europe.

9.2.4 Products Offered

ADS destinations

As explained in chapter 2, although there are exceptions to the general rule (see below), ADS trips are officially organised leisure group tours. Individual travel is not permitted under the ADS system. But business and technical groups, as well as individual business travellers, can visit non-ADS countries.

According to the requirements of the ADS scheme, all levels of tour are possible – from budget to luxury:

- In Shanghai, two of the agencies interviewed said they offered budget tours; the other two operate luxury tours.
- In Guangzhou, only one company said it offered luxury tours, with the other three operating only budget tours.
- In Beijing, two of the agencies said they specialised in business travel; the other two organise more in-depth leisure visits involving fewer, but more unusual, destinations.

One clear trend is suggested by the results of these interviews: the range and variety of holidays being offered are growing all the time.

The 12 agents were asked for their views on how ADS would likely develop in the years ahead, but it proved difficult to persuade them to make any comments on the subject. Government legislation dictates that only ADS group tourism is currently allowed and, while many of the agents expect to see changes to this scheme over time, they felt there was little point in speculating about which countries may be most affected by these changes.

Individual travel

Several companies mentioned that it is possible to arrange individual tours for customers who have had passports issued already, or who can obtain ordinary private passports. This applies to the following Chinese citizens:

- Those with family members in Europe.
- Those who have travelled previously on business to Europe and already have a visa.
- Those who have an individual financial guarantor in Europe.

Themed tours

A few themed tours are now being offered by some of the larger travel agencies. Tours were organised around the FIFA Football World Cup in 2006, for example, and there are regular skiing programmes, but the travel agents interviewed were vague about the availability of other themed tours.

One agent said that, until a couple of years ago: *"The Chinese market was very underdeveloped in this respect compared with Europe, and consumer demand for European tours was largely for 'photo tours' – seeing a lot of countries, taking a lot of photos (even if one cannot remember where they were taken), and coming back to China to show them off to one's friends."*

9.2.5 Booking Patterns and Preferences

There has been little overall change in the booking habits and preferences of the average Chinese tourist over the past five years. The following chart highlights the average booking lead-times.

Figure 9.2 How far in Advance Do Chinese Book their Holidays in Europe? (%)

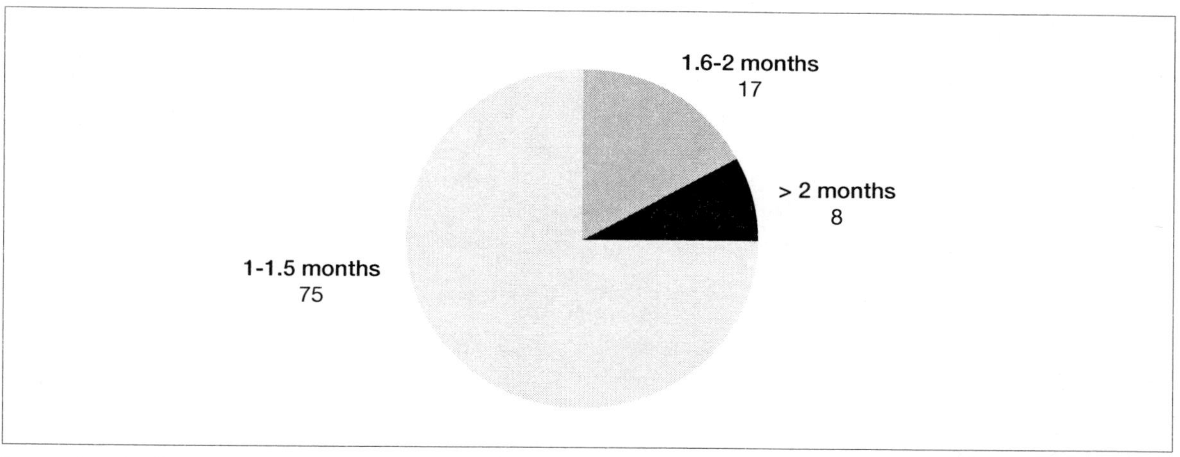

Source: Survey of Chinese Travel Agents by the European Tour Operators Association (ETOA) and Amber China Industry Insights, January-March 2006.

Leisure travel

According to the survey sample, the average lead-time for leisure bookings in the Chinese market is between one and two months. But bookings tend to be made further ahead for travel during public holidays – the so-called Golden Weeks. These holidays are in May, October and at Chinese New Year, which falls in late January/early February.

Business travel

The average lead-time for business trips is six weeks. Lead-times are driven by the visa application process. Those travellers who have visas already will usually book as late as two to three weeks in advance. But those who do not will need to allow one to two months. Since the Schengen visa became available, lead-times have shortened. However, Chinese visiting an additional non-Schengen country (e.g. the United Kingdom or some of the East European countries) need to allow a little more time.

Group sizes

The average size of leisure tour groups to Europe is 30-40 participants. Some of the travel agents interviewed mentioned groups of up to 50, but these are rare. Business groups range from 3-4 participants to as many as 20-30. There have been some much larger groups visiting Europe for 'business' – mainly incentive groups or trips to large conventions and other events.

Accommodation used

Three- and four-star hotels predominate. Scarcely any reference was made by the agents interviewed to either five-star hotels or bed & breakfast-style accommodation. When probed, all respondents said that they could offer tours using five-star hotels, but added that demand was low among ADS leisure groups.

Information sources used by Chinese travel agencies

Much of the information disseminated to their clients by Chinese travel agencies comes from tour operators in destination countries. One of the agents interviewed commented that the individual countries' NTOs also distribute brochures to travel agencies aimed at Chinese travellers.

Age groups

According to the agents in the survey sample, the average age of Chinese travellers to Europe is between 30 and 45. They added that 20-30 year-olds are likely to take a deeper interest than travellers in their 40s and 50s, whose main priority is to go to Europe once, take photographs, go shopping and come *"home to where the food is good".*

Frequency of travel to Europe

Most agents said they saw a high occurrence of repeat visits, and added that the second visit was generally intended to allow travellers to spend more time in their favourite country. Only one respondent in Shanghai and one in Guangzhou said they had not come across many people who wanted to return to Europe.

9.2.6 Most Popular European Countries

According to the travel agency survey, France and Italy are by far the most popular destinations among Chinese for both first and second visits to Europe. And within the two countries, the capitals Paris and Rome are the main attractions.

Many agents also mentioned Germany but, in this case, Chinese tourists had a more general desire to see the regions of the country than one particular site or city. Some agents also mentioned Switzerland and one mentioned Austria and the United Kingdom. Attractions that generate the most attention and are most often requested are iconic sites such as the Louvre, Notre Dame, the Eiffel Tower and Versailles Palace.

Figure 9.3 Which Country Is Most in Demand from Chinese Tourists? (%)

Country	%
Switzerland	16
United Kingdom	4
Russia	4
France	35
Italy	18
Germany	12
Austria	11

Source: ETOA/Amber Survey of Chinese Travel Agents, January-March 2006.

9.2.7 Visa Application Procedures

More detailed information on visa application procedures for different countries is provided in chapter 2, but this section highlights some of the main challenges facing travel agents trying to organise leisure tour groups and other types of trips to Europe – as reported during the interview phase of this study.

All but one of the travel agents interviewed stated that visas were the main operational barrier with regard to travel to Europe for Chinese groups, causing particular administrative difficulties for the agencies. According to one respondent in Guangzhou, when the tour members provide incomplete documents, consulates do not always give them a second chance to supply the missing information.

These requirements affect applications for visas regardless of the purpose of travel – whether ADS, private independent travel, or business travel.

Some of the information requested by consulates is considered to be very personal information. A senior manager at one of the largest travel agents in China – a Europhile with many years of experience operating and managing tours to Europe – said: *"There is no privacy for applicants. They are asked to provide a letter from their employer to prove they have leave for the proposed period of travel, and they are also asked to state where they will be going in the letter. This would never happen in Europe, which is a private society – people would be so offended!"*

Although this is not a standard requirement, travellers are sometimes asked to provide tax statements covering a period of six months to prove their financial status. The agents said that this had caused much indignation on the part of potential travellers. One of the respondents in Shanghai talked about professors from East China who had been refused visas because they lacked proof of their financial status. In China, a professor of engineering in a provincial capital on China's developed east coast can be earning as little as Rmb 4,000 (€ 385) per month, but salaries are rising and there are often other unofficial sources of income and year-end bonuses that go unchecked by the visa process.

According to the travel agents interviewed, another proof of financial status is credit cards. A respondent from an agency in Shanghai talked about individuals being asked to deposit original credit cards with the visa officials. Again, this leaves very little room for privacy and there is also an implication here that, without a credit card, applicants are not rich enough to travel. In a traditionally cash-based economy, a requirement for visa applicants to have credit cards appears to many Chinese to be an unnecessary barrier to their travel. Even the most westernised and affluent urban Chinese have only acquired credit cards in the past few years.

9.2.8 Image of Europe in China

Words associated with Europe

The 12 travel agents were asked to select five positive and five negative words that they would associate with Europe from a list provided to them. Their responses can be summarised as follows although, as indicated, they sometimes used phrases rather than single words:

Positive associations

Guangzhou	Shanghai	Beijing
Cultured	**Civilised**	**Well-planned**
Modern	**Beautiful**	Beautiful scenery
Ancient	Cultured	Classic
Beautiful	Modern	Clean
Civilised	Romantic	
Classic	Tasteful	
Clean	Well-organised	
Historic		
Humanity		

Negative associations

Guangzhou	Shanghai	Beijing
Arrogant	**Expensive**	Poor-quality Chinese food
Conservative	**Lack of understanding of Chinese people and China**	Dirty
Discriminating	Discrimination	Pickpockets
Distant people	Poor-quality accommodation	
Expensive	Slow-moving	
Luddite		
Old-fashioned		

Note: The words/phrases highlighted in bold are the associations cited the most frequently, or those considered by the respondents to be the most pertinent.

Describing Europe

The agents were then asked to give five positive and five negative images that they would use to describe Europe in general. Although they were asked to respond with concrete images, most could only manage to think of abstract qualities, and they found it difficult to come up with alternative responses, even when prompted by the interviewer. The request for negative images was difficult for them to answer. For all these reasons, only the descriptions are provided below – not the cities from which they come.

Positive images	Negative images
Civilised society	**Cold people**
Diversity	**Lack of knowledge about China**
Elegance	**Unsafe**
Law-abiding people	Accommodation is old and small
Wealth	Dirtiness of capital cities
Clean	Expensive
Clean environment	Far away
Comfortable standard of living	Misunderstanding of Chinese people
Fair	Too many languages
Good-quality drinking water	
Humanistic	
Impartial	
Modern	
Romantic	

Note: The words/phrases highlighted in bold are the associations cited the most frequently, or those considered by the respondents to be the most pertinent.

One of the negative images listed above is that of Europe being unsafe. In fact, it is the issue of safety in southern Europe that arose several times during the interviews. Respondents often had either personal experience or anecdotal evidence of pickpockets in some southern European cities, notably in Italy and Spain. One agent interviewed said: *"Safety is number one when travelling. Our clients often have stories told to them by friends that Spain and Italy are not that safe."*

Appeal of Europe to different age groups in China

No real pattern emerged from the responses to the questions on this topic. Several of the travel agents interviewed thought that Europe was an attractive destination for all age groups. Several focused on young people – *"They have a better knowledge of Europe than older Chinese"* – and a number highlighted older travellers – *"They are richer so have greater financial freedom".*

Overall image of Europe and its countries

It is one thing to associate words with Europe or to come up with terms that describe the continent in general, but what about Europe's overall image in China? The 12 travel agents were asked whether Europe and its regions conjured up specific images in China and, if so, what they were. Their responses included (not in order of importance):

- France: Arc de Triomphe, Eiffel Tower and Louvre in Paris
- Italy: Colosseum in Rome, gondolas in Venice
- Netherlands: Windmills
- Spain: Sagrada Familia basilica in Barcelona
- Switzerland: the Alps
- United Kingdom: Big Ben in London
- Greece: the Aegean Sea

Notable about this group of senior travel agents was their highly developed sense of Europe's regions – it is unlikely that customer-facing travel agents in the smaller cities would have a similar level of knowledge. The senior agents all thought that Europe could be divided up into different geographical regions for marketing purposes, and seven of the twelve believed that it *needed* to be divided up this way. Their suggestion was that the continent could be split easily into four: northern, eastern, southern and western Europe.

The respondents were also asked about the new Europe logo developed by ETC for its marketing activities, as well as the new pan-European website, www.visiteurope.com. A separate section of this report (9.9) is devoted to Chinese reactions to this logo.

The impact of global political relations on the image of Europe

The travel agents were asked whether they felt that global political relations affected the image of Europe. Of the total interviewed, nine said they did, two said not, and one said it was hard to tell.

Figure 9.4 Do Global Political Relations Affect the Image of Europe? (%)

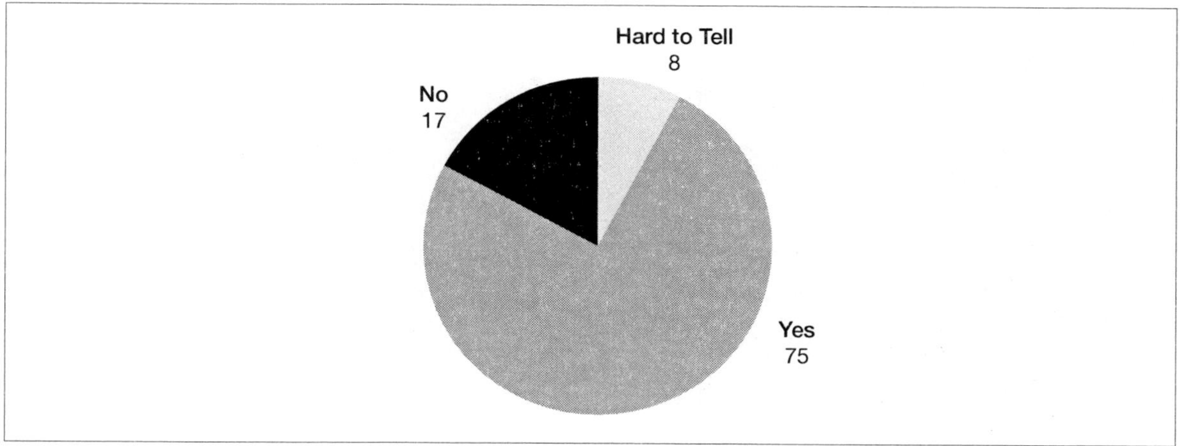

Source: ETOA/Amber Survey of Chinese Travel Agents, January-March 2006.

9.2.9 Europe's Main Competitors: The United States of America and Australia

Questions asking respondents to compare Europe with Australia and the United States of America were clearly difficult for the travel agents to answer. It was well understood that this was not a case of comparing like with like. All the travel agents in the survey group recognised that those travellers with a desire to see Europe had chosen the destination to some extent for its culture and history and that they would be unlikely to consider the United States of America or Australia as any kind of alternative.

That said, Europe was described as being more cultural, deeper, having a longer history, and being rich in heritage and art – with more beautiful architecture than that in Australia and the United States of America. One agent appreciated the combination of modern cities and countryside. Less positively, however, the agents regarded Europeans as more distant than nationals of the United States of America and Australia, and as less friendly and amusing.

Cost differences

Cost comparisons are always influenced by the choice of products and services being compared, and the respondents understood this. However, when asked to give a view on the respective costs of visits to Europe, the United States of America and Australia, their responses were as follows:

- Five agents said they felt that Europe was more expensive than the United States of America, while four thought prices were much the same in the two countries, and three declined to comment, saying the answer depended on the products and services being considered.
- Nine out of twelve agents said that Europe was more expensive than Australia. The remaining three, once again, would not be drawn.

Ease of travel and visa applications

The travel agents were asked to comment on the relative cost and ease of applying for visas to visit Europe, Australia and the United States of America. In addition, as a follow-up to the earlier question on the complexity of application procedures for European visas, they were asked to comment on the statement that the cost of getting a visa is a disincentive to travelling to Europe.

Europe did well in terms of the cost comparison with its two competing destinations, but it fared much less well on the other questions. It should be noted, however, that the travel agents' responses regarding the question of Europe being easier to travel to than the United States of America should be treated cautiously as their experience of travel to the United States of America was limited to organising business trips.

Figure 9.5 Ease of Obtaining Visas for Europe, Australia and the United States of America (%)

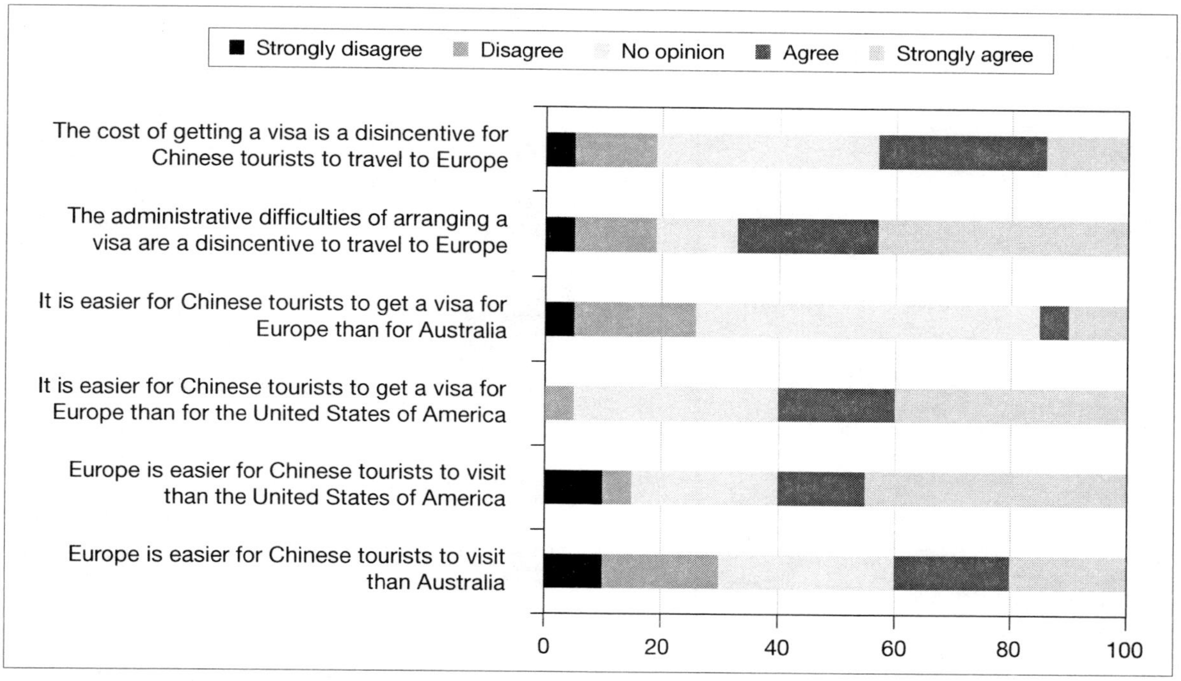

Strongly disagree
Disagree
No opinion
Agree
Strongly agree
The cost of getting a visa is a disincentive for Chinese tourists to travel to Europe
The administrative difficulties of arranging a visa are a disincentive to travel to Europe
It is easier for Chinese tourists to get a visa for Europe than for Australia
It is easier for Chinese tourists to get a visa for Europe than for the United States of America
Europe is easier for Chinese tourists to visit than the United States of America
Europe is easier for Chinese tourists to visit than Australia
0
20
40
60
80
100

Source: ETOA/Amber Survey of Chinese Travel Agents, January-March 2006.

9.2.10 Barriers to Travel to Europe

All but one respondent stated that visas were the main operational barrier to travel to Europe for Chinese groups. A number of other barriers were also cited, although they were clearly not considered significant. One respondent in Guangzhou, for example, mentioned flight tickets. Another noted that the difference between consumers' perceptions of their spending power and the reality had reduced their enjoyment of Europe.

As the following two graphs show, factors such as distance, language, the number of religious sites on itineraries and the need for additional visas to visit non-Schengen countries are not really perceived as barriers by the majority of travel agents interviewed.

Figure 9.6 Other Potential Barriers to Travel to Europe (%)

Strongly disagree
Disagree
No opinion
Agree
Strongly agree
There are too many religious sites on European itineraries
Distance is a barrier when travelling to Europe
Language is a barrier for Chinese travellers in Europe
Language is a barrier when doing business with China
0
20
40
60
80
100

Source: ETOA/Amber Survey of Chinese Travel Agents, January-March 2006.

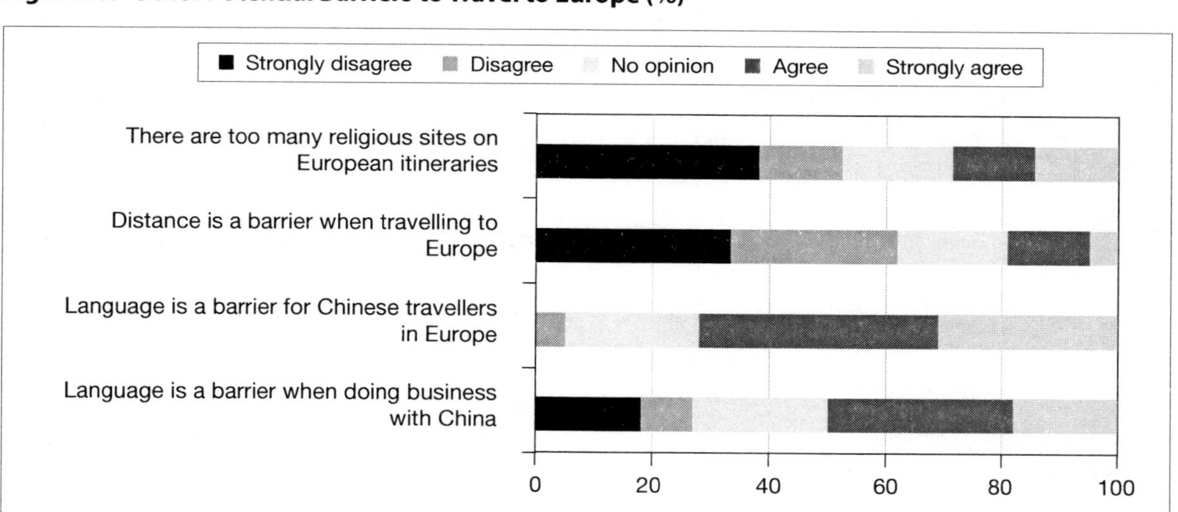

Figure 9.7 Having to Apply for an Extra Visa for Non-Schengen Countries Deters Chinese From Visiting Europe (%)

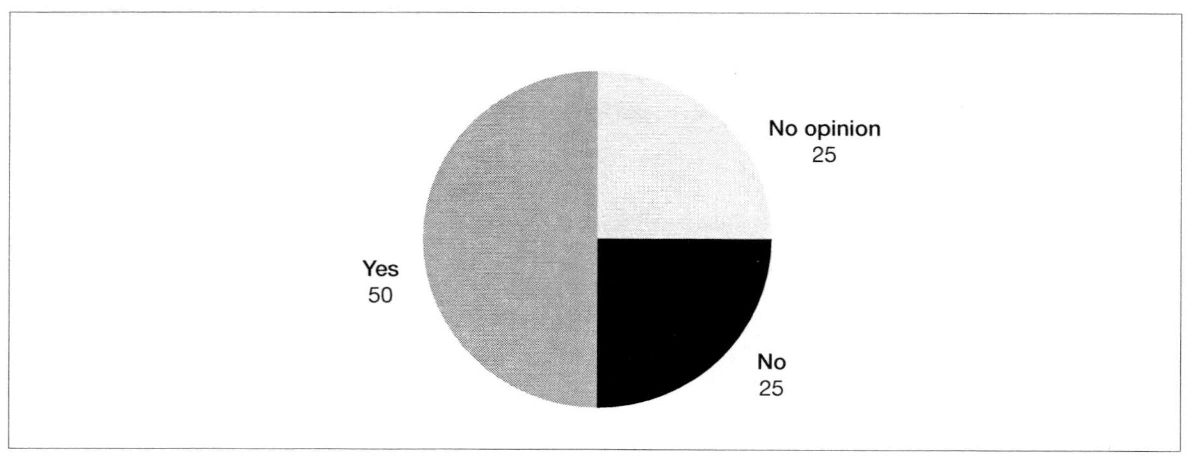

Source: ETOA/Amber Survey of Chinese Travel Agents, January-March 2006.

9.2.11 Selling Europe

The travel agents were asked which features of Europe would, in their opinion, help sell itineraries on the continent – and what would *not* help and should be avoided.

Useful	To be avoided
Architecture	Long coach journeys
Art	Small/less well-known countries
Cultural diversity	Too many churches
Cultural heritage	Too many museums
Customs	
Dining	
History	
Literature	
Nature	
Outdoor activities	
Scenery	
Shopping	

There was no notable difference in responses from agents, whether they came from Beijing, Guangzhou or Shanghai.

Changing perceptions of Europe and how to make it more welcoming

The agents were asked whether Chinese perceptions of Europe could be changed, at least partially, by marketing campaigns. If so, what form should these campaigns take?

The agents considered that the best form of campaign would be run through travel programmes on television and also through newspaper and magazine articles. Other initiatives could include:

- Competitions offering prizes such as discounts off the price of a package.
- Sponsored trips to Europe for Chinese journalists.
- More information for the travel trade.
- Advertising campaigns for Europe.

When asked what Europe could do to be more welcoming to Chinese tour groups, six respondents across all three cities (half of the survey sample) suggested that the visa application process should be simplified.

Information and brochures in Chinese about European cities and key tourist sites would greatly improve the value of a trip to Europe.

Evolution of the Chinese travel market to Europe

The panel of travel agents was asked what developments were likely to take place in the marketplace over the next five years. They identified the following:

- Smaller groups.
- Fewer destinations per tour.
- More first-time visitors.
- Lower-cost tour packages.
- Even lower margins (in a market that is already very competitive).
- Growth in the number of the Chinese middle class who can afford European travel.
- More visitors with a greater knowledge of Europe and, at the same time, continuing large numbers of visitors who will have had very limited exposure to Europe's culture and customs before their visits.
- Increased accessibility to outbound travel and the issuing of passports for residents of China's smaller cities and towns.
- More personalised tours with greater appreciation of culture.
- Dramatic increases in the number of visits to countries that lower visa requirements for Chinese tourists.
- The arrival of foreign travel agents in China will probably put some of the smaller, less profitable Chinese agencies out of business.
- Campaigns by foreign tour operators are likely to lead to improvements in the quality of brochures and information available.

9.3 Interviews with Tour Guides from China

9.3.1 Selection of Tour Guides

The 12 travel agents interviewed from Beijing, Shanghai and Guangzhou provided a list of Chinese tour guides who work in Europe with Chinese groups. From this list, a focus group of five guides was selected. The main criterion for their selection was that they had to have had at least two years experience in leading groups around Europe. The interviews were conducted in Shanghai. The questions on which the discussion was based can be found in annex VIII.

9.3.2 European Group Tour Characteristics

Frequency of tours

The guides generally visit Europe between two and three times a year, although some claimed to have led groups in Europe as often as 12 times in one year.

Size and profile of groups

The number of participants in each group ranges from 30 to 40. Most of the groups led by these guides consist of couples in their 40s who are not necessarily very well educated, but who have high disposable incomes.

Preferred activities

While travel agents making the bookings were unable to comment on the activities of groups once these are in Europe, tour guides see at first hand the ways in which most visitors to Europe choose to spend their time. And the favourite activity by far observed by the interviewees is shopping.

One of the focus group members was one of China's most experienced guides, having been to Europe over 30 times. He said: *"From the groups I have taken, the younger travellers like to see famous sights and nature, and the older tourists (those over 40) like to go shopping."*

Accommodation used

The focus group emphasised that the category of accommodation used is decided by consumers when they book their holidays. They also noted that many groups of travellers are disappointed by the accommodation offered in Europe. The most frequent reason for this is the size of room offered in the four- and five-star hotel categories – which is usually smaller than the equivalent in China, and also more expensive. (It is worth noting that the cost of five-star hotels in China is comparatively lower while rooms are generally more spacious.)

Another factor contributing to the Chinese visitors' disappointment is that hotels in Europe – at least the three- and four-star hotels usually selected – do not provide the same toiletries and accessories as hotels do in China. Slippers, combs, green tea, sewing kits, toothbrushes and toothpaste are just some of the things that are provided as standard in two- to four-star rooms in China, but not in Europe.

Information sources

The focus group felt that television programmes and travel magazines were generally the most important sources of information. Also cited were recommendations made by friends and colleagues. One guide mentioned the internet as a source of information for younger travellers.

9.3.3 Europe's Image in China

Overriding image of Europe

The tour guides were asked what they considered to be the overriding image of Europe in the eyes of Chinese travellers. The group came up with the following:

- Architecture
- Culture
- Eiffel Tower
- Elegance
- Good taste
- Style

Describing Europe

In addition to asking the guides what words they would use to describe Europe, they were also asked which words they overheard most frequently when their groups were talking about Europe. The two lists were rather different, as the following shows. The most popular words/phrases cited in each case are given below:

Guides' own descriptions	Reported travellers' descriptions
Eiffel Tower	Accessibility of public services
Gentlemen	Advanced
Modern	Beautiful
Rich in history and culture	Clean
Romantic	Fashionable
	Polite

Some misconceptions

The guides interviewed said they felt that Chinese travellers who had never been to Europe before harboured a number of common misconceptions. These included-expectations that:

- Hotels would be of a higher standard (because living standards are much higher than in China).
- The quality of Chinese food would be much better than it actually was.
- Europe would be more vibrant/lively at night.

None of these statements is necessarily a reflection of low standards or a lacklustre nightlife. They are more likely determined by the low prices that Chinese groups pay for their package holidays in Europe (one by-product of low prices is often modest hotel accommodation in suburban/out-of-centre locations), as well as by the comparison with similarly starred hotels in Asian cities.

Preferred destinations

The guides were asked which destinations their first-time visitors had most been looking forward to visiting, and which ones they liked best once they reached Europe. Their responses were as follows:

Most looked forward to	Most enjoyed
France	France (the number 1 choice)
Germany	Barcelona
Greece	Venice
Italy	Vienna
Spain	
Switzerland	

Preferred destinations by age of group

There was no consensus among the tour guides on this question. One guide said that younger people preferred France and that older people preferred Germany. Another guide felt that it was the older people who preferred France, while the younger ones liked Spain best. Two guides stressed how difficult it was to generalise on such questions. They said that Europe is so diverse that the reactions of different groups of visitors depend far more on the content of the itinerary than on any other factors (such as age).

Ease of travel

The tour guides felt that some countries were easier to travel in than others. Factors making travel easier included:

- The level of English spoken in the destination (Germany is seen as easier than Italy and France, where the level of English spoken is lower).
- Greater numbers of self-service restaurants.
- Countries with easier visa application processes (none was named).

Non-Schengen visas

The focus group was divided on whether or not the need for a non-Schengen visa would lower potential tourists' interest in a particular tour. Three of the five thought it would; the remaining two disagreed, saying that the decision on choice of countries to be included on tours was very much a matter for the travel agencies as they are the ones who have to apply for the visas.

Most effective promotional tools for attracting Chinese visitors to Europe

Guides are rarely responsible for promoting or selling tours; their role only starts once they have been sold. So when asked what might be the most effective promotional tool, the guides came up with a variety of responses, including the following:

- Television and radio advertisements.
- Travel magazines.
- Complimentary trips to Europe for members of the public (and perhaps for those who would not otherwise have a chance to go).

Many of the guides felt it important to emphasise in any promotional material the ease of obtaining a visa – this would allay potential travellers' fears on the issue.

9.3.4 Europe's Main Competitors

All five guides agreed that the main competitor for Europe was Australia. The reasons given were its:

- Opposing seasons to China's.
- Impressive scenery.
- Simpler visa application process.

Apart from Australia, South Africa, South-East Asia and the United States of America were all mentioned as competitors.

9.4 Interviews with Inbound Tour Operators in Europe

9.4.1 Methodology

Desk research, together with information provided by CNTA, earmarked five key European tour operators active in the Chinese market. Following a short telephone interview to confirm their suitability, these operators were invited to take part in this study as the Key Informant Group (KIG).

Members of the Key Informant Group (KIG):

- China Holidays
- Gullivers Travel Associates
- Kuoni Incoming Services
- Miki Travel
- Trafalgar Tours

In line with the project specifications, and taking the survey responses of the Chinese travel trade as a starting point, a semi-structured interview template was drawn up, consisting of both quantitative and qualitative questions, and sent electronically to each of the five European tour operators. Once their replies were received, follow-up interviews were conducted by telephone in order to discuss their responses in more detail and, where relevant, to collect additional data and comments.

The data collected from this group was robust and pertinent to the objectives of the study. Nevertheless, it was also decided to invite all other CNTA-approved European tour operators to express their views. A letter was sent to these operators attaching a questionnaire. In total, 47 responses were received, of which 18 were from operators sufficiently active in China to be included.

A copy of the questionnaire used for both the KIG and the other tour operators can be found in annex IX. The five members of the KIG and the 18 additional operators provided an interview sample of 23 companies.

Respondents were asked to rate their agreement on a scale of 1-5, with 1 implying 'strongly agree' and 5 implying 'strongly disagree'.

9.4.2 Destinations Offered

The following 24 countries are the European destinations available in the Chinese market through the tour operators contacted:

- Austria
- Belgium
- Czech Republic
- Denmark
- Estonia
- Finland
- France
- Germany
- Greece
- Hungary
- Iceland
- Ireland
- Italy
- Latvia
- Lithuania
- Netherlands
- Norway
- Poland
- Slovakia
- Spain
- Sweden
- Switzerland
- Turkey
- United Kingdom

The countries most frequently offered are Austria, France, Italy, Germany, Spain and Slovakia, while France and Germany are the most widely offered countries by members of the KIG (three companies out of five). A number of tour operators also include North Africa and Egypt in their European packages.

Number of countries offered per tour

Within the KIG, most operators offered tours visiting between three and six countries: two offered three or four countries; two others five or six. Taking the interview sample as a whole, one can identify a similar range. Eight operators said they offered five or six countries; seven offered three or four.

There was no real consensus on the most common combination of countries visited, but the most commonly cited appeared to be:

- France, Germany, Austria
- Italy, France, Benelux
- Spain, France, Italy
- Italy, Spain, Germany
- the United Kingdom alone
- Spain, France
- Czech Republic, Hungary, Austria, Germany

9.4.3 Products Offered

Level of quality

The tour operators were asked what categories of products they offered their customers in Europe – budget, standard, luxury and/or business. All categories are widely available, with budget and luxury tours predominating. Nearly half the companies questioned said they offered all four categories of tour product; three of the five KIG members offer all four. The following chart gives more detailed information.

Figure 9.8 Categories of Product Offered by European Tour Operators in the Chinese Market (%)

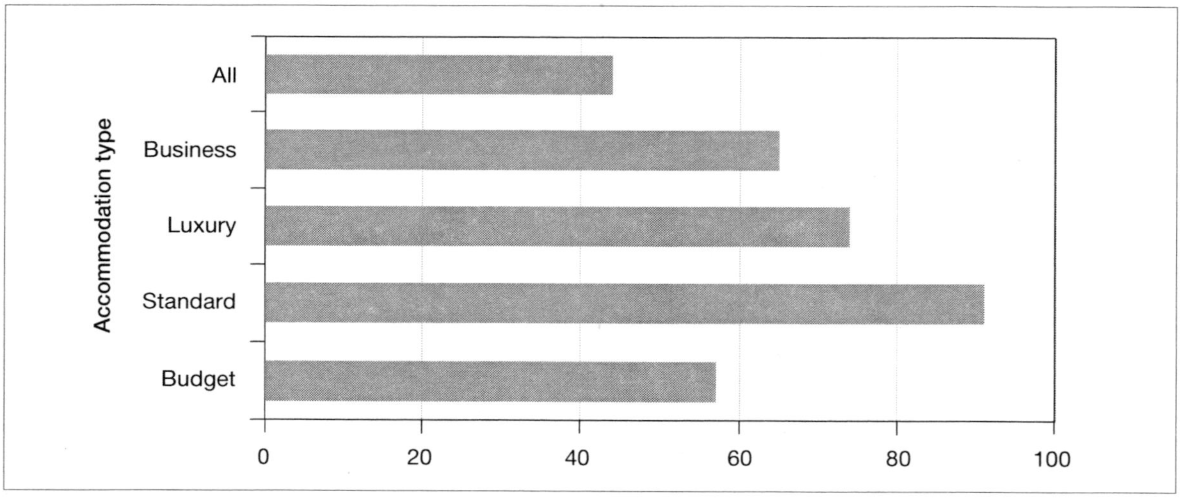

Source: ETOA Survey of European Tour Operators, April 2006.

Luxury is, of course, notoriously difficult to define. It can mean whatever people want it to mean. But for the Chinese market, it has to be viewed in the context of the exceptionally low prices secured for Chinese groups.

Type of tour

The European tour operators were asked what type of product they offered to their Chinese customers. If they offered more than just escorted tours, they were asked to give more details.

A total of 17 of the operators (74%) answered that they offer escorted tours, while 14 (61%) said they sell other types of package (instead or as well). Eight (35%) claimed to offer both.

The other types of products offered included:

- Business travel
- City tours
- City and beach tours in Spain
- Conference/congress travel
- Cultural tours
- Escorted tours for business delegations
- Fully independent trips (FIT travel)
- Gastronomy tours
- Individual tours tailored to customers' specifications
- Sporting events

Most of the tour operators – four of the five KIG members and 12 of the other operators – also said they offered packages that did not come under the ADS scheme.

Changes in demand for business and leisure travel

There was near unanimity – and complete unanimity among KIG members – that demand in the Chinese market for both leisure and business travel to Europe had risen over the past five years, at least up to April 2006. As many as 90% of the tour operators surveyed said that leisure demand had increased, while 82% said that business demand had risen.

9.4.4 Booking Patterns and Preferences

Leisure travel

The well-known Chinese trend to late booking was confirmed by the European tour operator interviews. Operators said that most bookings were received between two and four weeks before the time of travel.

Figure 9.9 How Far in Advance Do Your Chinese Customers Book Leisure Travel to Europe? (%)

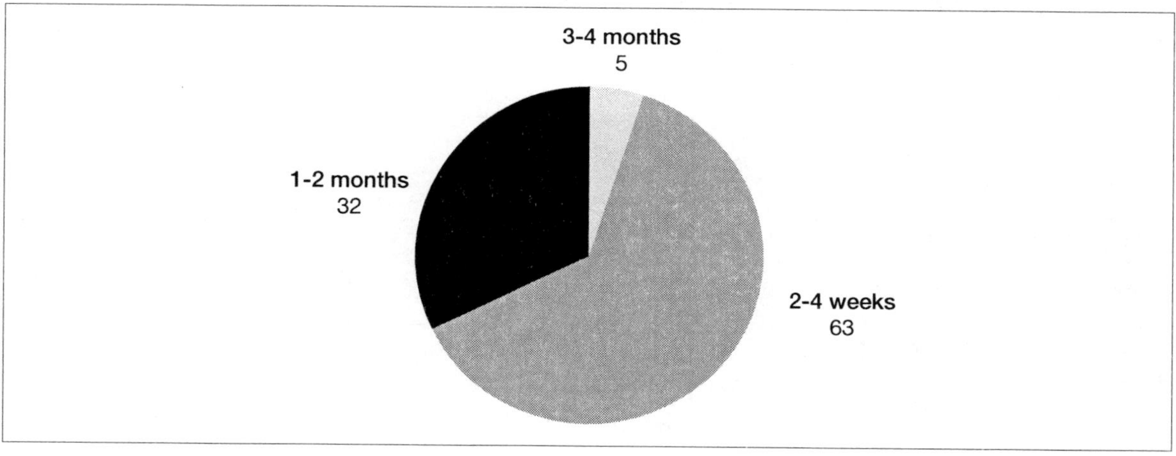

Source: ETOA Survey of European Tour Operators, April 2006.

Business travel

Some 50% of the tour operators questioned receive their business group bookings between two and four weeks in advance, with the remaining 50% enjoying three to four weeks advance bookings.

Group sizes

The typical size of the groups travelling to Europe is 11-30 participants. Only three of the 23 tour operators questioned mentioned average groups of more than 30; four said that groups averaged ten (or fewer) people.

No distinction was made between groups travelling for leisure or business.

Age groups travelling in Europe

The majority of groups comprised participants aged between 36 and 45 years old. This was the view of 13 (57%) of the 23 tour operators surveyed, including four of the five KIG members. The most common age range for the other groups was 46-55 years old.

Accommodation used

Tour operators were asked what type of accommodation was most popular with their customers – hotels, bed & breakfasts or hostels. Hotels were by far the preferred choice. All KIG members, without exception, said that their customers chose to stay in hotels. Of the other tour operators, only three said their customers stayed in bed & breakfasts. Not one reference was made to hostels. Three- and four-star hotels dominate the market. Of the total sample surveyed, tour operators said that 48% of travellers opt for three-star accommodation and 52% for four-star, while none of their customers opt for two- or five-star properties. The statistics for the KIG members are similar.

Figure 9.10 Which Categories of Hotel Are Most Used by Your Chinese Customers to Europe? (%)

Hotel category	%
2*	0
3*	48
4*	52
5*	0

Source: ETOA Survey of European Tour Operators, April 2006.

Frequency of visits to Europe

In general, the market for Europe is dominated by one-off visits. Ten (43%) of the European tour operators questioned said that fewer than 5% of their clients returned to Europe for repeat visits. This figure rose to 60% among the KIG members – or three of these five major players in the Chinese market. The travellers most likely to return are those aged between 36 and 45 years, as the next chart shows.

Figure 9.11 Which Age Groups of Your Chinese Customers Are Likely to Visit Europe more than once? (%)

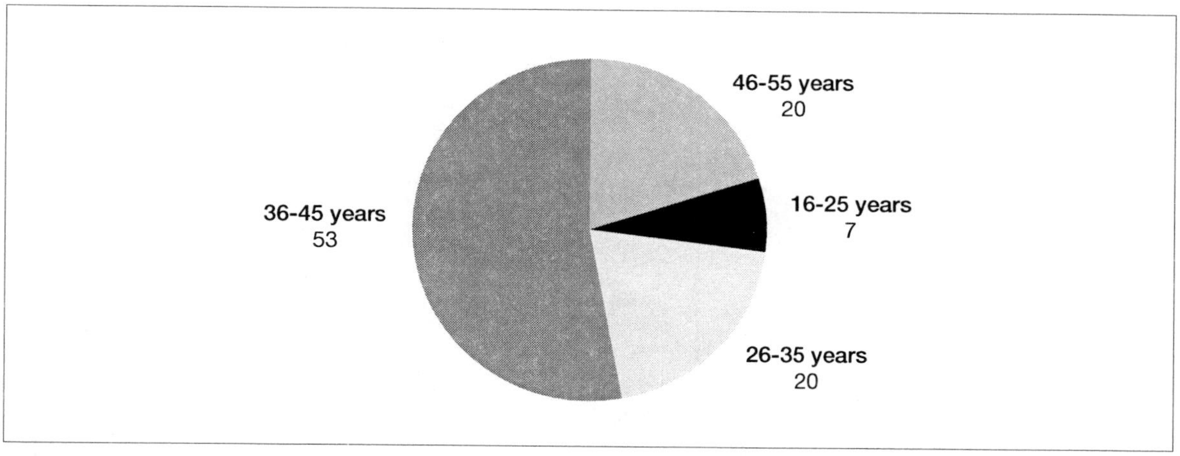

46-55 years
20
16-25 years
7
36-45 years
53
26-35 years
20

Source: ETOA Survey of European Tour Operators, April 2006.

Doing business with China

Overall, the European tour operators surveyed were fairly positive about their activities in China. While there were very mixed views on how easy it is to do business with China, the majority said it was profitable for them – despite the many obvious difficulties in working in this market.

Figure 9.12 Doing Business with China (%)

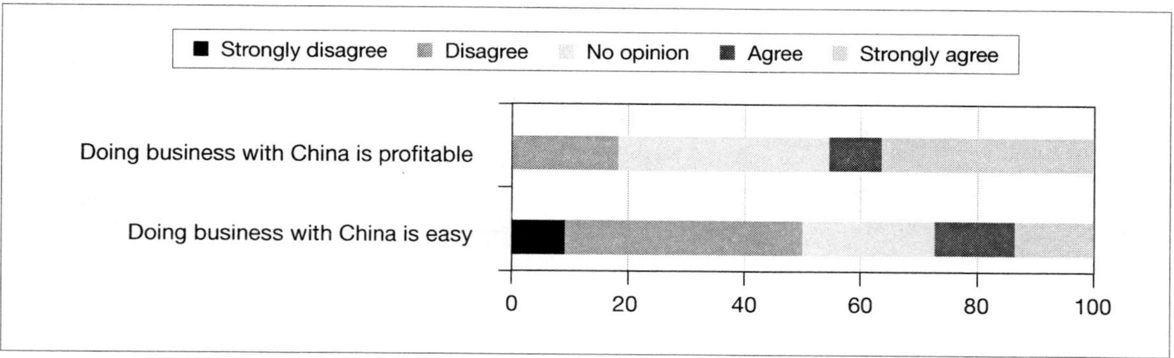

Source: ETOA Survey of European Tour Operators, April 2006.

9.4.5 ADS-approved Tour Operators

Nevertheless, despite the generally positive views on doing business in China, the ADS system is the subject of many complaints, particularly with regard to the ease with which businesses can get their names on the list of approved operators in Europe. The widely felt impression is that far too many inexperienced and 'informal' businesses have entered the market. While it is true that this market does seem to attract more than its fair share of such businesses, the fact that there is a register of 'approved' businesses is already extremely important.

The EU, which negotiated the ADS agreement for the Schengen countries, has let it be known that it would rather there were no lists at all. It believes that anyone who wishes to operate in China should be free to do so subject to normal trading rules – as in most other tourism markets – and so this is the guiding principle behind the operation of the lists in Europe. Nevertheless, the lists are required by CNTA regulations.

Figure 9.13 focuses on the ADS issue and how easy it is to become accredited. The tour operators interviewed were generally ambivalent on the subject, while 60% of the KIG group agreed it was too easy.

Figure 9.13 ADS Accreditation in Europe (%)

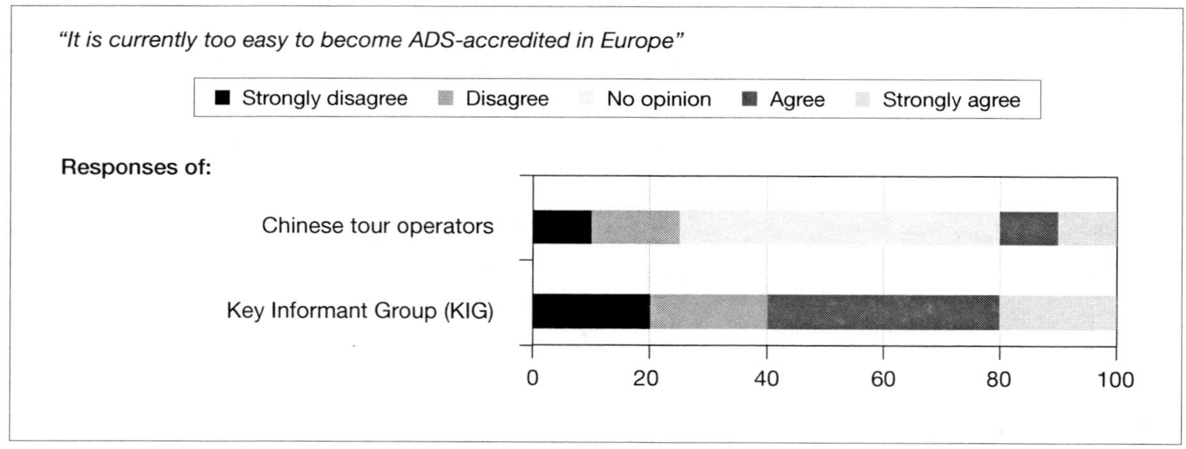

Source: ETOA Survey of European Tour Operators, April 2006.

9.4.6 Operational Difficulties Involved in Doing Business with China

Some of the potential pitfalls of doing business with China are discussed in more detail in chapter 7 but, as part of the required survey of European tour operators, companies in the sample were asked to list the operational difficulties they had encountered when organising trips to Europe. Among the problems they identified, the following are the most important:

- Bookings are placed at the very last minute.
- This enables Chinese travel agents to force tour operators, and their suppliers, to lower their prices to the point at which it is no longer economically viable to engage in this business in the long term.
- Last-minute bookings can lead to payment problems.
- The pressure on prices and the frequent changing of itineraries make it difficult to find accommodation of the standard expected by the Chinese travellers.
- The number of places expected to be visited in a very short time as part of the typical itinerary is excessive. Chinese travel agents seem unable or unwilling to understand the restrictions placed on itineraries by EU driving-hours legislation. (There is hope that the recent revisions to this legislation will give all operators a level playing field that allows them to implement realistic itineraries.)
- Difficulties with visas, guides, drivers, transport and budgets.
- Difficulties caused by the presence of different religions in the same group: sometimes groups are presented with food that individuals cannot eat.
- Chinese sales staff have insufficient knowledge of Europe.
- Some Chinese travel agencies request invitation letters for ADS groups. This is unnecessary.
- A lack of cultural understanding on both sides. The Chinese sometimes do not know how to behave in Europe; European suppliers are sometimes inflexible and unaccommodating.
- Unfair competition from small 'cash-paying' operators who, using minibuses, can by-pass normal operating restrictions.

9.4.7 Image of Europe

Words associated with Europe

The 23 tour operators were asked to give five positive and five negative words that they would associate with Europe. They answered as follows (the most frequently occurring words/phrases are highlighted in bold):

Positive	Negative
Culture	**Expensive**
History	**Food**
Food	**Language**
Scenery	Condescending and arrogant
Secure	Crime
Shopping	Old-fashioned
Traditions	Pollution
	Weather

How Europe is portrayed and the political issues

In response to the question: *"Do you portray Europe as a whole or as a diverse region with many countries?"*, 20 of the 23 tour operators surveyed (87%) said they portrayed the continent as a diverse region with many countries. Surprisingly, a much lower 60% of the KIG group gave the same response, although the sample was of course too small to be really meaningful.

Figure 9.14 Do Global Political Relations Affect the Image of Europe? (%)

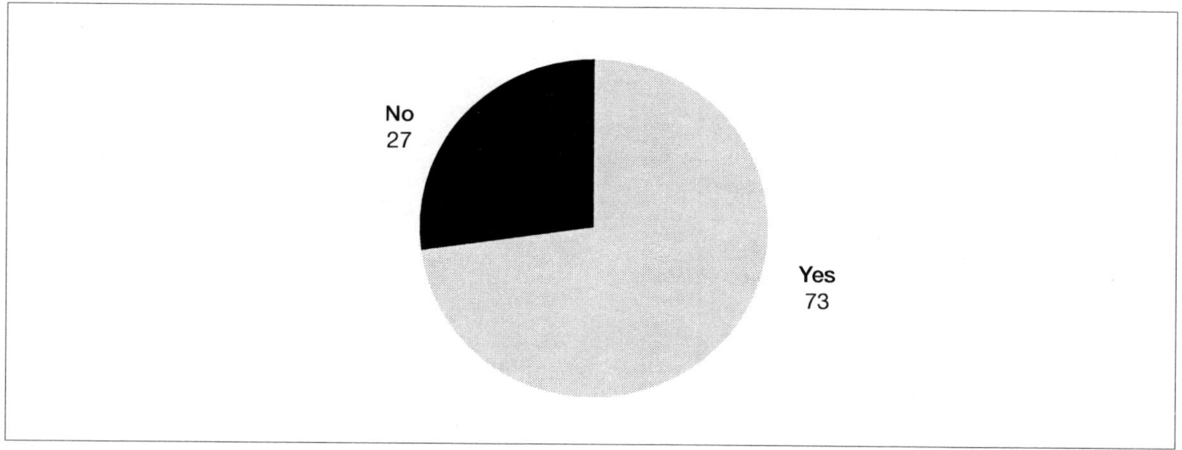

Source: ETOA Survey of European Tour Operators, April 2006.

The European tour operators surveyed were asked whether they felt that global political relations affected the image of Europe. Of the 22 who answered this question, 16 (73%) said that the image was affected by such political factors and six (27%) said that it was not. The pattern of responses among KIG members was similar.

9.4.8 Europe's Main Competitors: The United States of America and Australia

As already reported from the analysis of the survey among Chinese travel agents, the United States of America (even though it still lacks ADS status) and Australia are seen as two of Europe's main competitors in the Chinese market. There are certain perceptions of the two destinations that seem to predispose many Chinese in favour of these two important competitors.

Cost differences

Europe is seen by many of the European tour operators surveyed as being more expensive than both Australia and the United States of America.

The main difference between the two sets of findings is to be found in the strength of opinion on the comparison with Australia, perceived as the main alternative destination for Chinese visitors. Over half of the respondents agreed with the statement in the question – i.e. that Europe is more expensive than Australia – while 15 respondents had no opinion in the case of the United States of America. The table shows the detailed responses given to the statements and the number of tour operators making those responses.

Figure 9.15 Comparing the Cost of Europe, Australia and the United States of America (%)

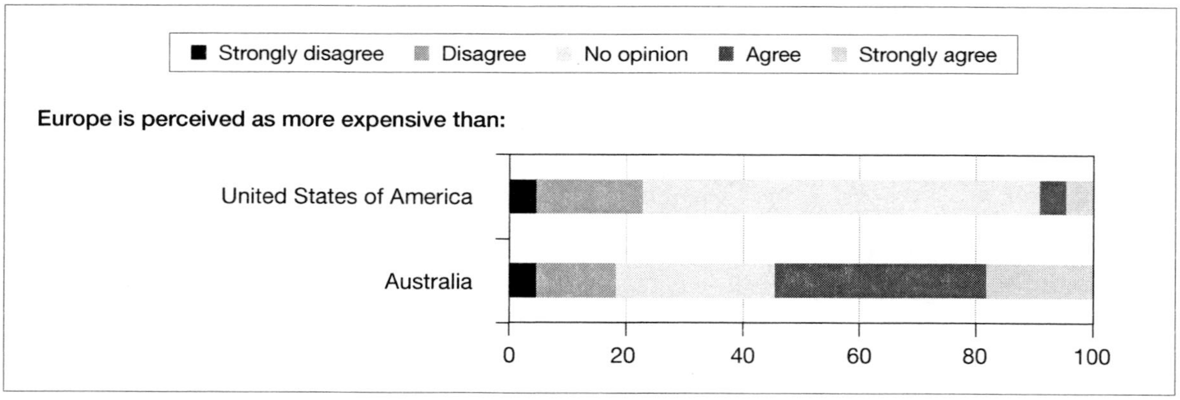

Note: Only 22 operators responded to this question.

Source: ETOA Survey of European Tour Operators, April 2006.

Ease of travel and visa applications

The European tour operators were asked to comment on the relative cost and ease of applying for visas to visit Europe, Australia and the United States of America. The objective was also to determine whether cost of a European visa was a disincentive to travel, as well as to compare the relative ease of travel to the three destinations. Most of the tour operators stated that the process of obtaining a visa should be made easier. One of them said that getting a visa for Italy was almost impossible.

The responses, summarised in figure 9.16, show that the cost and the administrative difficulties of obtaining/arranging for a visa are clear disincentives to travelling to Europe. Tour operators strongly agreed that Europe is easier to visit than the United States of America and, perhaps surprisingly, the majority think the same regarding Australia – i.e. that Europe is easier to visit than Australia. They also believe that it is easier to obtain a visa for Europe than for the United States of America but, as might be expected, it is less easy than for Australia.

Figure 9.16 Ease of Obtaining Visas and Travelling to Europe, Australia and the United States of America (%)

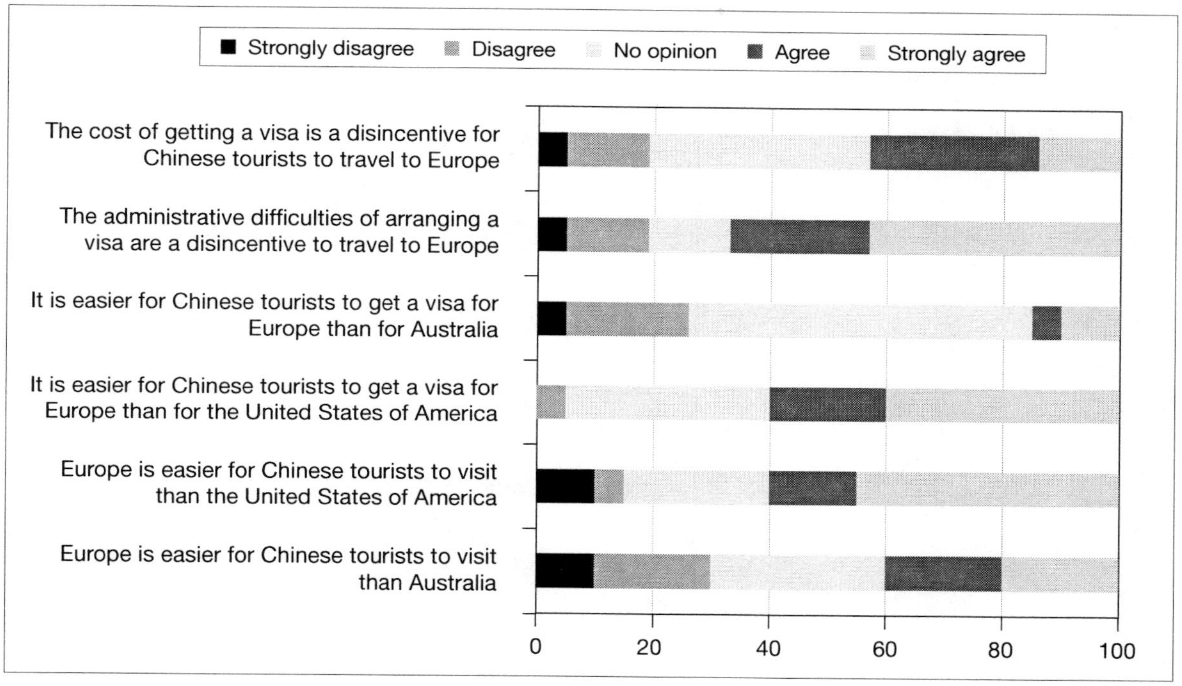

Strongly disagree
Disagree
No opinion
Agree
Strongly agree
The cost of getting a visa is a disincentive for Chinese tourists to travel to Europe
The administrative difficulties of arranging a visa are a disincentive to travel to Europe
It is easier for Chinese tourists to get a visa for Europe than for Australia
It is easier for Chinese tourists to get a visa for Europe than for the United States of America
Europe is easier for Chinese tourists to visit than the United States of America
Europe is easier for Chinese tourists to visit than Australia
0
20
40
60
80
100

Source: ETOA Survey of European Tour Operators, April 2006.

9.4.9 Barriers to Travel to Europe

Visa application procedures and the cost of visas may deter some Chinese travellers from visiting Europe, but there are other barriers, too. These include distance, language, the number of religious sites on itineraries and the need for additional visas to visit non-Schengen countries (such as the United Kingdom and Ireland). However, as the following two charts show, there is no real consensus on how important these barriers are, or whether they are even barriers at all. The exception, perhaps, is an agreement that language is a real barrier for Chinese travellers in Europe.

Figure 9.17 Further Barriers to Travel to Europe (%)

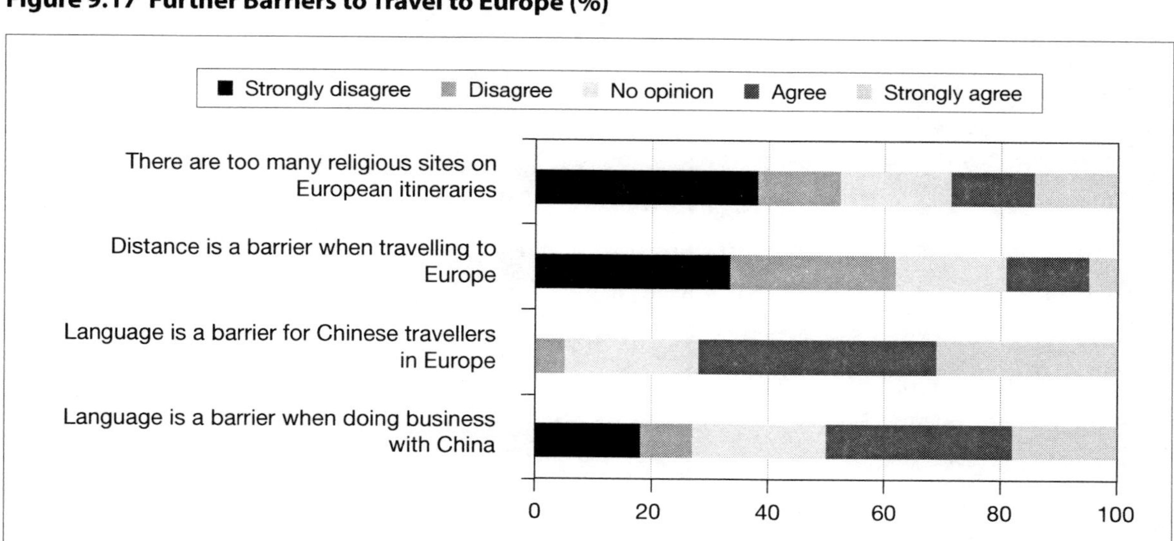

Source: ETOA Survey of European Tour Operators, April 2006.

Figure 9.18 Having to Apply for an Extra Visa for Non-Schengen Countries Deters People from Visiting Europe (%)

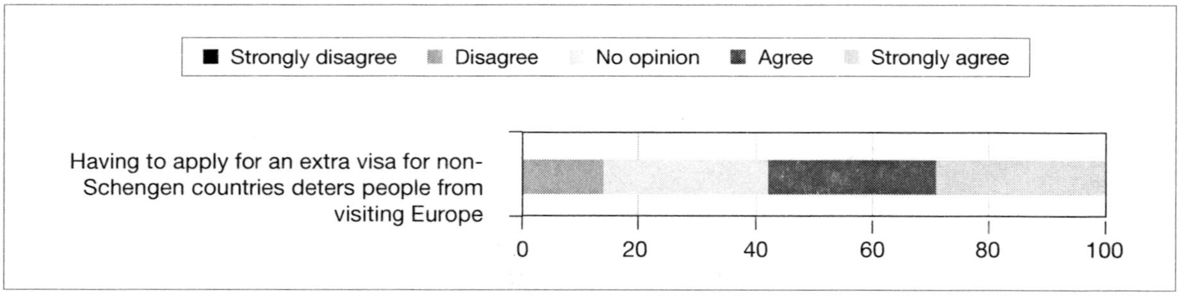

Strongly disagree | Disagree | No opinion | Agree | Strongly agree

Having to apply for an extra visa for non-Schengen countries deters people from visiting Europe

0 20 40 60 80 100

Source: ETOA Survey of European Tour Operators, April 2006.

The perception of Europe – and ways of changing it

For all the misgivings that have been reported in this study, it is also important to note a general neutrality on the part of the European tour operators as to whether Europe represents a value-for-money destination for Chinese tourists. As many as 47% said they had no opinion on the subject, with the balance almost equally split between those who agreed and those who disagreed with the statement.

More than two thirds (68%) of the tour operators interviewed said they felt that any negative associations with Europe could be changed, at least partly, by marketing campaigns.

Figure 9.19 The Perception of Europe – And Changing It (%)

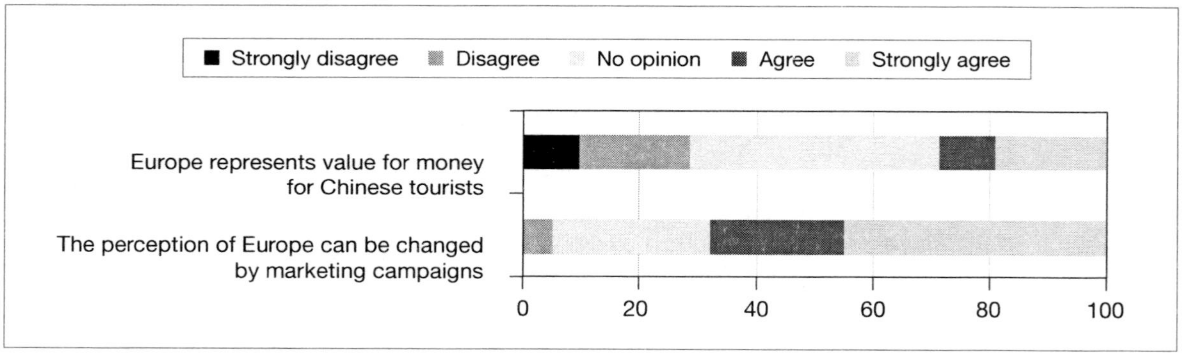

Strongly disagree | Disagree | No opinion | Agree | Strongly agree

Europe represents value for money for Chinese tourists

The perception of Europe can be changed by marketing campaigns

0 20 40 60 80 100

Source: ETOA Survey of European Tour Operators, April 2006.

Increasing awareness of Europe as a destination for Chinese travellers

The European tour operators were asked what they considered to be the most effective ways of increasing awareness of Europe as a destination for Chinese travellers. As part of this exercise, they were shown a list of possible methods and invited to indicate their agreement or disagreement with these methods. Figure 9.20 summarises their responses.

Figure 9.20 The most Effective Ways of Increasing Awareness of Europe as a Destination for Chinese Travellers (%)

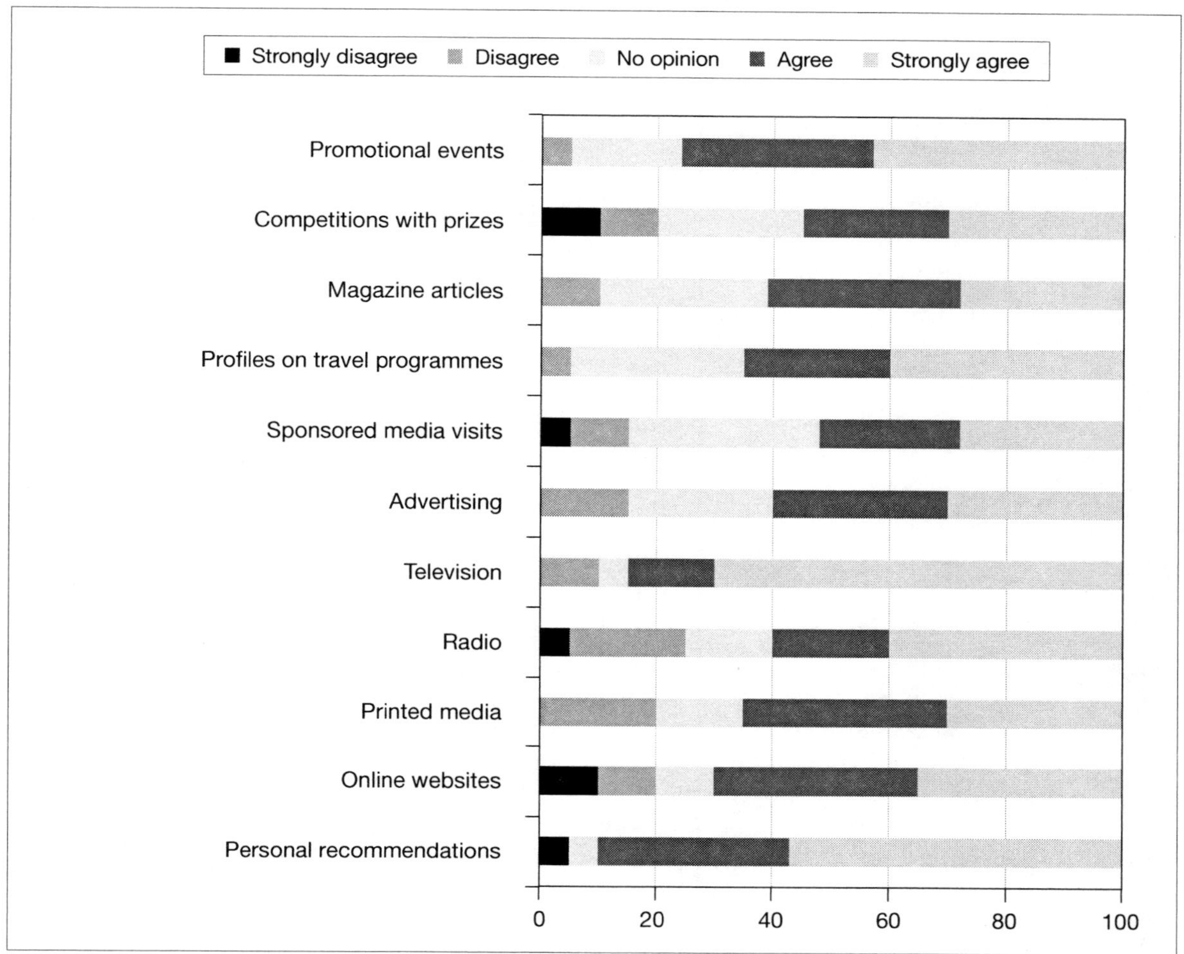

Source: ETOA Survey of European Tour Operators, April 2006.

9.4.10 Selling Europe

The tour operators were asked which features of Europe would, in their opinion, help sell tour group itineraries – and what would *not* help and should be avoided.

It can be seen that some of the claimed selling points contradict what was said by the Chinese travel agents. Examples of this are comments on history, monuments and cultural attractions. These statements are perhaps more a by-product of what all itineraries normally include than representing what is particularly appealing to the Chinese market. The features to be avoided are informed by what Chinese visitors dislike. No marketing plans would feature crime, poor customer service or Sinophobia, of course.

Positive	Negative
Big and famous cities	Cost/high prices
Brand-name shops and factories	Crime
British royal family	Customer service not as good as it could be
Culture/Europe as a cultural experience ("a completely different culture from China")	Dangerous, crowded places
Fashion/Europe as a fashionable place to visit ("Europe has a growing fashion-conscious middle class")	Mentioning negative political issues about China
Friendliness of people	Religious sites
Gastronomy	Remote countryside
Historical sites	Ruins
History	Selling Europe through unprofessional agents
Landscape diversity	
Monuments and museums	
Nature	
Quality of shops and businesses	
Relaxation and well-being opportunities (spas, etc.)	
Safety	
Scenery	
Shopping	
Sports – winter and summer	
Travel times – short travel times between countries	
Variety ("Barcelona is modern, Paris is cosmopolitan, Rome is cultural, London is diverse and Berlin is arty")	

Making Europe more welcoming for Chinese groups

It has already been seen that European tour operators believe the Chinese perception of Europe can be changed, at least partially, by marketing campaigns. But their views were also sought on what needs to be done to make Europe a more welcoming place for Chinese groups. Their suggestions included the following:

- Learning the Chinese language, culture and habits – this was mentioned six times.
- Making the visa process easier – this was mentioned four times.
- Competitive prices, flexibility to work with and accept Chinese travellers with open arms.
- Education of the front staff who deal with the China market.
- It is a young market and hoteliers and service suppliers need to realise that it will mature over years. Staff also need to grasp that the market is huge: service standards and needs will vary according to the type of tour taken.
- More varied itineraries are needed.
- More native speaking Chinese guides, more printed promotional material in Chinese, more products in the Chinese language.

- Direct consumer promotions.
- Service with a smile.

Evolution of the Chinese market for travel to Europe

The panel of European tour operators was asked what developments were likely to take place in the marketplace over the short term. The following are a selection of their comments:

- The Chinese market is currently very young and will start to mature. It is hoped that larger, 'reputable' companies will replace the more informal operators that currently account for a large share of the market.
- The Chinese industry needs more experience; Chinese travel agents do not yet fully understand Europe as a destination.
- The average number of countries visited per trip is currently eight countries. In the future, there will be fewer countries per itinerary, and more days spent in each country.
- Travellers will become more sophisticated and base their travel decisions on quality as well as price. Single- or dual-destination tours with longer stays in each city or destination will develop.
- More personalised programmes will be developed, providing more time in each country.
- A gradual increase in the number of tourists will require a better quality and greater variety of services.
- The numbers of groups will increase, for both business and leisure travel.
- Much of the current marketplace is dominated by tours paid for by government-run businesses. The share is predicted to decline, with a significant increase in self-funded tours.
- Growth (in the market) will come with an increased awareness of Europe. This improvement in understanding will lead to a more realistic approach to what can be covered in an itinerary.
- It will hopefully become easier to obtain a visa. Unless the visa requirements for Europe (especially Greece) improve, it will be very difficult for the Chinese to visit Europe.
- Consumer needs will increase dramatically as they become more experienced and more demanding travellers.

9.5 Interviews with European Hoteliers

Apart from the survey of European tour operators, a brief survey of some of the main hotel groups in Europe was also carried out. Some ten hotel groups were contacted by telephone and all agreed to answer questions put to them. The hotels involved nonetheless requested to remain anonymous. The interview questions – which were different from those used for the tour operators – are provided in annex X.

Main findings

The numbers of Chinese clients coming through European hotels has yet to reach a level at which they leave a significant traceable impact.

The only substantial reaction received from the hotel industry was their shock at the low prices demanded by wholesalers catering to the Chinese ADS market. Rates below € 20 per day can only be accepted at hotels substantially outside the main centres of attraction, and only at the last moment when no alternative business is available. The average lead-time of a booking being made at a hotel is two weeks.

"Dealing with the Chinese is extremely challenging," said one hotelier. *"The rate is low and it has to be applied to groups whose small size would not normally attract any reduction."* For reasons of cost and taste, groups also invariably dine out in Chinese restaurants. Thus, the Chinese spend the least of any of the categories of guest in their hotel.

Partly as a result of the very low yield from Chinese groups, few hotels in the categories usually requested by Chinese ADS tour groups (i.e. up to four-star hotels) have made any attempts to modify their services to meet specific Chinese needs. Some offer Chinese-speaking front-of-house personnel, but only because they happen to have that skill. *"No-one would go out and recruit Chinese speakers as there is no chance of any immediate return."*

There have been attempts by European hotel groups to court Chinese business and the non-ADS market. The returns in this area are referred to as *"better than the ADS groups, but that is not saying much".* Another hotel chain felt that: *"Business and FIT travel exists, but at small levels – and price is still a major factor."*

9.6 Summary of Travel Trade Interviews

9.6.1 The Pitfalls of Doing Business with China

China presents obvious difficulties for any foreign business, especially those from outside Asia. The most important of these are language, distance and time difference. These need no explanation.

Another concern is corruption. In a 2005 survey, the Berlin-based anti-corruption organization, Transparency International, placed China in the middle of the range in their measure of world corruption, ranking it at number 78 out of 159 countries surveyed. The Chinese Government is conscious of the need to improve this situation and is making great efforts to do so. Indeed, the same survey carried out the following year, in 2006, showed that it had moved up the listing to number 70 (out of 163). It is expected that the Olympic Games in 2008 will bring new levels of transparency and probity into public life.

Foreign tourism businesses have their fair share of challenges of operating in China. ETOA's survey of European tour operators and the experiences of its members more generally over the years highlight some of these.

Intense pressure on prices

For the uninitiated, the most vexing feature of selling tourism services in China is the ability of the Chinese to source the lowest possible prices.

In 2005, ETOA and the European Commission organised a symposium to discuss with European national government officials the implementation of Europe's ADS agreements. Central to the discussion was the question of wholesale prices achieved by Chinese agencies from European wholesale tour operators. Figure 9.21 shows the sharp drop in prices charged to Chinese tour group participants between 2003 and 2005. The slight hardening of the position since then has been due to output cost increases. Both diesel and hotel space have become more expensive.

Figure 9.21 Price per Person per Day (Full Board) for Chinese Groups Visiting Europe (€)

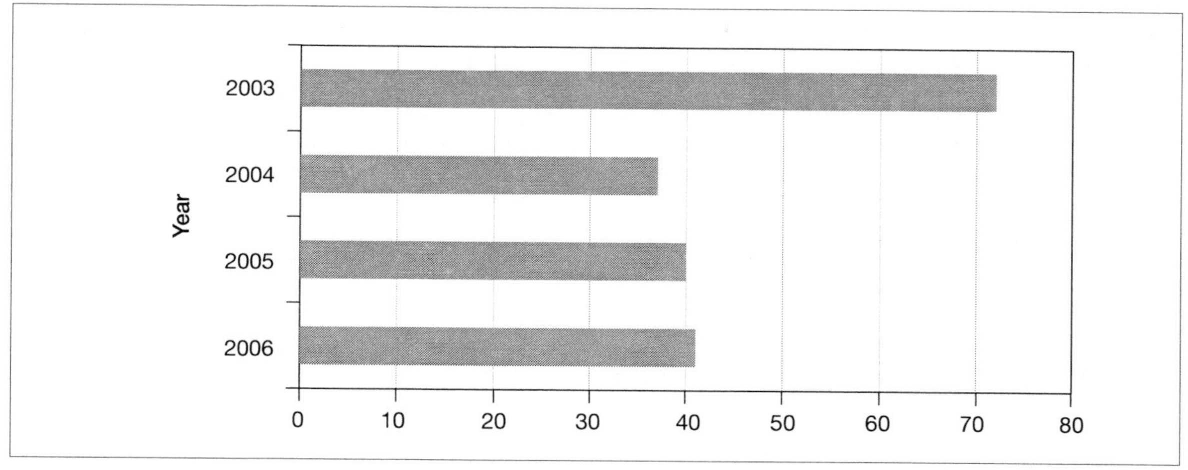

Source: ETOA Members' Survey, 2005.

These figures reflect the average of what was charged for a day on tour (inclusive of bed, board, transport and sightseeing). Given the range of services included in their packages, the business visitors' market was already highly competitive at the start of this decade. The subsequent development of leisure group business to ADS countries triggered a savage round of cost cutting from wholesale tour operators and their suppliers.

In its December 2005 newsletter for the travel trade, the Scandinavian Tourist Board (STB) – working for Denmark, Norway and Sweden in the Asia Pacific market – commented: *"In several European destinations, many land operators face hopeless competition from operators who provide land services for less than € 30 a day, including ground transport, meals and accommodation."*

9.6.2 Competition and Infringement of Regulations

The difficulty of adding value with the Chinese market

One factor that is helping to drive down prices is competition from Chinese operators based in Europe. It is very difficult for an established European tour operator to compete on price with a company that can supply a Chinese-speaking waiter driving a minibus.

The ability of Chinese agents to source services through the wider Chinese community has also been a feature of this evolving market. Tour operators find themselves competing with Chinese restaurants that are prepared to make their margin on the supply of food to the groups. Such restaurants can also draw on a pool of native Chinese speakers to look after their clients.

The STB newsletter spoke of the focus on low prices leading to a *"disregard for ensuring an attractive experience for the traveller"*. These issues will be resolved as the market matures, but it has proved exceptionally difficult for tourism companies to prove that they add value in China.

Blacklisting of Chinese travel agencies and tour operators

The number of ADS-approved travel agencies and tour operators blacklisted for infringing the ADS regulations is increasing. At one point in 2005, more than half of the registered operators in Shanghai were reportedly on CNTA's blacklist.

A home-grown problem

Another concern with the current ADS system is the lack of uniformity in the visa application process for the Schengen area (cf. chapter 2). Tour operators are confused by the variation in standards from one

European visa-issuing authority to another and regard some authorities as simply too difficult to work with. The tightening of the French Government's processing of visas in the first quarter of 2007 is one example. The late approval or rejection of visa applications by consulates could lead to European tours being cancelled.

9.7 Focus Groups with Consumers in China

9.7.1 Methodology

As the travel experience of Chinese consumers is still relatively limited, carrying out a representative survey of the potential consumers of European travel proved challenging. It was decided that the best way to meet this challenge was to conduct focus groups with two categories of consumer:

- Those who had been to Europe within the previous five years.
- Those who had not yet visited Europe, but who were seen as potential visitors.

The basic criteria used to select the interview sample were:

- Age: 25-40 years old.
- Salary range: Rmb 8,000 to Rmb 13,000 (€ 780-1,260).
- Education: graduate and above.
- Male to female ratio: 50:50.
- Privately employed.

Two further criteria were applied to the selection of the potential travellers' focus group:

- Participants were genuine prospects for travel, confident that they would take a holiday to Europe within the next three years.
- Participants were asked a minimum-salary 'screener' question to ensure that they all had the financial means to travel overseas.

One focus group for each of the two categories was held in each of the following three cities: Beijing, Shanghai and Guangzhou, giving a total of six focus groups. Each focus group had six members.

All focus groups were held between January and March 2006. The questionnaires used to guide the discussions can be found in annex XI.

9.7.2 Destinations Offered/Visited

Chinese who had already travelled to Europe in the past were asked how often they had visited the destination in the previous five years. Most had done so between one and three times. They were then asked which countries they had previously visited, and which ones they would most like to visit.

Countries visited	**Countries of interest to potential visitors**
France – *all had visited*	France – *most often cited*
Italy – *most often cited after France*	Italy – *most often cited*
Austria	Belgium
Belgium	Germany
Denmark	Spain
Germany	United Kingdom
Greece	
Luxembourg	
Netherlands	
Spain	
Sweden	
Switzerland	
United Kingdom	

All focus groups mentioned London, Paris and Rome as the principal cities that would attract them to Europe. Other cities mentioned were:

- In Beijing: Amsterdam and Brussels.
- In Guangzhou: Barcelona.
- In Shanghai: Florence.

Further motivations for all the focus groups were:

Attractions	**Other reasons for visiting**
Alps	Beautiful scenery and architecture
Arc de Triomphe	European culture and art
Colosseum	Experiencing the European lifestyle
Eiffel Tower	Shopping
Louvre	Taking photographs to send to friends and family

Repeat visits

All the respondents who had visited Europe previously wanted to visit it again. The most popular destinations for these planned repeat visits were:

- Czech Republic
- Greece
- Italy
- Spain

Respondents in Beijing also expressed interest in Russia and other former Soviet states. (Chinese people see these as part of Europe.)

Length of visit

Among those travellers who had been to Europe already, the length of stay and purpose of visit varied according to the city of the focus group being questioned:

City	Average length of stay	Comment by focus group
Beijing	Business trips: 5-7 days Leisure visits: 1-2 weeks	• Travellers are mostly business travellers. The length of the visa application process puts them off leisure travel.
Guangzhou	All visits: 2-3 weeks	
Shanghai	All visits: 2-3 weeks	• Those Chinese who had been once or twice to Europe had gone for leisure purposes and had paid for themselves. • Those who had been more than twice had done so on business and had had their trips paid for.

The least time spent by any one respondent on one visit was five days; the most time spent was three weeks. Students from all three cities (a few were included in the focus groups as they also had private employment) often took the opportunity of visiting other European countries during their vacations. For those who had not visited but planned to, the preferred length of stay was two weeks. This was true for respondents in all cities.

Timing of visits by previous travellers

The most popular periods for all focus groups in Shanghai and Guangzhou were the months of June to October. In Beijing, it was more a case of when they could get time off work. Honeymoons were also popular times to travel. The season of travel was a lesser consideration. All groups confirmed that they had a strong preference for travelling during the three main national holiday periods – the so-called 'Golden Weeks'.

Reasons for not travelling to Europe

The members of the focus groups of travellers who had not previously been to Europe were asked why they had not visited before. They gave three main reasons:

- Time – they did not have enough time off for travelling.
- Visas – they wanted to see two or three different countries on one trip, but decided that the visa application process was *"too much hassle"*.
- Money – they had insufficient financial resources.

The relative importance of these responses is shown in figure 9.22.

Figure 9.22 Reasons for not Travelling to Europe (%)

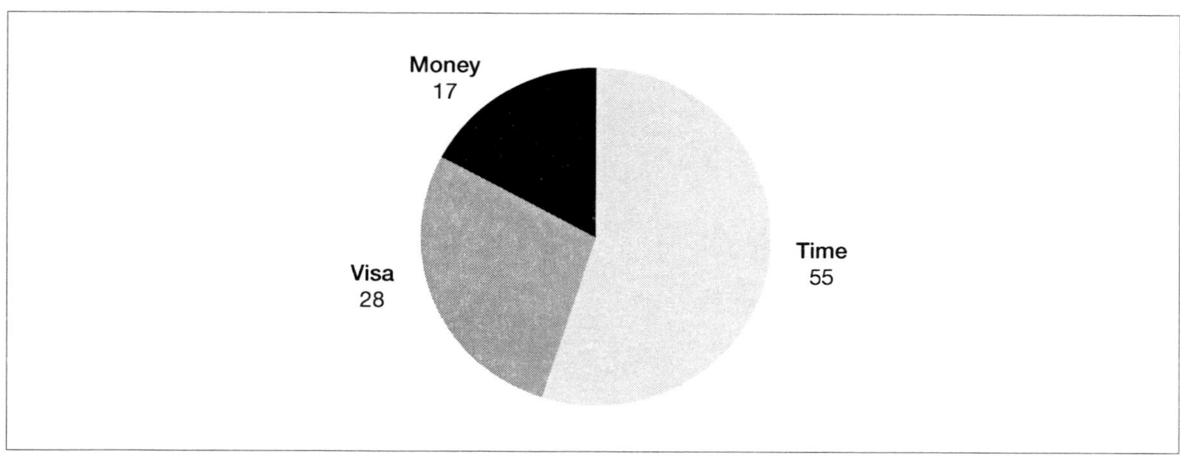

Source: ETOA/Amber Survey of Potential Travellers to Europe, January-March 2006.

Destinations already visited by potential travellers to Europe

Respondents who had not yet been to Europe had all visited Australia, South-East Asia and the United States of America.

9.7.3 Booking and Planning

How far ahead?

Respondents who had previously been to Europe said that they had spent, on average, three to six months planning their most recent visit to Europe. All cited the visa application process as the main reason for taking so long.

The focus groups that had not been to Europe envisaged shorter time delays for making their bookings. In Beijing and Shanghai, the would-be travellers to Europe stated that they would make their bookings between one and three months ahead of departure. Travellers in Guangzhou estimated average booking times of one to four months.

Information sources

All groups mentioned newspapers, magazines, television programmes and the internet as sources of information to consult. Other sources cited were video compact discs, DVDs and promotional leaflets.

Particularly highlighted were:

- *Zheng Da Zong Yi* – a long-running television programme on CCTV, which visits a different country every week and introduces its culture, sights and customs.
- *Traveller* magazine and the Chinese edition of *National Geographic.*
- A free newspaper (similar to *Metro* in Europe), which is distributed to commuters in Shanghai. Its lifestyle pages include both domestic and international travel promotions.

Travel agents preferred to the internet

Experienced and potential travellers alike were clear in their preference for booking through travel agents. Some 95% of previous leisure visitors in the three cities had booked this way; all would-be travellers said that they intended to.

There were several reasons given for favouring travel agents:

- Travellers in groups are not able to book hotels and tours independently.
- Agents assist with the visa arrangements.
- Given the requirement on them to submit sensitive private documents as part of the travel planning process, the Chinese interviewed were keen to meet face to face the person managing exchanges of large sums of money and handling visa applications.
- Few people in China had the international credit cards needed to make online bookings.
- There was a lack of trust in online bookings.

If the internet was used at all, respondents said, it was by those under the age of 40, 90% of whom used the internet at work and who regarded it as an information source. Older respondents – the most likely bookers of European travel – said they preferred more traditional sources of information, even if the family had a computer at home.

Despite this, respondents remained critical of one aspect of travel agents' services – they commented that customer-facing staff lacked knowledge about Europe. One respondent said: *"They were not able to cater for our needs at all and some of the tour routes are not attractive to us."*

Marketing

The focus groups agreed on the importance of marketing to influence the perception of Europe among Chinese people. They felt that the most effective forms of marketing were promotional campaigns and media – whether the internet, travel journals, or magazines. Other suggestions included:

- food festivals;
- promotional weeks for individual countries;
- cultural exchange programmes and activities;
- sponsored visits to Europe by journalists;
- television programmes that allow Chinese people to learn about Europe through the eyes of successful Chinese people who live there;
- newspaper columns on aspects of European life.

Although respondents were asked to give rankings in their responses to some questions – stating levels of agreement from 1-5 – these answers proved difficult to prompt.

9.7.4 Travel to Europe

Spending

The average spending on trips to Europe, including airfares, by those who had already been there was Rmb 15,000-30,000 (€ 1,460-2,920 or US$ 1,830-3,660). Those who had never been to Europe estimated that they would spend between Rmb 20,000-25,000 (€ 1,940-2,430 or US$ 2,440-3,050) on an average trip to Europe.

Taking shopping into account, this spend would rise to approximately Rmb 40,000-50,000 (€ 3,880-4,850 or US$ 4,880-6,100). Not knowing the exact prices of flights and accommodation, they found it hard to break these figures down any further.

Transport to Europe

The airlines used most often by previous visitors to enter Europe were Air China from Beijing and China eastern from Shanghai. (In 2006, both these carriers flew to all major European cities.) The port of entry mentioned most often was Frankfurt.

The would-be travellers intended to use Chinese airlines for their visits, too. Surprisingly, none of the travellers had any idea as to the availability of international airlines. Only in Beijing did the respondents mention that they had heard of Finnair and Virgin Atlantic Airways.

Travel within Europe

Respondents who had been to Europe before mentioned that economy-class air travel, trains and coaches were used by most tours. Public transport – trains, the underground/metro, buses – and coaches were the most popular forms of transport within Europe. None of the focus groups mentioned hire cars, but as long-haul vacations are almost exclusively in groups, this is hardly surprising.

Accommodation

Three-star hotels were generally chosen by respondents who had visited Europe on tour groups, while four- and five-star hotels were more often used by business visitors. The average price paid is € 80

(US$ 62) per night. This is of course the price paid to the agent and not what is received by the tour operator or hotel.

None of the respondents had any experience of bed & breakfast accommodation in Europe or, indeed, of any form of accommodation than hotels.

Focus group participants who had not yet travelled to Europe were asked what type of accommodation they would prefer to use. In Guangzhou, respondents said they would go for budget-class accommodation and agreed that staying in hostels could be an option. In Beijing, respondents said they preferred to stay in four- or five-star hotels, although they would *"also consider bed & breakfast accommodation"*. Safety featured highly in their responses, particularly in reference to some of Southern Europe's larger cities. In Shanghai, four- to five-star hotels and bed & breakfasts were the main choices.

Activities

The most popular activities enjoyed by respondents who had already been to Europe were:

- shopping;
- getting a feel for the typical European life;
- learning about the lives of famous Europeans known to Chinese people;
- leisurely afternoons in cafes;
- walking around with the crowds.

The Guangzhou focus group members said they had enjoyed:

- seeing famous architecture and museums;
- seeing famous sights and local cultural performances;
- tasting local food;
- walking in the streets;
- watching European life go by.

The respondents from Shanghai were especially keen on the visits they had made to smaller towns and regions where typical (more authentic) life had been on display.

Those who had not yet been to Europe were most looking forward to shopping and sightseeing. Guangzhou residents also mentioned cultural events. There were indications, in fact, that shopping might be less important to Guangzhou respondents than to those in Beijing and Shanghai. This is likely due to the city's proximity to Hong Kong, China, (one of Asia's main shopping destinations).

Travel preferences

Respondents who had been to Europe already were asked to say what their preferred type of travel to Europe was: individual or group; one country or many.

Responses to this were difficult to analyse as arrangements were the responsibility of travel agencies. This said:

- Young people who spoke English would prefer to travel independently.
- Non-English speakers prefer group travel.
- In future, they would like to travel with family and friends.
- They would not like to visit more than three countries in one trip. Guangzhou respondents went so far as to say that the programmes organised by the travel agencies are fixed so they had all found themselves *"stuck with a very fast trip to five or six countries"*.

9.7.5 Image of Europe

Words associated with Europe

All six focus groups were asked to give five positive and five negative words that they would associate with Europe. They answered as follows, sometimes using phrases rather than single words:

Positive	Negative
Artistic	Arrogant
Diverse culture	Conservative
Elegant	Reticent
Fairy-tale	Slow moving
Funky	Too traditional
Lasting appeal	
Lingering charm	
Prudence	
Rich in history	

Describing Europe

The focus groups were then asked to give five positive and five negative images that they would use to describe Europe in general.

Positive	Negative
Cultural diversity	Cold in response to other people
Elegant middle-aged women	Like *"a conservative man who is over-cautious, a little arrogant and slightly racist"*
Enjoyment (in middle age) of art and culture	Unsafe streets (in southern Europe)
The old and the new mixed together	
Wines	

Awareness of Europe

Respondents planning to visit Europe were most aware of the following:

- the Alps;
- Eiffel Tower;
- Louvre;
- Paris;
- Rome;
- Venice.

Respondents who had already been to Europe had been attracted by its:

- architecture and art of its cities;
- beauty and cleanliness;

- fashion;
- history and culture;
- modern design *(this one mentioned in Beijing);*
- 'noble' images;
- sculpture.

In Guangzhou and Shanghai, the focus groups were in complete agreement that France and Italy were the European countries of most appeal to Chinese people.

The impact of global political relations on the image of Europe

The focus groups were asked whether they felt that global political relations affected the image of Europe. They answered that they did not.

Two of Europe's main competitors – the United States of America and Australia

The focus groups were to give a view on the respective costs of visits to Europe, Australia and the United States of America.

Those that had been to Europe thought that accommodation was cheaper than in Australia and the United States of America. ETOA's researchers in China were puzzled by this because all other aspects of travel to Europe were thought to be more expensive. Price competition has driven down the cost of package tours to the extent that Europe seems comparatively cheap.

The opinions of those who had not been to Europe before were varied. Respondents in Guangzhou felt Europe would be cheaper than the United States of America, but they were not sure how it would compare with Australia. In Beijing, it was understood that travel to Europe was much more expensive than travel to Australia or to the United States of America.

Ease of visa applications

Europe and Australia were perceived to be easier than the United States of America for obtaining visas. Respondents felt that going to non-Schengen countries such as the United Kingdom was inconvenient, or more difficult, because of the visa application process (in other words, the requirement for a separate visa). Note that these responses were different from those given by the Chinese travel trade, which felt that the European visas were the most difficult to obtain.

9.7.6 Barriers to Travel to Europe

Visa applications

These consumers did not regard the cost of European visas as a barrier, but all but one of the focus groups did mention as a barrier the administrative difficulties of actually getting a visa.

Language

All groups of respondents thought that this was a minor barrier to travel. All respondents had a higher education level and so would have had access to English lessons to at least middle-school level. They are possibly not representative of the greater mass of middle-class Chinese tourists who are expected to visit Europe in the coming three to five years. Chinese discretion may not allow respondents to be totally honest about their levels of spoken English: the barrier could be more important than they were prepared to admit.

Distance

Among those who had not been to Europe, the distance between China and Europe was felt to be a barrier. But it was not mentioned at all by those who had been to Europe.

Number of religious sites on itineraries

None of the previous visitors or potential travellers felt that there were too many religious sites on the itineraries. This was in contrast to the Chinese travel agents, who said that Chinese tourists became exhausted by the numbers of such sites and would probably prefer tours that visited fewer churches and cathedrals.

9.8 Survey of Travellers on Coach Tours in Europe

9.8.1 Methodology

The questions for this survey were developed by ETOA in conjunction with ETC and UNWTO, and in line with the responses of the consumer focus groups in China. ETOA's consumer surveys' partner, Consumerdata, translated the questions into simplified Chinese.

The idea behind the survey was to analyse the perceptions of visitors before their trip and their views and reactions after the trip – an important insight into pre-travel perceptions and the reality actually experienced by Chinese visitors in Europe.

Distribution

A two-sided A5-size survey leaflet was produced and distributed to ETOA's tour operator partners in the study. These companies, all leading players in this market, were Gullivers Travel Associates, China Holidays and Kuoni Incoming Services. They disseminated the surveys to the tour managers leading their Chinese groups in Europe. The tour managers circulated the survey to the travellers at the end of their trips. 134 completed responses were collected and forwarded to Consumerdata for analysis.

An English version of the survey used, and a full breakdown of the data received, can be found in annex XII.

9.8.2 Responses

Previous visits to Europe

A relatively high proportion of those questioned had been to Europe at least once before. This is indicative of the type of sample rather than of the Chinese market as a whole.

It is not clear whether those who had been before had travelled on business or for leisure, but the likelihood is that these would have been business trips, since this would have been the usual method of visiting Europe before ADS became widely available.

Figure 9.23 Number of Previous Visits to Europe by Coach Travellers (%)

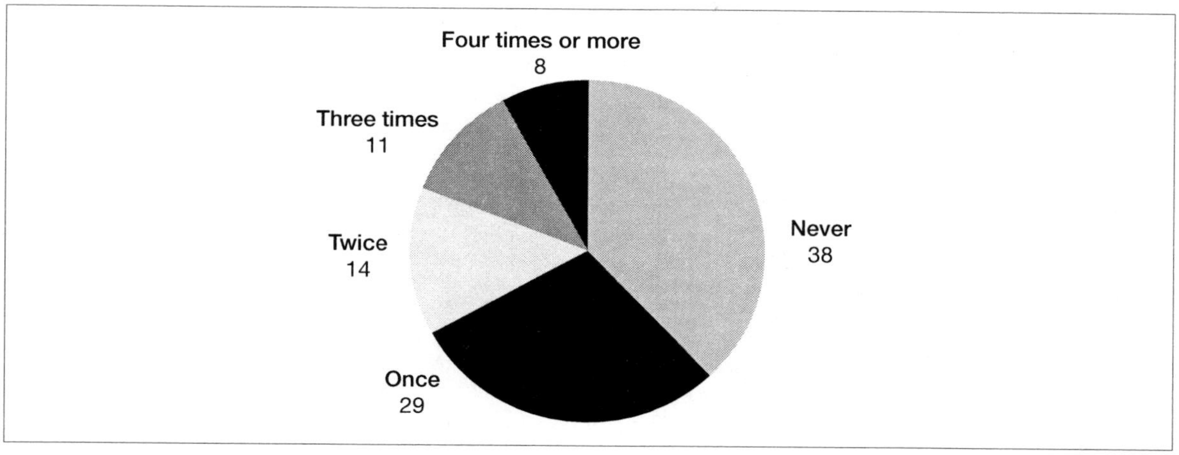

Four times or more
8
Three times
11
Twice
14
Once
29
Never
38

Source: ETOA Survey of Chinese Coach Travellers in Europe, 2006.

Perceptions of visitors before and after their trip

It would appear that Chinese visitors' perceptions of Europe as cultural, historical and scenic become stronger once they had visited the destination. Their impression of Europe's cleanliness and safety also becomes more positive. The biggest negative shift in perception, according to ETOA's survey of coach travellers in Europe, was over Europe's image as 'modern'. This could be because group coach tours tend to visit a high proportion of historical monuments and focus less on newer/modern areas of European cities.

There is also a suggestion in the data that the European shopping experience did not live up to their expectations. While the percentage of those who strongly agreed that *"Europe had good shopping"* did not change, the number of travellers who *disagreed* with this statement rose quite considerably after their trips and thus caused a drop in the rating for 'good shopping'. Respondents' perception of Europe as being 'good value for money' also fell once they had completed their trip – this may be linked to their disappointment with their shopping experiences.

It should be noted that, as with the travel trade surveys, respondents were asked to comment on a number of words to describe Europe. Their responses varied from 1 = 'strongly disagree' to 5 = 'strongly agree'. The following graph reflects the breakdown of responses (weighted).

Figure 9.24 How Valid Are the Following Terms When Used to Describe Europe? (%)

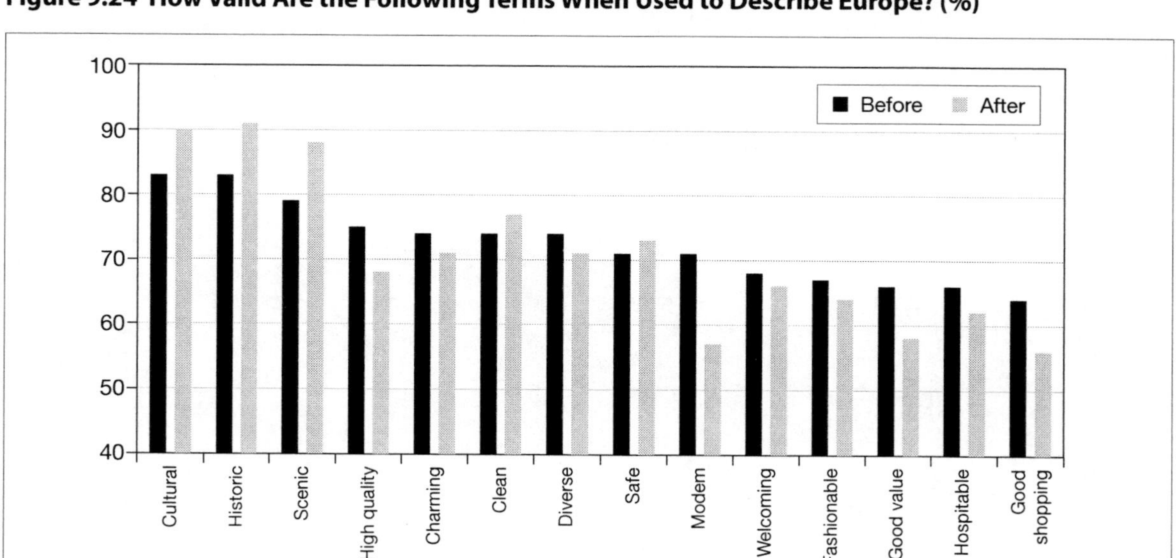

Source: ETOA Survey of Chinese Coach Travellers in Europe, 2006.

Describing Europe

The respondents were asked to describe the image they had of Europe in one word. The evidence above that European history and scenery have the greatest impact on Chinese visitors is borne out by the fact that the two words cited most often were 'beautiful' and 'historic'. 'Clean', 'elegant' and 'cultural' were also mentioned frequently.

'Welcoming' is not the overriding image of Europe among Chinese travellers. This word did relatively well in the perceptions question (see figure 9.24), but in this part of the survey, only 1% of respondents said they would use 'friendly' to describe Europe in one word.

Word	Responses (%)	Word	Responses (%)
Beautiful	24	Friendly	1.0
Historic	15	Fairytale	0.4
Clean	12	Eclectic	0.4
Elegant	11	Arrogant	0.4
Cultural	10	Charming	0.4
Modern	8	Noble	0.0
Conservative	4	Fashionable	0.0
Artistic	2	Diverse	0.0
Traditional	2	Funky	0.0
Slow	1		

Chinese travellers and European food

Most respondents ate European food on their trip, but only a minority of those surveyed – 44% – had several 'European' meals. This supports the assertions made in the travel trade interviews that Chinese visitors prefer to eat Chinese food when in Europe.

Figure 9.25 Proportion of Those Who Ate European Food on Their Trip (%)

Category	%
Not at all	10
Once	46
Several times	44

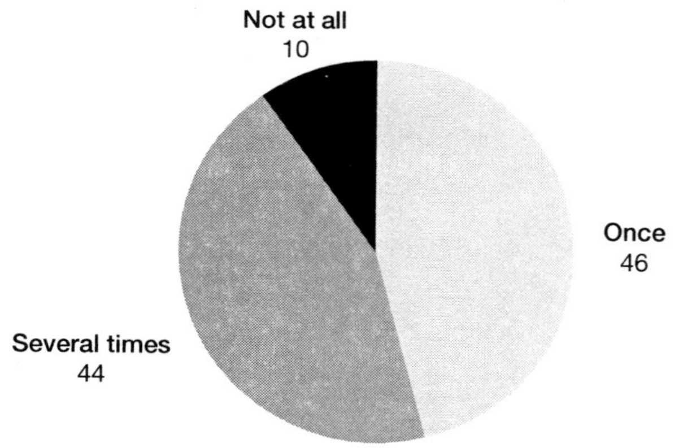

Source: ETOA Survey of Chinese Coach Travellers in Europe, 2006.

This limited experience of European food could also be the reason why a trip to Europe did little to alter Chinese visitors' perceptions of it. While respondents thought it was less 'strange' at the end of their trip, the other perceptions remained almost unchanged. One suggestion made was that European menus should show numbered photographs of the different dishes.

Figure 9.26 Perceptions of European Food Before and After the Trip (%)

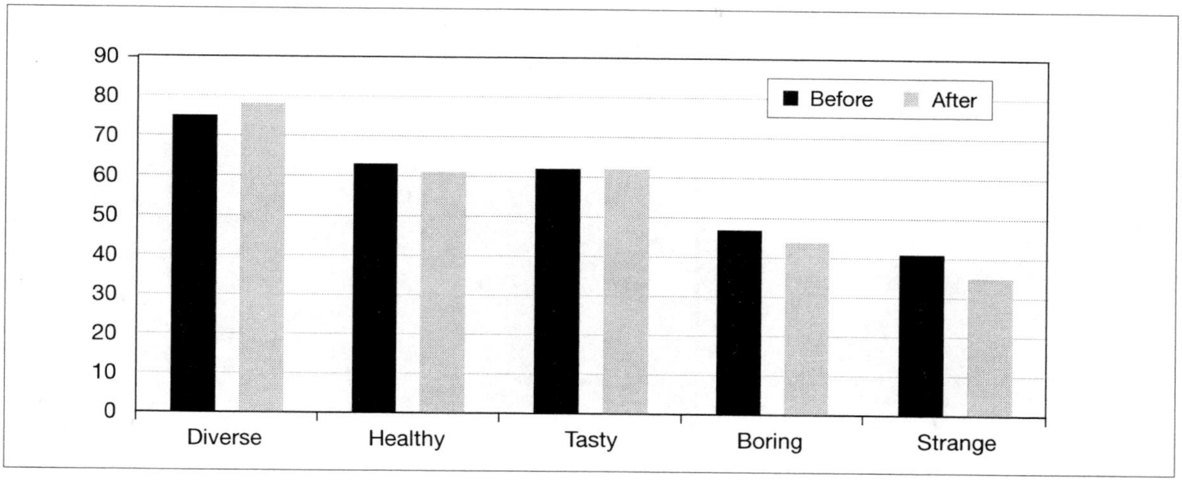

Before After

90 80 70 60 50 40 30 20 10 0

Diverse Healthy Tasty Boring Strange

Source: ETOA Survey of Chinese Coach Travellers in Europe, 2006.

Satisfaction of Chinese visitors with their trip

Almost all the visitors surveyed said that they were either *"very satisfied"* or *"satisfied"* with their trip. Indeed, 93% of them said they would return for another visit. Nobody at all was *"dissatisfied"* or *"very dissatisfied"*.

Figure 9.27 Visitor Satisfaction Ratings (%)

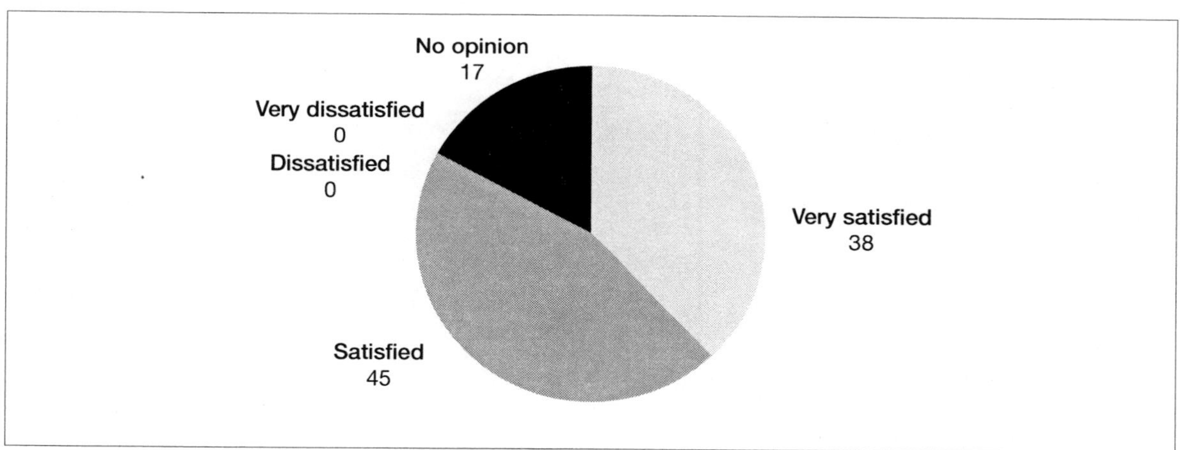

Source: ETOA Survey of Chinese Coach Travellers in Europe, 2006.

The number of countries visited on the trip

It was surprising to learn that most respondents had visited only one country during their trip to Europe. As with the earlier finding that a relatively high proportion of those questioned had been to Europe at least once before, this new finding appears to be indicative of the sample rather than of Chinese visitors in general: it contained a higher-than-average number of visitors on their second visit to Europe.

"Four or more" was the next most common response. Few of those surveyed had visited only two or three countries.

Figure 9.28: Number of European Countries Visited on This Trip (%)

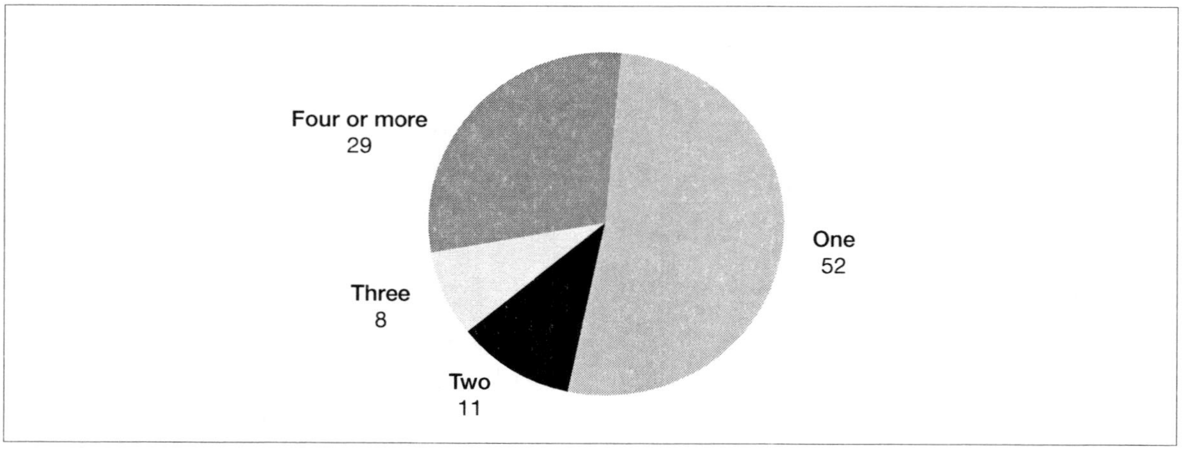

Four or more 29
One 52
Three 8
Two 11

Source: ETOA Survey of Chinese Coach Travellers in Europe, 2006.

Length of stay in Europe

Six to ten days was easily the most common length of stay. Stays of 10-15 days came in second place in the survey. This concurs with the results from both the consumer focus groups and the travel trade.

Figure 9.29 Length of Stay in Europe (%)

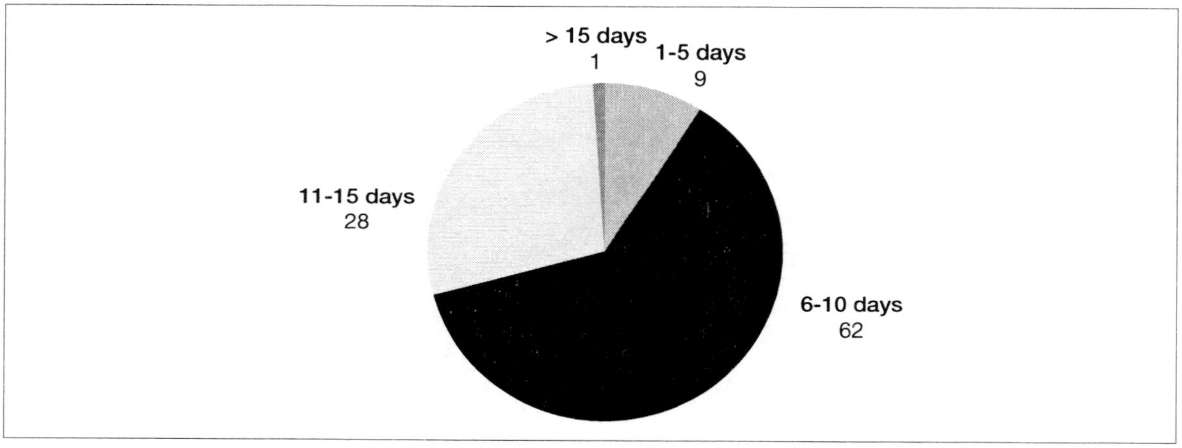

> 15 days 1
1-5 days 9
11-15 days 28
6-10 days 62

Source: ETOA Survey of Chinese Coach Travellers in Europe, 2006.

Visitors' region of origin in China

Most of the 134 respondents surveyed came from Shanghai (67%). Some 13% came from Beijing and 7% from Guangzhou. The remaining 13% came from regions other than the three main traffic-generating regions of China.

Spending by Chinese groups in Europe

The question on expenditure brought widely varying results, but it was clear that most visitors spent less than Rmb 10,000 overall (€ 9,700).

Figure 9.30 Expenditure in Europe (Rmb)

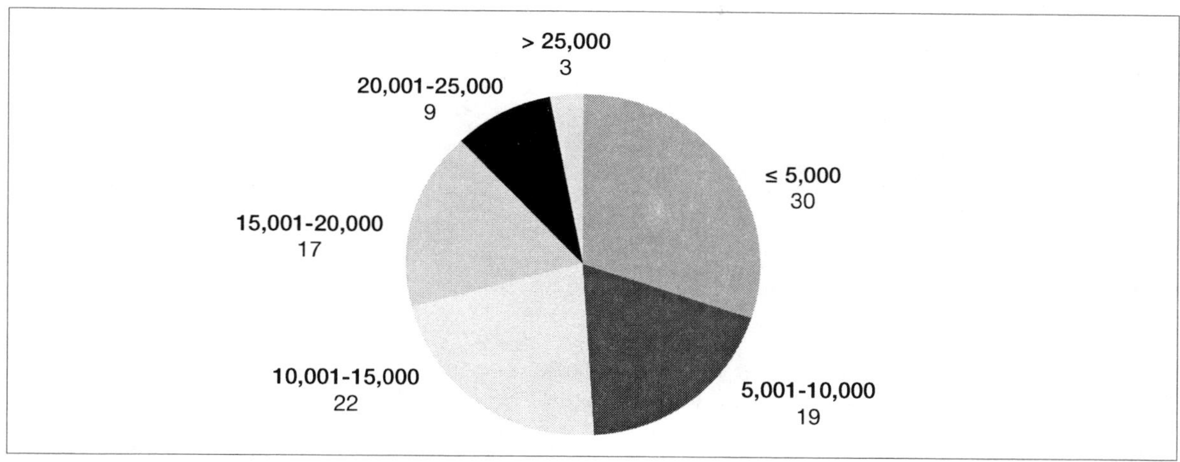

Note: In 2006, the average exchange rate was Rmb 10.20 to € 1.

Source: ETOA Survey of Chinese Coach Travellers in Europe, 2006.

Overall assessment

Overall, the Chinese coach travellers' responses were very positive about the experience of visiting Europe. But responses to questionnaires such as these are naturally positive. Clients, whatever their origin, usually want to reassure the tour manager collecting the forms that he/she has done a good job – and has happy clients. Veiled in such common courtesy it is possible that people's expectations were 'met' rather than 'exceeded'.

9.9 Survey on ETC's 'Europe' logo

9.9.1 Methodology

As part of this study, survey respondents were also asked for their views on ETC's 'Europe' logo. The objective was to determine in particular whether they thought the logo was good for the image of Europe, whether they understood the English language on the logo and whether one image was, in their opinion, sufficient to describe Europe.

The following questions were put to all groups interviewed for the different surveys, with the exception of the Chinese coach tourists actually travelling around Europe.

9.9.2 Is the Logo Good for the Image of Europe?

Support for the 'Brand Europe' logo was not strong among any of the groups.

Many of the Chinese travel agents commented that they did not really understand what the 'wings' motif represented and so were unsure whether it could successfully represent the image of Europe. The first impressions of the consumer focus groups were also that they did not know what the logo was supposed to be.

The reactions of the Chinese tour guides and European tour operators were slightly more positive. The guides thought that about half of their customers would understand the logo; only four (19%) of the 22 European companies who expressed an opinion disagreed that the logo was good for the image of Europe. Nine (41%) of the companies had no opinion on the matter.

Other comments on the logo from the Chinese travel agents and consumer focus groups were criticisms implying that the logo was not memorable. One leading Chinese agent said: *"The logo doesn't leave me with any great impression."*

Consumers were critical of the logo's design. One said: *"The colour and the font are not at all creative and don't represent the diversity of culture in Europe."* Another said: *"I don't know what the picture is and the colour seems very dull to represent Europe."*

9.9.3 English Language on the Logo

The Chinese travel agents, guides and consumer focus groups commented on this issue.

All the agents said that they could understand the strap-line but they were all adamant that it would have to be translated if it were to be effective in China. They pointed out that many Chinese travellers to Europe were unable to understand basic English phrases. They said that, while it was true that the number of English speakers in China was increasing, it was unlikely that non-English-speaking Chinese over the age of 35 would ever learn.

This belief that the strap-line would need to be translated in order to be effective was shared by the consumer focus groups. Once they understood the words used, most respondents interpreted them positively and understood them to mean that there was much to see in Europe. However, there was one respondent in Shanghai who interpreted the words negatively: *"My understanding is that this means Europe is endless and boring."*

All five guides interviewed said that they understood the English-language strap-line.

9.9.4 Is One Image Sufficient to Describe Europe?

The general consensus on this question was that one image was not enough.

Six (50%) of the Chinese travel agents shared this view. They believed that the diversity of Europe would be best represented by a number of images. They suggested that the most appropriate way of highlighting Europe's diversity would be to divide up the continent into geographical regions (north, south, east and west) and then to identify an iconic piece of architecture – or a person – to represent each one.

Only three of these travel agents thought one image was enough. Three had no opinion on the subject.

The consumer focus groups also believed that one image was not enough and that several images would work better. And they, too, suggested dividing Europe into geographical regions: in their case, north, west and central.

The 22 European tour operators who answered this question clearly had reservations about the single logo for the whole of Europe. Only 38% thought that one image was sufficient to describe Europe, while 38% disagreed and 24% had no opinion. A more detailed breakdown is given below:

Figure 9.31 One Image Is Sufficient to Describe Europe (%)

	Completely disagree	Disagree	No opinion	Agree	Completely agree
Views of European tour operators	24	14	24	28	10

Source: ETOA Survey of European Tour Operators, April 2006.

As to what *should* feature on a logo of Europe from the Chinese point of view, four of the twelve Chinese travel agents suggested the EU symbol/flag (see below) because they saw this as something that tourists would instantly associate with Europe. Respondents from the consumer focus groups also mentioned the EU flag as a suitable symbol of Europe. (Their other suggestions included the Eiffel Tower, the Mona Lisa, Roman pillars and Venus de Milo.)

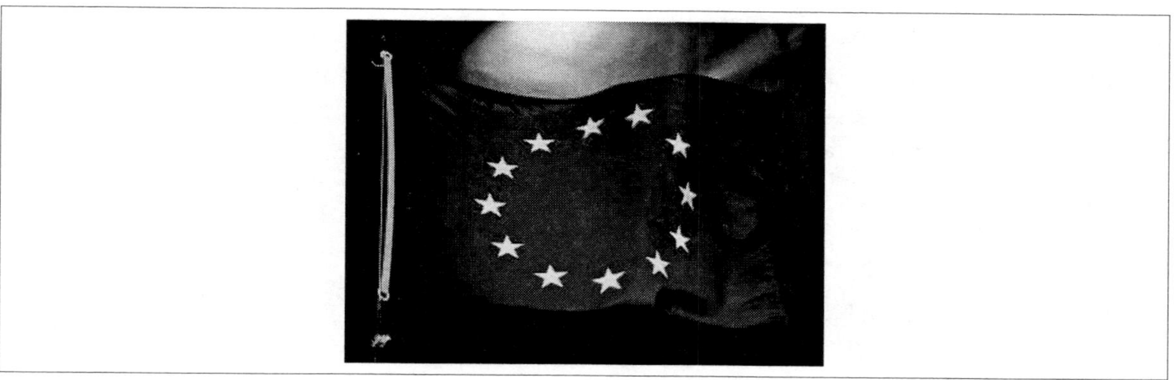

It seems likely that those suggesting the EU flag did not understand that ETC's 'boundaries' go beyond those of the European Union.

9.10 Summary of the Research Findings

9.10.1 A Challenging Market

The travel trade interviews and focus groups confirm that China is a growing market for Europe, but that this growth is still from a very low base. Moreover, demand is – and will for some time continue to be – concentrated in the three greater city regions of Beijing, Shanghai and Guangzhou, and for a relatively small number of European countries.

In terms of marketing, the interviews and focus groups also highlighted the fact that China represents a unique challenge. Unlike North America, it is culturally discrete. The average citizen of the United States of America speaks, eats and thinks in a similar way to Europeans. Europe thus represents a cultural and ancestral 'homeland'. This informs both their approach to a European vacation – what they imagine they are going to enjoy – and their experience of one. Stratford-upon-Avon, the Parthenon and the Sistine Chapel all carry a profound appeal to a common cultural heritage. The Chinese market does not experience anything like these impulses.

With regard to the images and words associated with Europe, there were similarities in responses between those respondents who were yet to visit Europe and those who had already done so. This may be because the type of travel under discussion – primarily Approved Destination Status (ADS) tour groups – was concentrated on those sights and attractions which are most famous and, therefore, likely to be most familiar to anyone who has not yet visited them. First-time, or less-frequent, travellers are clearly likely to buy tours that consist of attractions of which they have heard and want to see.

9.10.2 Europe's Attractions

The three main tourism generating regions in China all had similar views about what makes Europe attractive. This homogeneity should facilitate marketing and promotions by Europe's national tourism organizations (NTOs) in the future and would seem to make it unnecessary to tailor specific marketing messages for individual Chinese cities.

Europe's luxury shopping, scenic and historical/cultural attractions feature highly in both travel agents' and potential clients' perceptions of Europe. Like all emerging markets, highly recognisable sights are a major motivator in attracting clients. When little is known generally about a destination or location, familiar sights/icons become even more important.

Another motivating factor is the perception of Europe's 'otherness'. Travel agents in China thought it a good idea to promote Europe through food festivals. This might seem surprising given the fact that, according to the research findings, few Chinese eat more than one 'European-style' meal when in Europe.

Even when buying group tours, travellers remain individuals. As the market matures, there will be an increase in the number of experienced travellers who are open to take more intensive single-country tours. But, in China, as in all large emerging markets, there will always be a vast pool of potential first-time visitors.

Despite some recognition of individual countries and of regional distinctions, Chinese still generally regard Europe as a single, unified destination. Any promotional work carried out by the NTOs should take this fact into account. Europe's image and positioning in China should be concentrated and well defined.

Great caution should be exercised in developing sub-brands. The market will change as access to information improves and more Chinese travel abroad and, especially, outside Asia. But the proportion of Europhiles who have extensive travel experience will remain small as a share of the total market – even thought the absolute volume is likely to grow fast. But first-time travellers will continue to make up the vast bulk of the market.

9.11 Recommendations

9.11.1 Importance of Joint Efforts

The proportion of China's population who are able to travel to Europe will remain extremely small for several years. Even in the medium term, a European vacation will be a niche product appealing to a small proportion of an affluent elite. According to the travel trade interviewed in China, this makes it even more important for NTOs to work together to try to attract the Chinese market.

Among the core recommendations made by these travel agents as to ways of enhancing Europe's potential as a tourism destination for Chinese, the following were the most important:

- improve Europeans' understanding of how Chinese travel agencies operate;
- supply more information in Chinese, both in China and to Chinese tourists in Europe;
- pay very careful attention when designing marketing brochures, etc – the appropriate style and layout are just as important as the language used;
- take professional advice from local expertise in China as to the best way of adapting the visiteurope.com website for the Chinese market;
- compile a list of European NTO offices in China, and encourage them to work together in multi-country promotions.

The internet is growing in importance as a tool with which Chinese consumers investigate the possibilities of a vacation. The development of visiteurope.com as a Chinese-language site is of central importance. It both reflects the use that the Chinese make of the internet and mirrors their idea of Europe being 'one destination with many regions'.

9.11.2 Specific Recommendations from the European Travel Trade

In general, the research showed that the travel trade – in Europe and China – felt the following:

- Currently available data on the Chinese market is poor. Individual countries must try to differentiate between Chinese visitors and 'other Asians'. Data from visa issuing authorities would also be very useful for the travel trade in China, as well as for suppliers.
- China has grown as a source market to Europe during a period of declining demand from the United States of America and Japan. This has enabled Chinese groups to access distressed inventory. If the Japanese and Americans were to return to Europe in great numbers, prices of accommodation, restaurants and attractions would inevitably rise, leading to a reduction in demand from China.
- Europe is perceived as an expensive destination, so it is important to devise some way of increasing the prestige of visiting Europe so that price becomes less of a constraint. If the goal for the industry is more visits from the Chinese middle class, this can be a long-term project.
- Despite increased use of the internet and of information channels such as television and newspapers, word of mouth has genuine authority in Chinese culture. A rumour that a particular visa issuing office is asking personal questions can be sufficient to deter waves of groups from entering a country. One attack on a Chinese individual can blight a destination. How this can be countered by European NTOs remains a difficult question to answer, as it is not easy to allay fears without attracting attention to them.
- More effort must be made to make Chinese groups feel welcome. One negative impression that is gaining ground is the perception that Europe is unfriendly and lacking in understanding. One way of countering this is to ensure that more information is available in Chinese to visitors – in particular, explanations as to European customs and mores.

The Chinese market to Europe is currently neither large, in terms of its actual value and or short-term growth potential, nor easy to tap. The short-term prospects for Europe as a destination remain uncertain. But as China grows into being an economic super-power, finding a way to appeal to the potential Chinese visitor is one of the most pressing questions facing the European travel industry.

Annex I

Countries with Approved Destination Status (ADS)

Figure I.1 Countries with Approved Destination Status, as at April 2007

Country	Date[a]	Country	Date[a]
Asia Pacific			
Hong Kong, China	1983	Indonesia	2002
Macao, China	1983	Nepal	2002
Thailand	1988	India	2003
Malaysia	1990	Maldives	2003
Singapore	1990	Pakistan	2003
Philippines	1992	Sri Lanka	2003
Republic of Korea	1998	Lao PDR	2005
Australia	1999	Fiji	2006
New Zealand	1999	Mongolia	2006
Brunei	2000	Papua New Guinea	2006
Cambodia	2000	Tonga	2006
Japan	2000	Vanuatu	2006
Myanmar	2000	Bengal	2007
Vietnam	2000		
Europe			
Malta	2002	Greece	2004
Turkey	2002	Iceland	2004
Croatia	2003	Ireland	2004
Germany	2003	Italy	2004
Hungary	2003	Latvia	2004
Austria	2004	Liechtenstein	2004
Belgium	2004	Lithuania	2004
Cyprus	2004	Luxembourg	2004
Czech Republic	2004	Netherlands	2004
Denmark	2004	Norway	2004
Estonia	2004	Poland	2004
Finland	2004	Portugal	2004
France	2004	Romania	2004

Country	Date[a]	Country	Date[a]
Slovakia	2004	Switzerland	2004
Slovenia	2004	Russian Federation	2005
Spain	2004	United Kingdom	2005
Sweden	2004	Andorra	2007
Americas			
Cuba	2003	Peru	2005
Antigua and Barbuda	2005	Bahamas	2006
Barbados	2005	Ecuador	2006
Brazil	2005	Grenada	2006
Chile	2005	St Lucia	2006
Dominica	2005	Argentina	2007
Jamaica	2005	Trinidad and Tobago	2007
Mexico	2005	Venezuela	2007
Africa and Middle East			
Egypt	2002	Lesotho	2005
Morocco	2003	Madagascar	2005
South Africa	2003	Namibia	2005
Ethiopia	2004	Algeria	2006
Jordan	2004	Benin	2006
Kenya	2004	Cameroon	2006
Mauritius	2004	Cape Verde	2006
Seychelles	2004	Gabon	2006
Tanzania	2004	Ghana	2006
Tunisia	2004	Mali	2006
Tunisia	2004	Mozambique	2006
Zambia	2004	Nigeria	2006
Zimbabwe	2004	Uganda	2007
Botswana	2005	United Arab Emirates	2007

a) Date at which ADS came into effect. A number of other countries have signed Memorandums of Understanding with the Chinese Government regarding ADS, e.g. Monaco and Bulgaria, but their respective agreements have not come into effect.

Note: Until July 1997 ADS was officially only for visits to friends and relatives (VFR tourism).

Source: China National Tourism Administration (CNTA).

Annex II

Schengen Countries

In June 1985, five European Union member countries signed a treaty to end international border checkpoints and controls. These were Belgium, France, Germany, Luxembourg and the Netherlands. Other countries joined over the following years – all of which EU members except Iceland and Norway – taking the total to 15 by 1996.

On May 2004, on their accession to EU membership, the following countries also signed the Schengen Agreement: Czech Republic, Estonia, Hungary, Latvia, Lithuania, Poland, Slovakia, Slovenia, Malta and Cyprus. All except Cyprus are set to implement the Treaty sometime during early 2008. Bulgaria, Switzerland and Romania have also signed the Agreement, but have not formally declared when they will implement it.

Figure II.1 Signatories to the Schengen Agreement

Country	Date[a]	Country	Date[a]
Belgium	1998	Norway	1996
France	1998	Sweden	1996
Germany	1998	Czech Republic	2008
Luxembourg	1998	Estonia	2008
Netherlands	1998	Hungary	2008
Italy	1990	Latvia	2008
Greece	1992	Lithuania	2008
Portugal	1992	Poland	2008
Spain	1992	Slovakia	2008
Austria	1995	Slovenia	2008
Denmark	1996	Malta	2008
Finland	1996	Cyprus	na
Iceland	1996		

a) Date at which membership came/is due to come into effect.

Source: European Commission.

Annex III

Scheduled Airlines Operating between China and Europe, 2003-2006

Figure III.1 European Airports Served Directly from China, 2003-2006

Code	Airport	Code	Airport
AMS	Amsterdam	IST	Istanbul
ARN	Stockholm	KBP	Kiev
BUD	Budapest	LHR	London Heathrow
CDG	Paris Charles-de-Gaulle	MAD	Madrid
CPH	Copenhagen	MUC	Munich
DME	Moscow Domodedovo	MXP	Milan Malpensa
DUS	Düsseldorf	SVO	Moscow Sheremetyevo
FCO	Rome Fiumicino	VCE	Venice
FRA	Frankfurt	VIE	Vienna
HEL	Helsinki	ZRH	Zurich

Source: The Airline Codes Web Site (www.airlinecodes.co.uk).

Figure III.2 Scheduled Airlines Operating from Guangzhou to Europe, January 2003-2006

Airline	Destination	Departures/week				Seats/week (one-way)			
		2003	2004	2005	2006	2003	2004	2005	2006
Air France	CDG	0	5	5	5	0	1,300	1,095	1,095
China Southern Airlines	CDG	0	0	4	8	0	0	1,168	2,341
China Southern Airlines – Regional	CDG	0	0	4	3	0	0	200	150
Lufthansa	FRA	0	0	0	6	0	0	0	2,070
Finnair	HEL	0	0	0	3	0	0	0	861
Total		**0**	**5**	**13**	**25**	**0**	**1,300**	**2,463**	**6,517**

Sources: Pacific Asia Travel Association (PATA); SRS Analyser.

Figure III.3 Scheduled Airlines Operating from Guangzhou to Europe, August 2003-2006

Airline	Destination	Departures/week				Seats/week (one-way)			
		2003	2004	2005	2006	2003	2004	2005	2006
Air France	CDG	0	7	7	3	0	1,533	1,820	739
China Southern Airlines	CDG	0	4	4	6	0	1,520	1,168	1,599
Lufthansa	FRA	0	0	7	7	0	0	2,415	2,415
Finnair	HEL	0	0	0	4	0	0	0	1,148
Total		**0**	**11**	**18**	**20**	**0**	**3,053**	**5,403**	**5,901**

Sources: PATA; SRS Analyser.

Figure III.4 Scheduled Airlines Operating from Beijing to Europe, January 2003-2006

Airline	Desti-nation	Departures/week				Seats/week (one-way)			
		2003	2004	2005	2006	2003	2004	2005	2006
China Southern Airlines	AMS	2	4	5	11	760	1,520	1,460	3,058
KLM Royal Dutch Airlines	AMS	4	3	7	7	1,112	834	1,946	1,946
Air China International	ARN	2	2	3	4	422	428	642	856
Hainan Airlines	BUD	0	0	3	3	0	0	660	630
Air China International	CDG	3	5	0	0	909	1,608	0	0
Air France	CDG	7	7	7	10	1,890	1,890	2,170	2,868
SAS Scandinavian Airlines	CPH	7	7	7	7	1,827	1,806	1,806	1,806
LTU International Airways	DUS	0	0	1	0	0	0	340	0
Air China International	FCO	0	0	0	4	0	0	0	1,309
Air China International	FRA	7	7	7	7	2,606	2,315	2,315	2,606
Lufthansa	FRA	7	7	7	7	2,730	2,800	2,730	2,730
Finnair	HEL	5	3	5	5	1,435	861	1,435	1,435
Turkish Airlines	IST	3	5	5	5	813	1,355	1,355	1,355
Aerosvit Airlines	KBP	0	1	1	1	0	230	230	230
Air China International	LHR	4	4	5	5	1,212	1,208	1,509	1,608
British Airways	LHR	3	3	4	5	726	726	968	1,210
Air Comet	MAD	0	0	0	2	0	0	0	788
Air China International	MUC	0	0	2	4	0	0	428	1,380
China Eastern Airlines	MUC	2	2	0	0	574	574	0	0
Lufthansa	MUC	0	0	3	3	0	0	741	741
Air China International	MXP	4	3	4	0	1,212	909	1,309	0
Aeroflot	SVO	7	7	7	7	2,056	2,037	1,981	1,596
Air China International	SVO	3	3	3	4	633	1,035	1,035	1,725
Austrian Airlines	VIE	3	3	4	4	771	831	1,031	1,092
SWISS International Air Lines	ZRH	3	0	0	0	870	0	0	0
Total		**76**	**76**	**90**	**105**	**22,558**	**22,967**	**26,091**	**30,969**

Sources: PATA; SRS Analyser.

Figure III.5 Scheduled Airlines Operating from Beijing to Europe, August 2003-2006

Airline	Desti-nation	Departures/week				Seats/week (one-way)			
		2003	2004	2005	2006	2003	2004	2005	2006
China Southern Airlines	AMS	4	3	4	14	1,520	1,140	1,168	3,934
KLM Royal Dutch Airlines	AMS	3	7	7	7	834	1,946	1,946	1,946
Air China International	ARN	2	4	4	4	428	856	856	856
Hainan Airlines	BUD	0	0	3	3	0	0	660	630
Air China International	CDG	5	7	7	7	1,610	2,113	2,111	2,503
Air France	CDG	7	7	14	14	1,890	2,744	3,663	4,060
China Eastern Airlines	CDG	0	2	0	0	0	574	0	0
SAS Scandinavian Airlines	CPH	4	7	7	7	800	1,806	1,806	1,806
LTU International Airways	DUS	0	1	3	0	0	387	1,020	0
Air China International	FCO	0	0	4	7	0	0	1,212	2,121
Air China International	FRA	7	7	7	11	2,606	2,800	2,606	4,180
Lufthansa	FRA	7	7	7	7	1,680	2,800	2,730	2,730
Finnair	HEL	4	7	6	7	1,148	2,009	1,722	2,009
Turkish Airlines	IST	3	5	5	7	813	1,355	1,355	1,687
Aerosvit Airlines	KBP	0	2	2	3	0	460	460	690
Air China International	LHR	5	7	7	7	1,608	2,115	2,113	2,606
British Airways	LHR	3	5	6	7	726	1,210	1,452	1,694
Air Comet	MAD	0	0	2	0	0	0	788	0
Air Europa Líneas Aéreas	MAD	0	0	2	2	0	0	506	598
Air China International	MUC	0	2	4	7	0	428	1,380	2,415
China Eastern Airlines	MUC	2	0	0	0	574	0	0	0
Lufthansa	MUC	0	3	3	7	0	720	741	1,729
Air China International	MXP	3	4	0	0	909	1,212	0	0
Aeroflot Russian Airlines	SVO	7	7	7	14	1,976	2,037	1,793	3,220
Air China International	SVO	3	5	5	7	1,035	1,725	1,725	2,415
Austrian Airlines	VIE	3	6	6	7	795	1,866	1,586	1,594
Total		**72**	**105**	**122**	**158**	**20,952**	**32,303**	**35,399**	**44,825**

Sources: PATA; SRS Analyser.

Figure III.6 Scheduled Airlines Operating from Shanghai to Europe, January 2003-2006

Airline	Desti-nation	Departures/week				Seats/week (one-way)			
		2003	2004	2005	2006	2003	2004	2005	2006
KLM Royal Dutch Airlines	AMS	3	4	6	7	834	1,946	1,946	1,946
SAS Scandinavian Airlines	CPH	0	0	6	6	0	0	1,806	1,806
LTU International Airways	DUS	0	0	0	0	0	0	0	0
Air China/Lufthansa	FRA	11	7	7	14	2,800	2,730	2,730	4,180
Shanghai Airlines	FRA	0	0	0	7	0	0	0	1,407
Finnair	HEL	0	3	5	4	0	861	1,435	1,435
Turkish Airlines	IST	0	0	5	5	0	0	1,355	1,355
Aerosvit Airlines	KBP	0	0	5	5	0	0	690	690
Virgin Atlantic Airways	LHR	3	4	9	16	726	968	2,177	2,177
British Airways	LHR	0	0	4	4	0	0	968	968
China Eastern Airlines	LHR	0	0	0	5	0	0	1,380	1,380
Air Europa Líneas Aéreas	MAD	0	0	0	3	506	0	0	500
Air China International	MXP	0	2	3	3	0	428	909	909
Blue Panorama	MXP	0	1	0	0	0	0	1,455	2,037
Alitalia	MXP	0	0	5	7	0	0	0	0
China Eastern Airlines	SVO	0	2	2	2	0	574	574	574
Aeroflot Russian Airlines	SVO	0	4	4	4	0	920	920	920
Lufthansa	MUC	0	0	7	7	0	0	2,730	2,730
China Eastern Airlines	CDG	7	7	7	7	2,009	2,009	2,009	2,009
Air China International	CDG	2	3	3	3	428	642	642	642
Air France	CDG	5	6	7	14	1,350	1,620	1,890	3,663
Air China	FCO	0	2	0	0	0	422	0	0
Air China/Austrian Airlines	VIE	0	0	1	3	0	0	257	771
Blue Panorama	VCE	0	0	1	0	0	0	196	0
Total		**31**	**45**	**87**	**126**	**8,653**	**13,120**	**26,069**	**32,105**

Sources: PATA; SRS Analyser.

Figure III.7 Scheduled Airlines Operating from Shanghai to Europe, August 2003-2006

Airline	Destination	Departures/week				Seats/week (one-way)			
		2003	2004	2005	2006	2003	2004	2005	2006
KLM Royal Dutch Airlines	AMS	4	7	7	7	834	1,946	1,946	1,946
SAS Scandinavian Airlines	CPH	0	3	6	6	0	800	1,806	1,548
LTU International Airways	DUS	0	1	1	2	1,020	387	387	680
Air China/Lufthansa	FRA	14	11	7	7	5,460	4,290	2,730	2,800
Finnair	HEL	0	5	4	4	0	1,435	1,148	1,148
Turkish Airlines	IST	0	0	5	5	0	0	1,355	1,355
Aerosvit Airlines	KBP	0	0	5	0	0	0	460	0
Virgin Atlantic Airways	LHR	4	5	7	5	968	1,210	1,694	1,433
China Eastern Airlines	LHR	4	4	4	4	1,148	1,148	1,148	1,148
British Airways	LHR	0	0	5	5	0	0	1,455	1,210
Air Europa Líneas Aéreas	MAD	0	0	2	2	0	0	580	506
Blue Panorama	MXP	0	0	1	0	574	574	574	0
Air China International	MXP	0	3	2	2	0	0	196	606
Alitalia	MXP	0	0	5	5	0	0	1,890	1,070
Aeroflot Russian Airlines	SVO	0	5	4	6	0	825	660	1,410
China Eastern Airlines	SVO	0	2	2	0	0	574	574	0
Lufthansa	MUC	0	0	7	7	0	0	2,730	1,729
China Eastern Airlines	CDG	7	7	7	7	2,009	2,009	2,009	2,240
Air China International	CDG	3	3	3	3	642	642	642	903
Air France	CDG	12	7	7	7	3,132	1,827	1,827	1,890
Air China International	FCO	0	3	0	2	0	633	0	606
Air China/Austrian Airlines	VIE	0	6	5	5	0	1,620	1,350	1,150
Blue Panorama	VCE	0	0	1	0	0	0	196	0
Total		**50**	**72**	**97**	**91**	**15,787**	**22,097**	**29,577**	**25,388**

Sources: PATA; SRS Analyser.

Figure III.8 Scheduled Airlines Operating from Hong Kong, China, to Europe, January 2003-2006

Airline	Desti-nation	Departures/week				Seats/week (one-way)			
		2003	2004	2005	2006	2003	2004	2005	2006
Cathay Pacific Airways	AMS	5	5	5	7	1,245	1,245	1,245	1,701
KLM Royal Dutch Airlines	AMS	7	7	7	7	1,946	1,946	1,946	1,946
Air France	CDG	7	7	7	7	1,890	1,890	1,930	2,090
Cathay Pacific Airways	CDG	7	7	7	7	2,723	2,709	2,681	2,681
Transaero Airlines	DME	0	1	0	0	0	225	0	0
Cathay Pacific Airways	FCO	4	5	5	5	996	1,245	1,245	1,215
Cathay Pacific Airways	FRA	7	7	7	7	2,723	2,709	2,681	2,681
Lufthansa	FRA	7	7	7	7	2,730	2,800	2,730	2,730
British Airways	LHR	14	14	17	21	4,914	4,914	5,967	7,371
Cathay Pacific Airways	LHR	18	21	21	28	6,162	7,161	7,105	8,764
Qantas Airways	LHR	0	0	3	4	0	0	1,182	1,576
Virgin Atlantic Airways	LHR	7	7	7	7	2,177	2,177	2,177	2,177
Lufthansa	MUC	3	0	3	5	741	0	741	1,235
Aeroflot Russian Airlines	SVO	3	4	4	4	660	920	908	920
SWISS International Air Lines	ZRH	7	7	6	6	2,030	1,750	1,500	1,500
Total		**96**	**99**	**106**	**122**	**30,937**	**31,691**	**34,038**	**38,587**

Sources: PATA; SRS Analyser.

Figure III.9 Scheduled Airlines Operating from Hong Kong, China, to Europe, August 2003-2006

Airline	Desti-nation	Departures/week				Seats/week (one-way)			
		2003	2004	2005	2006	2003	2004	2005	2006
Cathay Pacific Airways	AMS	5	5	7	7	1,245	1,245	1,743	1,701
KLM Royal Dutch Airlines	AMS	7	7	7	7	1,946	1,946	1,946	1,946
Air France	CDG	5	7	7	10	1,350	1,890	1,890	2,827
Cathay Pacific Airways	CDG	7	7	7	10	2,709	2,681	2,681	3,410
Transaero Airlines	DME	0	1	0	0	0	225	0	0
Cathay Pacific Airways	FCO	4	5	5	7	1,548	1,915	1,915	2,681
Cathay Pacific Airways	FRA	7	7	11	10	2,709	2,681	3,677	3,410
Lufthansa	FRA	7	7	7	7	2,800	2,800	2,730	2,730
Finnair	HEL	0	0	3	5	0	0	861	1,435
Turkish Airlines	IST	0	0	0	2	0	0	0	542
British Airways	LHR	14	17	21	21	4,914	5,967	7,371	7,371
Cathay Pacific Airways	LHR	18	21	21	28	6,414	7,105	7,105	8,893
Qantas Airways	LHR	0	0	3	7	0	0	1,182	2,758
Virgin Atlantic Airways	LHR	7	7	7	7	2,177	2,177	2,177	2,177
Lufthansa	MUC	0	3	3	7	0	720	741	1,729
Aeroflot Russian Airlines	SVO	4	6	3	5	920	1,356	690	1,150
SWISS International Air Lines	ZRH	5	7	7	7	1,450	1,750	1,750	1,750
Total		**90**	**107**	**119**	**147**	**30,182**	**34,458**	**38,459**	**46,510**

Sources: PATA; SRS Analyser.

Leading Outbound Travel Agencies in China

Beijing	China Travel Service (CTS) Head Office Tel.: +86 (0) 10 646 1259 Fax: +86 (0) 10 6461 2597 Email: gwc@bj.china.com
	China Comfort Travel Co. Tel: +86 (0) 10 6594 0881 Fax: +86 (0) 10 6594 0891 Email: cct2001@263.com
	China Youth Travel Service (CYTS) Tel: +86 (0) 10 5815 8272/ 8813 Fax: +86 (0) 10 5815 8826 Email: info@cytsonline.com
Shanghai	JinJiang Tours Ltd. Tel: +86 (0) 21 6466 2828 Fax: +86 (0) 21 6466 2297 Email: jjj@jjtravel.com
	HuaTing Overseas Tourist Company Tel: +86 (0) 21 6248 5469 Fax: +86 (0) 21 6248 5470 Email: httravel@public.sta.net.cn
Guangdong	GZL International Travel Service Tel: +86 (0) 20 8107 3490 Fax: +86 (0) 2 8109 8082 Email: gztcbgs@public.guangzhou.gd.cn
	China Travel Service (CTS) Tel: +86 (0) 20 8333 6888 Fax: +86 (0) 20 8333 2247 Email: webmaster8@gdcts.com
	China International Travel Service (CITS) Tel: +86 (0) 755 8233 8822 Fax: +86 (0) 755 8232 9832 Email: citssz@public.szptt.net.cn

Annex V

Chinese Public Holidays in 2007

New Year	1 January
Spring Festival, Chinese New Year	18-20 February
International Women's Day	8 March
Labour Day	1 May
Golden Week	1-4 May
National Youth Day	4 May
Tibet Liberation Day	23 May
International Youth Day	1 June
Army Day	1 August
National Holiday/Day	1-3 October

Annex VI

Travel Trade Events in China, 2007-2008

Event	Location	Date	More information
2007			
Guangzhou International Travel Fair (GITF)	Guangzhou	30 March-1 April	
World Travel Fair (WTF)	Shanghai	22-25 March	www.worldtravelfair.com.cn
Incentive Travel & Conferences, Meetings (IT&CM China)	Shanghai	23-25 April	www.itcmchina.com
China Outbound Travel and Tourism Market (COTTM)	Beijing	14-16 May	www.cottm.com
Beijing International Travel Expo (BITE)	Beijing	21-23 June	
Asia Luxury Travel Market (ALTM)	Shanghai	18-21 June	www.altm.com.cn
China Incentive Business Travel and Meetings Exhibition (CIBTM)	Beijing	3-5 July	www.cibtm.travel
China International Travel Mart (CITM)	Kunming	1-4 November	
China Business Travel Forum (CBTF)	Shanghai	4-5 December	www.cbtf.cn
China Outbound Travel Congress (COTC)	Beijing	10-11 December	www.chinaoutboundcongress.com
2008			
World Travel Fair (WTF)	Shanghai	27-30 March	www.worldtravelfair.com.cn
Guangzhou International Travel Fair (GITF)	Guangzhou	30 March-1 April	
Incentive Travel & Conferences, Meetings (IT&CM China)	Shanghai	9-11 April	www.itcmchina.com
China Outbound Travel and Tourism Market (COTTM)	Beijing	14-18 April	www.cottm.com
Asia Luxury Travel Market (ALTM)	Shanghai	16-18 June	www.altm.com.cn
Beijing International Travel Expo (BITE)	Beijing	19-21 June	
China International Travel Mart (CITM)	Shangai	20-23 November	

Annex VII

Questionnaire for Interviews with Travel Agents in China

Face-to-face or telephone interviews of approximately 30-40 minutes each in length were conducted in Chinese with interviewees drawn from the CNTA list of approved outbound tour operators/travel agents. The interviews were based on the following questionnaire:

Visits

1. Which destinations do you offer?
2. Which destinations do you offer in Europe?
3. How many destinations are on average included in a tour to Europe? What is the most common combination of destinations?
4. What category of product do you offer in Europe (e.g. luxury, tourist class, etc.)? Please describe.
5. What type of product do you offer to Europe (e.g. escorted tour, individual travel)? Please describe.
6. Is your product ADS or non-ADS?
7. What is your opinion of the ADS procedures in different European countries?
8. How far in advance do customers book leisure travel to Europe?
9. How far in advance to customers book business travel to Europe?
10. For each of the above questions, have there been any changes in demand during the last five years? ('up', 'down' or 'stayed the same' is sufficient). Please describe.
11. What is the average size of your groups?
12. What type of accommodation is used (if hotels, which category)?
13. Do you experience operational difficulties when organising trips to Europe? If yes, please describe.
14. What administrative difficulties do you experience with arranging visas for your clients?
15. Do you see a willingness to repeat visits to Europe among your customers and, if so, in what circumstances? Why would they visit Europe a second or third time?
16. Which destinations are in highest demand (both country-wise and places within those countries)? Have there been any changes in the last five years?
17. Which themes do you use when selling tours and packages to Europe?
18. Have you been to Europe personally? If so, to which countries?
19. What is your main source of information about Europe?
20. Are there particular age groups or types of people that tend to visit Europe for leisure more than once?

Image of Europe

1. What, for you, is the image of Europe?
2. Which five positive words would you use to describe Europe in general?
3. Which of these is the strongest?
4. Which five negative words would you use to describe Europe in general?
5. Which of these is the strongest?
6. Which five positive images would you use to describe Europe in general?
7. Which of these is the strongest?
8. Which negative images would you use to describe Europe in general?
9. Which of these is the strongest?
10. Is the image of Europe appealing to all age groups? In your opinion, and based on your experience of selling travel to Europe, which age group does it appeal to most?
11. Does the image of Europe influence travel decisions? If so, how?
Show Europe logo now and translate if necessary.

On a scale of 1-5, rate your agreement to the following sentence
(1 = completely disagree, 5 = completely agree):

12. The new logo for Europe is good for the image of Europe in China (1-5 rating)
13. Do you understand the English language on this logo?
14. Should there be more images for Europe or is one sufficient?
15. If Europe and the individual countries have many images, what are these images? Please describe any images mentioned along with their associated countries.
16. Can Europe be divided into different geographical areas, each with a specific individual image? Do you portray Europe as a whole or as a diverse region with many countries?
17. Do global political relations affect the image of Europe? Yes/No
18. How is Europe perceived compared with the United States of America and Australia? Please give details.
19. Is Europe perceived as more, less, or equally expensive than/as the United States of America?
20. Is Europe perceived as more, less or equally expensive than/as Australia?
21. Europe is easier to travel to than the United States of America? (1-5)
22. Europe is easier to travel to than Australia? (1-5)
23. It is easier to get a visa for Europe than for the United States of America. (1-5)
24. It is easier to get a visa for Europe than for Australia. (1-5)
25. Having to apply for an extra visa for non-Schengen countries puts clients off visiting Europe. (Yes/No/No opinion)
26. The cost of getting a visa is a disincentive to travel to Europe. (1-5)
27. The administrative difficulties of arranging a visa are a disincentive to travel to Europe. (1-5)

28. Language is a barrier when travelling to Europe. (1-5)
29. Language is a barrier to doing business with Europe. (1-5)
30. Distance is a barrier when travelling to Europe. (1-5)
31. There are too many religious sites on European itineraries. (1-5)
32. Doing business with Europe is easy. (1-5)
33. Doing business with Europe is profitable. (1-5)
34. Europe represents value for money for Chinese travellers. (1-5)
35. Which features of Europe help sell European itineraries? Please give details.
36. In your opinion, which features should be avoided when selling Europe?
37. Could the perception of Europe be changed, at least partially, by marketing campaigns?
38. What would be the best way to do this? Please rate the effectiveness of the following ideas:
    - Promotional events
    - Competitions with prizes
    - Magazine articles
    - Profiling on travel programmes
    - Sponsored journalist visits
    - Advertising
        - TV
        - Radio
        - Printed media
        - Online
39. What can Europe do to be more welcoming to Chinese groups?
40. What developments will we see in the Chinese tourism industry over the next five years? How will consumer needs change?

Annex VIII

Questionnaire for Interviews with Tour Guides in China

A group of five tour guides in Shanghai, all of whom have been guiding groups to Europe for at least two years, was interviewed. Interviews were based on the following questionnaire:

Visits

1. How many European countries have you visited personally? Which ones?
2. How many trips in total have you made to Europe in the past five years?
3. What is the average size of your groups?
4. What type of clients make up your groups? Singles, couples, with children, retired? Please give approximate percentages.
5. How important is clients' shopping in Europe to you?
   Rate from 1-5 where 1= poor and 5= excellent.
6. Are your clients generally satisfied with their visits to Europe? If not, why not? Is there anything they miss?

Image of Europe

7. In your opinion, what is the overriding image of Europe among Chinese travellers?
8. Is there a specific site or attraction that motivates your clients to visit Europe?
9. Is there any difference according to age regarding what is interesting in Europe? Please give details.
10. Is Europe more suited to a certain age group of tourist? If so, approximately how old?
11. What are some of the main misconceptions about Europe for travellers who have yet to visit Europe?
12. Which are the preferred destinations before tourists travel to Europe? Which countries do they think they are going to like best?
13. On their return, which are the favourite countries or cities?
14. Does this preference vary by age of tourist? If so, how?
15. Are the opinions of Europe for Chinese tourists formed from TV images, printed information or friends' stories, or other? Please describe.
16. If a marketing campaign were to be launched to attract larger numbers of Chinese to Europe, what would be the most effective method or placement of the campaign? Please use your imagination!
17. What are the other countries/destinations that compete with Europe for Chinese travellers? In your experience, do Chinese group tourists prefer Australia or the United States of America to Europe? If so, why?

18. Can Europe be described by one image? If so, what would that be?

On a scale of 1-5, rate your agreement to the following sentence
(1 = completely disagree, 5 = completely agree).
Show Europe logo now and translate if necessary.

19. The new logo for Europe is good for the image of Europe in China
20. Comments.
21. Do you understand the English language on this logo?
22. Approximately what % of your clients do you think would understand the English language on this logo?
23. Can you name the adjectives you hear most from Chinese travellers talking about Europe?
24. Are there countries that are easier for you to travel through than others? If so, which ones and why?
25. Having to apply for an extra visa for non-Schengen countries puts people off visiting Europe. (Yes/No/No opinion)
26. What can Europe do to be more welcoming to Chinese groups?

Annex IX

Questionnaire for Interviews with Inbound Tour Operators in Europe

The European Travel Commission and World Tourism Organization have commissioned an important study on the image of Europe for Chinese travellers. Your views and activities as a tour operator are vital to assisting the industry in this growing market.

Please state the name of your organization, your name and email address.

Name of organization:

Your name: Your email address:

With reference to Chinese travellers to Europe please answer the following questions in all three sections.

Visits

Q1. Which countries in Europe do you offer to Chinese travellers? Please list below:

....

Q2. How many destinations are, on average, included in the tours you offer? Please *select one* of the following.

1-2 3-4 5-6 7-8 9+

Q3. What is the most common combination of countries? Please list below:

....

Q4. Which category of product do you offer the Chinese in Europe? Please *select one or more* of the following:

Economy Standard Luxury Business

Q5. What type of product do you offer the Chinese visitor in Europe? Please *select one or more* of the following:

Escorted tours Other types of tours (Please specify) ....

....

Q6. Do you offer non-ADS products? Please answer YES or NO:

Yes No

Q7. On average how far in advance do Chinese customers book leisure travel to Europe? Please *select one* of the following:

2-4 weeks 1-2 months 3-4 months 5-6 months 6+ months

Q8. On average, how far in advance do Chinese customers book business travel to Europe? Please *select one* of the following:

1-2 weeks 3-4 weeks 5-6 weeks 7-8 weeks 9+ weeks

Q9. Have there been any changes in demand by the Chinese for leisure travel to Europe during the last five years? Please *select one* of the following:

Increased Decreased No change

Q10. Have there been any changes in demand by the Chinese for business travel to Europe during the last five years? Please *select one* of the following:

Increased Decreased No change

Q11. What is the average size of your groups? Please *select one* of the following:

1-10 11-20 21-30 31-40 41-50 51+

Q12. What is the most common age range of your groups? Please *select one* of the following:

5-15 yrs 16-25 yrs 26-35 yrs 36-45 yrs 46-55 yrs 56+ yrs

Q13. What type of accommodation is most commonly used? Please *select one* of the following:

Hostels Bed & Breakfasts Hotels

Q14. If hotels, which category is most commonly used? Please *select one* of the following:

2* 3* 4* 5*

Q15. What percentage of customers return for repeat visits? Please *select one* of the following:

0-5% 6-10% 11-15% 16-20% 21+%

Q16. Are there particular age groups that tend to visit Europe for leisure more than once? Please *select one* age group:

5-15 yrs 16-25 yrs 26-35 yrs 36-45 yrs 46-55 yrs 56+ yrs

Image and perception of Europe

Q17. In your opinion, which five positive words would you use to describe Europe? Please list below:

....

Q18. Which of these is the strongest? ....

Q19. In your opinion, which five negative words would you use to describe Europe? Please list below:

....

Q20. Which of these is the strongest? ....

Q21. Do you portray Europe as a whole or as a diverse region with many countries? Please *select one* of the following:

Europe as a whole Europe as a region with many countries

Q22. In your opinion, do global political relations affect the image of Europe? Please answer YES or NO:

Yes No

On a scale of 1-5 rate your agreement to the following statements where 1 = completely disagree and 5 = completely agree). Please *select* the most appropriate number for each statement.

Q23. Europe is easier for Chinese tourists to visit than the United States of America.

1 2 3 4 5

Q24. Europe is easier for Chinese tourists to visit than Australia.

1 2 3 4 5

Q25. Doing business with China is easy.

1 2 3 4 5

Q26. Doing business with China is profitable.

1 2 3 4 5

Q27. It is currently too easy to become ADS-accredited in Europe.

1 2 3 4 5

Q28. Language is a barrier when doing business with China.

1 2 3 4 5

Q29. Language is a barrier for Chinese travellers in Europe.

1 2 3 4 5

Q30. Chinese tourists perceive Europe as more expensive than the United States of America.

1 2 3 4 5

Q31. Chinese tourists perceive Europe as more expensive than Australia.

1 2 3 4 5

Q32. It is easier for Chinese tourists to get a visa for Europe than for the United States of America.

1 2 3 4 5

Q33. It is easier for Chinese tourists to get a visa for Europe than for Australia.

1 2 3 4 5

Q34. Having to apply for an extra visa for non-Schengen countries puts clients off visiting Europe.

1 2 3 4 5

Q35. The cost of getting a visa is a disincentive for Chinese tourists to travel to Europe.

1 2 3 4 5

Q36. The administrative difficulties of arranging a visa are a disincentive to travel to Europe.

1 2 3 4 5

Q37. Distance is a barrier when travelling to Europe.

1 2 3 4 5

Q38. There are too many religious sites on European itineraries.

1 2 3 4 5

Q39. Europe represents value for money for Chinese tourists.

1 2 3 4 5

Q40. The perception of Europe can be changed, at least partially, by marketing campaigns.

1 2 3 4 5

Q41. What would be the most effective way of increasing awareness of Europe as a destination for Chinese travellers? Please *select* the most appropriate number for each method.

1 = not effective at all 5 = extremely effective

Promotional events	1	2	3	4	5
Competitions with prizes	1	2	3	4	5
Magazine articles	1	2	3	4	5
Profiling on travel programmes	1	2	3	4	5
Sponsored journalist visits	1	2	3	4	5
Advertising	1	2	3	4	5
Television	1	2	3	4	5
Radio	1	2	3	4	5
Printed media	1	2	3	4	5
Online websites	1	2	3	4	5
Personal recommendations	1	2	3	4	5

Q42. What developments will we see in the Chinese tourism industry over the next five years? How will consumer needs change?

....

....

This is the Europe logo.

On a scale of 1-5 rate your agreement to the following statements (where 1 = completely disagree and 5 = completely agree).

Please *select* the most appropriate number for each statement.

Q43. The logo for Europe is good for the image of Europe in China.

1 2 3 4 5

Q44. One image is sufficient to describe Europe.

1 2 3 4 5

Your views

Q45. What operational difficulties have you experienced when organising trips to Europe, if any?

....

Q46. In your opinion, which features of Europe help sell European itineraries?

....

Q47. In your opinion, which features of Europe should be avoided when selling Europe?

....

Q48. What can Europe do to be more welcoming to Chinese groups?

....

Thank you very much for your time in completing this very important questionnaire.

Annex X

Questionnaire for Interviews with European Hotels

1. Do you accommodate Chinese groups?
2. If not, why not?
3. If yes, do they have any particular requirements?
5. What is their food and beverage spend?
6. Are there any areas in which Chinese visitors could modify/improve their behaviour?
7. Are there any particular areas with which Chinese groups express disappointment?
8. Do you have any specific features in your hotel that have been introduced because of their appeal to Chinese visitors (such as Chinese television programmes)?
9. How far in advance do they book?

Annex XI

Questionnaires for Consumer Focus Groups in China

Focus groups 1 – Consumers who have travelled to europe within the last five years

Focus groups were conducted in Beijing (6), Shanghai (6) and Guangzhou (6).

Visit

1. How many times have you visited Europe in the last five years?
2. Which European countries/cities have you visited? (Include details on multi-destination trips.)
3. Have you also visited other overseas destinations in the last five years? If so, where, how often, when and for what reason? (e.g. North America, Australia)
4. How long did your stays in Europe last?
5. What was the purpose of your visit to Europe? (Business, holiday, business and holiday combined VFR, convention, incentive trip, study visit, health reasons, to work in Europe). If for leisure, what type of holiday was it and how was it booked?
6. Why did you choose Europe as a destination? Was there a specific site or attraction that made you want to visit Europe? If so, which one?
7. How far in advance did you book travel to Europe? How did you book it, e.g. through a travel agent, via the internet, by phone, etc.?
8. How long did you spend planning your most recent trip to Europe?
9. Which airport was your gateway into Europe?
10. Do you plan to travel to Europe again?
11. If not, why not, and what would persuade you to visit it again?
12. If yes, which countries do you plan to visit next time and why?
13. Are you publicly or privately employed?
14. What destinations outside China, other than Europe, have you visited in the last five years?

Time and cost in Europe

15. What was the total amount you spent in Europe (in Rmb). Please break this down into airfares, pre-paid packages and spending during the trip.
16. Which airline did you use?
17. What form of transport did you use in Europe (plane, train, bus, hire car)?
18. What type of accommodation did you use in Europe (if hotels, which category)?

19. What time of year did you travel (month)?
20. What was the approximate cost for the trip to Europe (in Rmb)?
21. What activities did you enjoy most on your latest trip to Europe? E.g. shopping, historical sites, cultural events, gambling, entertainment.
22. Did you eat any European food? If so, which European food did you enjoy?
23. What is your preferred type of travel to Europe? Individual or group, single destination or multi-destination trips?
24. How would you rate the quality of service in the hospitality and travel trade in Europe, where 1 = excellent and 5 = very poor. Please explain using specific examples if needed.
25. Did Europe cater to you needs and live up to your expectations? If not, why not?
26. On a scale of 1-5, where 1 = 'not at all important' and 5 = 'very important', how important are travel agents and tour operators to consumers?
27. What is the most famous destination in Europe to you?
28. Which countries are 'must see' destinations in Europe?
29. List the countries in Europe which you would consider to be well known.
30. What is the image of European countries in China? Please describe.
31. What are Europe's biggest selling points in your opinion? Please list by country if possible.
32. Do global political relations affect the image of Europe? Yes/No
33. What are the main advantages of Europe in comparison to other regions? Please describe.
34. How is Europe perceived compared with the United States of America and Australia? Please give details.
35. Do you perceive Europe as more, less or equally expensive than/as the United States of America?
36. Do you perceive Europe as more, less or equally expensive than/as Australia?
37. Europe is easier to travel to than the United States of America. (1-5)
38. Europe is easier to travel to than Australia. (1-5)
39. It is easier to get a visa for Europe than for the United States of America. (1-5)
40. It is easier to get a visa for Europe than for Australia. (1-5)
41. Having to apply for an extra visa for non-Schengen countries puts me off visiting Europe. (Yes/No/No opinion)
42. Which five positive words would you use to describe Europe in general?
43. Which of these is the strongest?
44. Which five negative words would you use to describe Europe in general?
45. Which of these is the strongest?
46. Which five positive images would you use to describe Europe in general?
47. Which of these is the strongest?

48. Which five negative images would you use to describe Europe in general?
49. Which of these is the strongest?
50. What is your most preferred destination within Europe? Please state reasons.

On a scale of 1-5, rate your agreement to the following sentences
(1= completely disagree, 5 = completely agree).

51. Language is a barrier when travelling to Europe. (1-5 and please explain why).
52. Distance is a barrier when travelling to Europe. (1-5)
53. There are too many religious sites on European itineraries. (1-5)
54. The cost of getting a visa is a disincentive to travelling to Europe. (1-5)
55. The administrative difficulties of arranging a visa are a disincentive to travelling to Europe. (1-5)
    Show Europe logo now and translate if necessary.
56. What is your first impression of this logo?
57. What does this logo tell you about Europe?
58. Do you understand the English language on this logo?
59. The new logo for Europe is good for the image of Europe in China. Agree? (1-5)
60. Should there be more images for Europe, or is one sufficient?
61. If Europe and the individual countries have many images, what are these images to you? Please describe any images mentioned along with their associated countries.
62. Can Europe be divided into different geographical areas, each with a specific individual image?
63. Could the perception of Europe be changed, at least partially, by marketing campaigns?
64. What would be the best way to do this? Please rate the effectiveness of the following ideas:
    - Promotional events
    - Competitions with prizes
    - Magazine articles
    - Profiling on travel programmes
    - Sponsored journalist visits
    - Advertising
        - TV
        - Radio
        - Printed media
        - Online

Focus groups 2 – Consumers who intend to travel to europe within the next three years

These groups consisted of people with realistic potential for travel and existing travel plans, i.e. people who were confident they will be able to take a holiday in Europe during the next three years and who have the required minimum income levels. Focus groups were conducted in Beijing (6), Shanghai (6) and Guangzhou (6).

Visit

1. Which countries in Europe would you most like to visit? Please rate each one based on how much you would like to visit it, with 1 being the lowest and 5 being the highest scores.
2. Which cities in Europe would you most like to visit? Please rate each one based on how much you would like to visit it, with 1 being the lowest and 5 being the highest scores.
3. Is there a specific site or attraction that makes you want to visit Europe? If so, which one?
4. If you were to travel to Europe, would you be travelling individually, as a couple, as a family or with a group?
5. What would be the purpose of the trip to Europe (preferred experiences i.e. cities, culture, getting to know people, countryside/landscapes, events/happenings, shopping, VFR, ethnic and business)?
6. What time of year would you prefer to travel (month)?
7. How long would you take to plan the trip (how many months in advance)?
8. What would be the time of booking the trip (how many months in advance)?
9. How far is this determined by administrative problems, e.g. obtaining a visa?
10. What sources of information would you use when planning the trip (what newspapers and magazines do you read, which channels/programmes do you watch on television, etc.)?
11. What is the importance of these information sources in planning your overseas travel?
12. How often do you use the internet? For what purpose? Would you buy travel services online or book a European holiday online?
13. Where would you be most likely to book a European holiday?
14. Why have you not visited Europe in the past?
15. Are you publicly or privately employed?
16. Which destinations outside China and other than Europe have you visited?

Time and cost in Europe

17. What would be your preferred means of transport in Europe (plane, train, bus, hire car)?
18. What would be your preferred length of stay in Europe?
19. Which countries do you plan to visit in Europe?
20. What are your preferred holiday activities? E.g. shopping, historical sites, cultural events, gambling, entertainment.

21. What would be your approximate travel budget for a European holiday? Please list expenditure for the trip to/in Europe (airfare and accommodation) and other spending (e.g. shopping) separately please (in Rmb).
22. What type of accommodation would you use – deluxe hotel, first class, tourist class, hostel?
23. Luxury is important to me when travelling – answer 1-5, where 1 = strongly disagree and 5 = strongly agree.
24. Do you believe that Europe would cater to your needs? If not, why not?

Image of Europe

25. Of which destinations in Europe are you most aware? Which are the most famous? Please name countries and cities or regions/landmarks and list reasons for this.
26. Which countries are 'must see' destinations in Europe?
27. What is the general image of European countries in China?
28. In your opinion, what are the major selling points of Europe (or of individual European countries)?
29. Do global political relations affect the image of Europe? Yes/No
30. What are the main advantages of Europe in comparison to other regions? Please describe.
31. Do you perceive Europe as more, less or equally expensive than/as the United States of America?
32. Do you perceive Europe as more, less or equally expensive than/as Australia?
33. Europe is easier to travel to than the United States of America. (1-5)
34. Europe is easier to travel to than Australia. (1-5)
35. It is easier to get a visa for Europe than for the United States of America. (1-5)
36. It is easier to get a visa for Europe than for Australia. (1-5)
37. Having to apply for an extra visa for non-Schengen countries puts me off visiting Europe. (Yes/No/No opinion)
38. Which five positive words would you use to describe Europe in general?
39. Which of these is the strongest?
40. Which five negative words would you use to describe Europe in general?
41. Which of these is the strongest?
42. Which five positive images would you use to describe Europe in general?
43. Which of these is the strongest?
44. Which five negative images would you use to describe Europe in general?
45. Which of these is the strongest?
46. Which are your top three preferred destinations within Europe? Please state a reason in each case.

47. Which airline would you prefer to travel on for your planned trip to Europe?

48. Does your proposed trip to Europe depend on your travelling during Chinese public holidays? How important is time in general for a trip to Europe? Please explain.

49. What would be your preferred leisure activities on your coming trip to Europe?

50. What is your preferred arrangement for travelling to Europe? (Individual or group trip, single or multi-destination?

On a scale of 1-5, rate your agreement to the following sentences
(1= completely disagree, 5 = completely agree).

51. Language is a barrier when travelling to Europe. (1-5)

52. Distance is a barrier when travelling to Europe. (1-5)

53. There are too many religious sites on European itineraries. (1-5)

54. The cost of getting a visa is a disincentive to travelling to Europe. (1-5)

55. The administrative difficulties of arranging a visa are a disincentive to travelling to Europe. (1-5)
    Show Europe logo now and translate if necessary.

56. What is your first impression of this logo?

57. What does this logo tell you about Europe?

58. Do you understand the English language on this logo?

59. The new logo for Europe is good for the image of Europe in China. Agree? (1-5)

60. Should there be more images for Europe, or is one sufficient?

61. If Europe and the individual countries have many images, what are these images to you? Please describe any images mentioned along with their associated countries.

62. Can Europe be divided into different geographical areas, each with a specific individual image?

63. Could the perception of Europe be changed, at least partially, by marketing campaigns?

64. What would be the best way of doing this? Please rate the effectiveness of the following ideas:

    - Promotional events
    - Competitions with prizes
    - Magazine articles
    - Profiling on travel programmes
    - Sponsored journalist visits

Annex XII

Questionnaire for Survey of Coach Travellers in Europe

The European Travel Commission and the World Tourism Organization have commissioned a study on the image of Europe for Chinese travellers. Now that you are at the end of your trip, we would be very interested to hear your thoughts on Europe. Please take a few moments to answer these questions, and hand them back to your tour guide.

1. Before this trip, how many times had you visited Europe during the last five years?

   Never Once Twice Three times Four or more times

2. Before coming on this trip, what did you think Europe would be like? Please rate on a scale of 1-5, with 5 meaning 'strongly disagree' and 1 meaning 'strongly agree':

   - Historic
   - Cultural
   - Scenic
   - Diverse
   - Good shopping
   - Welcoming
   - Fashionable
   - Safe
   - Clean
   - Good value for money
   - High quality
   - Hospitable
   - Modern
   - Charming

3. At the end of your trip, what is your perception of Europe? Please rate on a scale of 1-5, with 5 meaning 'strongly disagree' and 1 meaning 'strongly agree':

   - Historic
   - Cultural
   - Scenic
   - Diverse
   - Good shopping
   - Welcoming

- Fashionable
- Safe
- Clean
- Good value for money
- High quality
- Hospitable
- Modern
- Charming

4. Now that you have been to Europe, can you describe your image of Europe in one word? Please select one only:

   - Beautiful
   - Clean
   - Noble
   - Arrogant
   - Modern
   - Fashionable
   - Fairytale
   - Historic
   - Conservative
   - Diverse
   - Cultural
   - Charming
   - Elegant
   - Artistic
   - Eclectic
   - Traditional
   - Slow
   - Friendly
   - Reticent
   - Funky

5. What was your perception of European food before your trip? Please rate on a scale of 1-5, with 5 meaning 'strongly disagree' and 1 meaning 'strongly agree':

   - Diverse
   - Tasty

- Healthy
- Boring
- Strange
- I had no thoughts about it

6. Did you eat any European food during your trip?
   - Yes, once
   - Yes, several times
   - No, not at all

7. If you ate any European food, what was your perception of it after your trip? Please rate on a scale of 1-5, 5 meaning 'strongly disagree' and 1 meaning 'strongly agree'.
   - Diverse
   - Tasty
   - Healthy
   - Boring
   - Strange

8. Would you come back to Europe for another visit? Yes/No

9. How satisfied were you with your European trip? Please rate on a scale of 1-5, with 5 meaning 'very dissatisfied' and 1 meaning 'very satisfied'.

10. How many European countries have you visited on this trip? One, two, three, four or more?

11. How long was your trip to Europe? Please select one: 1-5 days, 6-10 days, 10-15 days, more than 15 days.

12. Which region of China are you from? Please select either: Beijing, Shanghai, Guangzhou, other.

13. Approximately how much have you spent while in Europe (in Rmb)?
    - < 5,000
    - 5,001-10,000
    - 10,001-15,000
    - 15,001-20,000
    - 20,001-25,000
    - > 25,000

Figure XII.1: Detailed responses from coach traveller survey (sample size: 134)

Q1 How many times had you visited Europe previously?

Never	Once	Twice	Three times	4 or more
44	34	17	13	10

Q2 Before travelling, what did you think Europe would be like?

	Strongly disagree	Disagree	No opinion	Agree	Strongly agree
Historic	1	2	15	35	59
Scenic	0	1	24	41	45
Good shopping	7	5	41	39	23
Fashionable	5	1	40	34	23
Clean	0	2	32	43	31
High quality	0	4	25	40	32
Modern	3	3	38	25	35
Cultural	0	1	19	38	60
Diverse	1	2	27	52	28
Welcoming	4	4	36	44	24
Safe	1	3	33	47	26
Good value	4	5	34	46	19
Hospitable	3	5	35	31	21
Charming	0	2	34	47	33

Q3 After travelling, what is your perception of Europe?

	Strongly disagree	Disagree	No opinion	Agree	Strongly agree
Historic	0	4	7	8	77
Scenic	0	0	18	5	64
Good shopping	12	8	27	5	23
Fashionable	6	4	34	5	26
Clean	0	2	26	9	36
High quality	3	3	28	8	24
Modern	10	7	35	7	22
Cultural	0	0	16	3	65
Diverse	1	4	29	13	29
Welcoming	3	5	37	11	26
Safe	1	0	30	5	28
Good value	4	5	41	6	14

	Strongly disagree	Disagree	No opinion	Agree	Strongly agree
Hospitable	4	3	36	4	19
Charming	1	4	35	7	33

Q4 Having been to Europe, please describe its image in one word?

Image	Answers	Image	Answers
Beautiful	26	Clean	13
Noble	0	Arrogant	1
Modern	9	Fashionable	0
Fairytale	1	Historic	16
Conservative	4	Diverse	0
Cultural	11	Charming	1
Elegant	12	Artistic	4
Eclectic	1	Traditional	4
Slow	2	Friendly	2
Reticent	2	Funky	0

Q5 What was your perception of European food before your trip?

	Strongly disagree	Disagree	No opinion	Agree	Strongly agree
Diverse	6	5	16	37	46
Tasty	5	15	31	31	21
Healthy	6	6	34	41	16
Boring	20	13	43	21	10
Strange	26	14	34	15	8
No thoughts	21	2	24	11	6

Q6 Did you eat European food during your trip?

Once	Several times	Not at all
57	54	13

Q7 If 'Yes', what was your perception of European food after your trip?

	Strongly disagree	**Disagree**	**No opinion**	**Agree**	**Strongly agree**
Diverse	8	1	15	6	49
Tasty	1	10	36	11	18
Healthy	0	7	43	9	15
Boring	12	20	39	14	4
Strange	29	14	29	14	2
No thoughts	21	2	24	11	6

Q8 Would you return for another visit?

Yes	**NO**
99	8

Q9 How satisfied were you with your European trip?

Very dissatisfied	**Dissatisfied**	**No opinion**	**Satisfied**	**Very satisfied**
0	0	18	46	40

Q10 How many European countries have you visited on this trip?

Once	**Twice**	**Three times**	**4 or more**
56	12	9	31

Q11 How long was your trip to Europe?

1-5 days	**6-10 days**	**10-15 days**	**15+ days**
11	71	33	1

Q12 Which region of China are you from?

Beijing	**Shanghai**	**Guangzhou**	**Other**
15	75	8	14

Q13 Approximately how much have you spent on your European trip (in Rmb)?

< 5,000	**5,001-10,000**	**10,001-15,000**	**15,001-20,000**	**20,001-25,000**	**> 25,000**
34	22	26	20	11	3

Annex XIII

ETC Member Organizations
(August 2007)

Austria	Austrian National Tourist Office (ANTO)
Belgium	Flanders: Tourist Office for Flanders (TV)
	Wallonia: Office de Promotion du Tourisme Wallonie-Bruxelles (OPT)
Bulgaria	Bulgarian State Tourism Agency
Croatia	Croatian National Tourist Board (CNTB)
Cyprus	Cyprus Tourism Organisation (CTO)
Czech Republic	CzechTourism
Denmark	VisitDenmark
Estonia	Estonian Tourist Board (ETB)
Finland	Finnish Tourist Board (MEK)
France	Maison de la France (MDLF) / French Government Tourist Office
Georgia	Department of Tourism and Resorts
Germany	German National Tourist Board (DZT)
Greece	Greek National Tourism Organization (GNTO)
Hungary	Hungarian National Tourist Office (HNTO)
Iceland	Icelandic Tourist Board
Ireland	Tourism Ireland and Fáilte Ireland
Italy	Italian State Tourist Board (ENIT)
Latvia	Latvian Tourism Development Agency
Lithuania	Lithuanian State Department of Tourism
Luxembourg	Luxembourg National Tourist Office (ONT)
Malta	Malta Tourism Authority (MTA)
Monaco	Monaco Government Tourist Office
Montenegro	National Tourism Organization of Montenegro
Netherlands	Netherlands Board of Tourism and Conventions (NBTC)
Norway	Innovation Norway
Poland	Polish Tourist Organisation (POT)
Portugal	Turismo de Portugal (Portugal Tourism)
Romania	Ministry of SMEs, Trade, Tourism and Liberal Professions

San Marino	Ministry for Tourism, Sport, Transport, Telecommunications and Economic Cooperation
Serbia	National Tourism Organisation of Serbia
Slovakia	Slovak Tourist Board
Slovenia	Slovenian Tourist Board
Spain	Spanish Tourist Office (Turespaña)
Sweden	VisitSweden
Switzerland	Switzerland Tourism
Turkey	Ministry of Tourism
Ukraine	National Tourist Organization of Ukraine
United Kingdom	VisitBritain

List of Acronyms

ADS	Approved Destination Status
ANTO	Austrian National Tourist Office
CAAC	Civil Aviation Authority of China
CCTV	Official Chinese television new network
CNAC	China National Aviation Corporation
CNNIC	China Internet Network Information Centre
CNTA	China National Tourism Administration
DZT	German National Tourist Board
ETC	European Travel Commission
ETOA	European Tour Operators' Association
EU	European Union
IPS	International Passenger Survey (United Kingdom)
NTA	National Tourism Administration
NTO	National Tourism Organization
OECD	Organisation for Economic Co-operation and Development
PATA	Pacific Asia Travel Association
SARS	Severe Acute Respiratory Syndrome
SARs	Special Administrative Regions (i.e. Hong Kong, Macao)
SEZ	Special Economic Zone
STB	Scandinavian Tourist Board
TFWA	Tax Free World Association
UNWTO	World Tourism Organization
WTO	World Trade Organization

Bibliography

ACNielsen China (September 2007), *The Significance of China as a Travel Generator,* presentation made at Raven Fox Events' European Travel Partnership Symposium.

ACNielsen (2006), *China Trend Watch* (Online), available: http://www.acnielsen.com.

Air China (2006), *About Us* (Online), available: http://www.airchina.com.cn/en/zj/1_1.htm (18-7-2006).

Arlt, W. G. (2006), *China's Outbound Tourism,* Routledge, London.

BBC News (2006), *Country Profile: China* (Online), available: http://news.bbc.co.uk/1/hi/world/asia-pacific/country_profiles/1287798.stm#facts (21-7-2006).

BBC News (11 May 2005), *Boeing Wins Large 737 China Order* (Online), available: http://news.bbc.co.uk/1/hi/business/4535923.stm (18-7-2006).

Breaking Travel News (9 June 2006), *Cathay Buys Dragonair in Share Deal* (Online), available: http://www.breakingtravelnews.com/article/2006060908511439 (24-7-2006).

Central Intelligence Agency (2006), *The World Factbook – China,* CIA, Washington (Online), available: https://www.cia.gov/cia/publications/factbook/geos/ch.html (17-7-2006).

Centre for Asia Pacific Aviation (CAPA), various reports and presentations.

Chan, C. (2001), *China,* Odyssey Publications Ltd., Hong Kong, p. 350.

'China and the Internet – The Party, the People and the Power of Cyber-Talk' (2006), *The Economist* (Online), 27 April, available: http://www.economist.com/world/displaystory.cfm?story_id=6850080 (21-7-2006).

'China Eastern Airlines to Beef Up Fleet Capacity' (January 2005) (Online), available: http://english.sina.com/business/1/2005/0126/19348.html (18-7-2006).

China Highlights Travel Service (2006), China Eastern Airlines Corporation (Online), available: www.chinahighlights.com/china-airline/china_eastern_airlines.htm (18-7-2006).

China International Travel Mart (CITM) (Online), available: http://www.citm.com.cn/en/index.php (6-1-2006).

China Internet Network Information Centre, cited in *China Daily* (April 2006), *China's Internet: Behind the Attractive Statistics* (Online), available: http://www.chinadaily.com.cn/en/doc/2004-01/17/content_299888.htm (21-7-2006).

China Internet Network Information Centre (2004-2006), various reports, CNNIC, Beijing.

China National Tourism Administration (2006), *About CNTA* (Online), available: www.cnta.com/lyen/index.asp 18-7-2006.

China National Tourism Administration (2005), *China Tourism Annual Report 2005,* CNTA Beijing.

China National Tourism Administration (1999-2005), *China Tourism Statistics Almanac,* Beijing

China Outbound Tourism Research Project e. V. (2006), *How to Enter China's Tourism Market* (Online), available: http://www.china-outbound.com/Downloads/How_to_enter%20Chinas_Tourism_Market.pdf (8-7-2006).

China Outbound Travel and Tourism Market (COTTM) (Online), available: http://www.cottm.com/ (6-1-2006).

China Radio International (CRI) (April 2006), *Air China Says Net Profit Rose 0.9 pct* (Online), available: http://en.chinabroadcast.cn/855/2006/04/19/262@79116.htm (22-5-2006).

China Southern Airlines (January 2006), *China Southern Cracks 44 million Pax Mark* (Online), available: http://www.cs-air.com/en/news/2006/01/002.htm (19-5-2006).

China Southern Airlines (2006), *Company Profile: China Southern Overview* (Online), available: http://www.cs-air.com/en/nhsj/01/depa_info/index.htm (19-5-2006).

Civil Aviation Administration of China (2004-2005), *CAAC Statistics,* CAAC, Beijing.

de Burton, S. (11 November 2005), 'The Chinese Market: Swiss Make Measured Return to Mark Time in Beijing's Forbidden City', *Financial Times* (Online), available: http://news.ft.com/cms/s/285d85ce-5135-11da-ac3b-0000779e2340,dwp_uuid=ffa2aa5c-ee23-11d9-98e5-00000e2511c8.html (17-7-2006).

Deutsche Bank AG (21 August 2006), *China Travel* (PowerPoint presentation), Beijing.

Dujiang and Daibin (2005), *Annual Report of China Outbound Tourism Development 2004,* China Tourism Education Press, Beijing.

Economist Intelligence Unit (2006), *Country Report Briefings – China,* EIU, London.

Embassy of the People's Republic of China in the United Kingdom, *China Public Holidays (2006-2007)* (Online), available: http://china.embassyhomepage.com/chinese_public_holidays_china_embassy_london_uk.htm (8-1-2007).

Europa Publications, *The Europe World Year Book 2004,* Europa Publications, London.

European Travel Commission (2006), *Benchmarking Study on NTO Budgets, 2006,* ETC, Brussels.

European Travel Commission (2006), *ETC New Media Review* (Online), available: http://www.etcnewmedia.com/review/.

European Travel Commission (2006), *Market Insights – China,* ETC, Brussels.

European Travel Commission / World Tourism Organization (2003), *Chinese Outbound Tourism* (Online), available: www.etc-corporate.org/resources/uploads/chinastudy.pdf (8-1-2007).

German National Tourist Board (DZT), *Market Studies on China,* DZT.

'Golden Weeks Losing Lustre Among People' (19 November 2004), *China Daily* (Online), available: http://www.chinadaily.com.cn/english/doc/2004-11/19/content_393145.htm (20-7-2006).

Goldkorn, J. (9 December 2004), *'USA to Get 'Approved Destination Status' for Chinese Tourists'* (Online), available: http://www.danwei.org/internet/usa_to_get_approved_destinatio.php (18-7-2006).

Graddol, D. (1997), *The Future of English?* (Online), available: http://www.britishcouncil.org/learning-research.htm (16-2-2007).

ICT Group (2006), available: http://www.ictgroup.com/.

International Air Transport Association (15 December 2004), *IATA International Cargo and Passenger Forecasts 2004-2008* (Online), available: http://www.iata.org (18-12-2006).

International Monetary Fund (2007), *Overview of the World Economic Outlook Projections, July 2007,* IMF, Washington.

International Monetary Fund (2006), *World Economic Outlook September 2006* (Online), available: http://www.imf.org/external/pubs/ft/weo/2006/02/pdf/weo0906.pdf (16-2-2007).

International Monetary Fund (2005), *World Economic Outlook September 2005* (Online), available: http://www.imf.org/external/pubs/ft/weo/2005/02/index.htm (16-2-2007).

International Passenger Survey (IPS), *United Kingdom National Statistics* (Online), available: http://www.statistics.gov.uk/ (18-12-2006).

International Travel Expo Hong Kong (2006), *The 21st International Travel Expo (ITE) Hong Kong* (Online), available: www.itehk.com (6-1-2006).

Internet World Stats (2006), *Top Ten Internet Countries* (Online), available: http://www.internetworldstats.com/top20.htm (21.12.2006).

'Largest Cities of the World – By Population' (2000), *Times Atlas of the World (2000),* 10th edition (Online), available: www.worldatlas.com/citypops.htm (17-7-2006).

Laurent, C., *The Consumer Market of China to 2011,* Global Demographics (formerly Asian Demographics), Hong Kong.

Martinsen, J. (22 February 2006), *Newsstand Sales Figures for Beijing, Shanghai and Guangzhou* (Online), available: http://www.danwei.org/media_and_advertising/newsstand_sales_figures_for_be.php (21-7-2006).

McKinsey Global Institute (2006), *From 'Made in China' to 'Sold in China' – The Rise of the Chinese Urban Consumer* (Online), available: http://www.mckinsey.com/mgi/publications/china_consumer/index.asp (16-2-2007), p. 37.

Merrill Lynch and Capgemini (2006), *World Wealth Report 10th Anniversary, 1997-2006* (Online), available: http://www.ml.com/media/48237.pdf (16-2-2007).

Merrill Lynch and Capgemini (2004), *World Wealth Report 2004* (Online), available: http://www.ml.com/media/48237.pdf (16-2-2007).

National Bureau of Statistics of China (2005), *China Statistical Yearbook (2005),* China Statistics Press, NBSC, Beijing.

National Intelligence Council (2005), *Mapping the Global Future: Report of the NIC's 2020 Project* (Online), available: http://www.dni.gov/nic/NIC_globaltrend2020.html (19-2-2007).

'Online Shopping and Messages Service Began to Prevail' (18 January 2004), *People2people Net* (Online), available: http://p2pnet.net/story/580 (21-7-2006).

Pacific Asia Travel Association (20 March 2006), Report prepared for ETOA on Scheduled Airlines from Beijing, Guangzhou, Shanghai and Hong Kong to Europe, 2003-2006, PATA, Bangkok.

Pacific Asia Travel Association (2005-2007), various publications and presentations (cited in this report).

'Passports' (2004), *Shanghai Star* (Online), available: http://app1.chinadaily.com.cn/star/ (5-1-2006).

Qu Xiaodong and CCW Research General Manager (2006), cited at *C114 News,* available: http://www.c114.net/cn-c11404 (20-12-2006).

Reporters without Boarders (2006), *China – China's Burgeoning Internet* (Online), available: http://www.rsf.org/article.php3?id_article=10749 (21-8-2006).

Scandinavian Tourist Board (2006), *China White Paper,* STB, Tokyo.

Scandinavian Tourist Board, Tokyo (2004), *Chinese Outbound Travel Market 2004,* STB, Tokyo.

SRS Analyser (2007), *Airline Traffic Data to/from China.*

Tax Free World Association (TFWA), *Conference Spells Out True Potential of Asia Pacific Region* (Online), available: http://www.tfwa.com/duty_free/uploads/media/17_05_2005_04.pdf (18-7-2006).

Tax Free World Association (TFWA) and ACNielsen (2005), *2005 Chinese Traveller Study* (Online), available: http://www.tfwa.com/duty_free/Chinese_Traveller_Study.749.0.html (7-7-2006).

The World Bank (2004), *Fighting Poverty: Findings and Lessons from China's Success* (Online), available: http://econ.worldbank.org/WBSITE/EXTERNAL/EXTDEC/EXTRESEARCH/0,contentMDK:20634060~pagePK:64165401~piPK:64165026~theSitePK:469382,00.html (14-12-2006).

Tourism Australia (2006), *Markets: China* (Online), available: www.tourism.australia.com (18-7-2006).

TourMIS (July 2006), *Tourism in Europe: Nights and Arrivals* (Online), available: http://www.tourmis.info.

'Trade Shows Alphabetical List', *Events Eye (2006)* (Online), available: www.eventseye.com/ (6-1-2006).

The Travel Business Partnership (2004), 'The China Outbound Travel Market', *Travel Markets* (Issue 21, October-November 2004), London.

Transparency International (2005) (Online), available: http://www.transparency.org/policy_research/surveys_indices/cpi/2006

United Nations Department of Economic and Social Affairs Population Division (2005), *World Urbanization Prospects,* UN, New York.

United Nations Population Division (2002), *World Population Prospects,* UN, New York.

United States Department of Commerce, Commercial Service (2004), *Cable TV Market in China* (Online), available: http://www.buyusainfo.net/docs/x_2737062.pdf (23-2-2007).

Visa International Asia Pacific, various publications and presentations (cited in this report).

VisitBritain (2006), *China Market and Trade Profile* (updated January 2006) (Online), available: http://www.tourismtrade.org.uk/Images/Profile_China_tcm12-22105.pdf (18-7-2006).

VisitBritain (October-November 2005), *Asia Pacific Market Intelligence Report, China* (Online), available: http://www.tourismtrade.org.uk/MarketIntelligenceResearch/ (6-1-2006).

Wang, Y. (2006) (teacher at the Tianjin University of Science and Technology and former student of University of Oxford), personal comment.

Ward, N. ed (2005), *Whitaker's Almanac 2006*, A&C Black, London.

Wikipedia (2007), *Mandarin Linguistic* (Online), available: http://en.wikipedia.org/wiki/Mandarin_language (8-1-2007).

Wikipedia (2006), *China Eastern Airlines* (Online), available: http://en.wikipedia.org/wiki/China_Eastern_Airlines (18-7-2006).

Wong, D. (10 June 2005), 'Singapore's Millionaires Increase at Fastest Pace in the World', *Bloomberg.com* (Online), available: http://www.bloomberg.com/apps/news?pid=10000080&sid=aAyXEXQ8laDo&refer=asia (17-7-2006).

World Tourism Organization (2006), *China – The Asia and the Pacific Intra-regional Outbound Series,* UNWTO, Madrid.

World Travel Guides (2006), *China Travel Guide – Public Holidays* (Online), available: http://www.worldtravelguide.net/country/58/public_holidays/Far-East-Asia/China.html (8-1-2007).